I0476714

The Dream Breaker

The Dream Breaker

Volume 3

Larry Denis Campbell

Copyright@2015 by Larry Denis Campbell.

All rights reserved. No part of this publication may be reproduced, distributed or transmitted in any form or by any means, including photocopying, recording, or other method. Electronic or mechanical, without prior permission of the publisher, except in brief quotations embodied in critical reviews and certain other non commercial uses permitted by copy right law. For permission, requests, write to the publisher addressed 'Attention Permissions Co-coordinator, at the address below;

Larry Denis Campbell/ Dead Set Publishing.
larrycampbell09@gmail.com

Book Layout C 2015 BookDesignTemplates.com

Ordering Information.
Quantity Sales. Special Discounts are available.
For details, contact the publisher at the address above.

Guilty, or Not Guilty / Larry Campbell–1st Edition
Printed via CreateSpace and available on Amazon

This book has been supported by www.doityourselfpublishing.com.au
ISBN: 1515184455
ISBN 13: 9781515184454
Library of Congress Control Number: 2015912319
CreateSpace Independent Publishing Platform
North Charleston, South Carolina

How To Win A Trial against Police Verbalization.
*'**Boob.**' (bu;b) Slang. ~ n. **1.** 'An ignorant or foolish person.*

To Sir Colin Bennett QC (Member of Parliament.)

A man of formidable courage and true charity.

I mention Mrs Josephine Marty who told me to be a good boy, and to always fight for what is right.
And.....to never give in.

I thank all the supportive prisoners and staff for being there, when the going was really tough.'

'Especially Jack.'

A LAWFUL KIND OF PERJURY

I was once a very quiet, *as well as a decent young man,* who for reasons well documented in our many older neglected prison files, had carelessly and bodily thrown myself at the blue uniformed line of authority. An authority that had violently ruled the political roost. *An authority that broke the same legally written laws, that I, once did.*

I will say, that I am not a person who is at all qualified in writing books, or even professionally *'able'* in the art of writing, *but,* I do have a very important tale to convey to those who may wish to save other people. *Or,* to change certain laws that are unjust, and seriously unfair. In doing so, it may probably save your own children, *someday,* from a great harm. As well as prevent a most terrible one sided type of; *'Injustice.'*

I feel the tale must be told, even if it tends to embarrass both myself, and my relatives, for I do believe, that ignorance should never ever find a home to wallow in. Furthermore, I do not wish anyone to harbour such pain of long a past ignorance that had once been placed upon my once young, *and still then,* developing shoulders.

Now, one minor act of unlawful perjury by a government official, a legal man, *or a policeman,* can often change the direction in a man's life. *The route of his family tree?* It may cause the destruction of his compassion, as well as his *or her* relationship with other human beings. *Perjury in fact,* can change the outcome of a trial, and put a man in prison, for the rest of his life.

That is, for something he did not do.

I do most *certainly* know, that to be so wrongfully convicted, *or, 'incarcerated,'* because of some official person who speaks untruthfully, it could indeed demoralize a whole family, *and or,* create a situation of depression, insanity, and even death.

In that 1970's, Public Service dominated State of Queensland, *many long years ago,* all this unexpected misnomer had really happened, and perjury had soon set in motion an unlawful set of circumstances, that eventually led to the fall of an incumbent corrupt government. A Government, that had so *arrogantly* held power for more than thirty years.

I, *a lowly prisoner,* had in fact challenged this practice of an ongoing State legal perjury, that was then being committed by the; **Police, the Prosecution,** and the lofty arrogant predominant Judiciary. *Meaning, in the State of Queensland, Australia.*

Regina Vs Larry Denis Campbell; 1969 to 1971; (Resulting in fourteen jury acquittals. That is, with the eventual aid of certain good men of honor within the legal fraternity. Good men, who when provoked, had risen as one to force the truth to be told.) 'Legal Aid, Queensland Australia.'

These amazing untold events took place while I was to be continually ignored and or incarcerated in Boggo Road Gaol, for over one and a half years. *That is, while dealing with the above mentioned matters for almost a total, of a non-legal-custodial period of years. Mainly because of inappropriate police perjury.*

All this happened under the nose of the Law Society, and of those Sunday Sun Newspapers, who bravely spoke of my ordeal in; 'This Week in Court.' which was the only voice in the wilderness of 'Judicial Wrongdoing.'

It is not my intention to defame, or to insult a legal people, but simply to bring notice to citizens, that, if a police force is corrupt, so will be the machinery that supports them.

'If you do not acknowledge injustice, 'Officially,' then it does not exist.' LDC.

This is my true story of my unrelenting and determined perseverance over the biased Queensland Legal System. *It is your story,* as well as mine.

It explains of what really goes on behind closed doors.

That is, in places like the Queensland Remand System.

Known to many as the; 'Dream breaker.'

LDC.

It is not what you know, or whom you know,
But, it is what you know about, 'whom,'
That really matters in the State of Queensland.
LARRY DENIS CAMPBELL.

CONTENTS

Locked in from main compound.

INTRODUCTION BY THE AUTHOR

had, *in the 60's and 70's,* found that the Remand Yard of Boggo Road Gaol was an emotional place of motion, where personalities clashed, *both, in the egoistical sense, and the legal sense.* It was, *and never has at all,* been an easy place to survive morally, where the mellow, the soft, or the emotionally drained human beings, appear to flourish. I guess, that in some ways, it can be likened to a Court room, *where, once you dare bow your head, you are done like a Sunday dinner.*

As it were, thousands of good decent men and youth have passed through those *dour* unemotional yards in any twelve week period you care to mention, *so do please believe me when I suggest,* that some men and youth have had their dreams and beliefs broken beyond repair. *But,* for some, there is laughter, love, sex and friendship. *As well as being a place to repair their bodies, and to gather in ones sick and outraged and seriously damaged soul.*

To me, the Remand yard was a diversion that had prevented me from getting on with my life, *but,* by my having a dream, as well as an inner will-power that I felt could not be broken, I used what I could get, *barter or steal,* to achieve my own goals. *Crime is a diversion,* just as is sex, and or of our watching violence, or football, is a diversion, and, this writing is something that will hopefully divert young people from killing or hurting themselves. It is about *'the balance in your life'* and not ever allowing anybody or anything to destroy your dream. Not even if they have raped you or abused you, *lied about you,* defamed you, destroyed your way of life, *and or,* left you penniless lonely and unwanted? Because, for people who do truly have a dream, *there is always the future,* and if you *persevere,* no one in the whole world can take your future away from you.

I for one am in deep debt to my brother, Bruce Graham Campbell, who refused to believe that my life could not be salvaged from the ashes of childhood ruin. *And total defeat.*

To my brother Bruce, there is not only my deepest gratitude, but great love and respect for being a true man of family, and an example for all genuine Australians to; *never give up on your own,* no matter what they do. *Or, what they might say about you.*

Larry Campbell 2016   Larrycampbell09@gmail.com

CHAPTER 1

A VIEW FROM THE YARD

Out in general society, *I had,* among others, met the smart the dumb the rich the poor the good looking, *and also,* the extremely rude people, who on the surface, make our world, so damned diverse. *And so damned interesting.* What most people had in common, was that they had all forever appeared to rudely manipulate, trick, cheat, accumulate, pretend, show off, seduce, *and,* be liked by each other, at or any cost at all that it took to be popular. *And of course, emotionally desired.* Deny it if they wish, but if there was no law at all against certain behavior, then most rude Australian men and women soon found a way to do as they wished, *when they wished,* no matter who it was that they could hurt shame or embarrass in some unfair way.

In prison, there too was much the same type of people, except, that they would use *violence, anal rape, and official backing,* to achieve their goals. But, what was so amazing to me, *was,* that in both of those similar worlds, there were men and women of exceptional honour, of honesty, ethics, sensitivity, and of common decency. There were also those who could see the long term consequence of taking advantage of men and women with less integrity, *or innocence,* than others in the same situation. And, there were others who did not care an iota about any human being. *Living or dead.*

As it were, you quickly became an excellent salesman, a seducer, a leader, or an organizer, *as well as a follower of anyone with a genuinely good idea.* Or, you had quietly worked on toward your goal, without, taking any advantage of anyone at all.

Which meant, that you were quite exceptional.

Rare as the latter type people may be seen by others, *as a true individual,* you are, *if considered such a person,* often looked upon as a breath of fresh air in a harsh stale and ignorant prison world. A concrete existence that urgently needed smarter straightforward and clear thinking people in your corner. *So as to change the dourness of what once was.*

For me, I was not at all a clear thinking person, *nor very honest,* and the recipe for my then lack of social ethics is my having too many self-concerned people in my formative years. A type of people who embraced a sense of entitlement as if this whole community was theirs to tread on, *at will.*

At the same time, there were caring giving loving and genuinely unselfish human beings, in my earlier life. *Genuine people who set an amazing example for me.*

'Generosity, is a venue of healing.' *A tidbit by the Author.*

There once were quite a few decent people who had made that major underlying difference between my spending my life inside a filthy prison, or my eventually being married. Also, *in time,* loved by my own children. *I mean, if a view in our life changes, so does the person inside of us continue to change. Regardless of what the dumbest politicians in the world differ to suggest.*

Of course, being arraigned on charges of break and enter, in the year 1969, was the final end result of running with the pack. *While stupidly leaving common sense in the schoolroom.* Along of course with my suspect integrity in a local Woolworth store when*, hot greed as a motivating force*, had decided my future childhood directions. *As well as my future way of life.* One thing was quite certain, I was not raised to be a thief, liar, or a manipulator, but many of my past childhood disruptions, *and emotional confusions,* can do wonders in its creating such sickening rebelliousness in the mind and hearts of all lost young offenders.

As it was, *ten years later at the age of twenty six,* I was soon floundering out of my depth, *as those much tougher police got sick of me,* and had decided once and for all to put a stop to my cold blatant disregard for taking other good people's property. *As well as their own teenage daughter's respectability.* Daughters of all walks of life who had appeared to follow the advice of the tawdry criminal element, *rather,* than the advice of concerned parents who tend to offer to their rebellious and *virtually* insane children; 'Nothing at all.. Unfortunately for the criminals, *(and indirectly, for an ignorant society,)* those police workers had been so trained to; lie, cheat, verbalize, manipulate, steal, and do to those many offenders, what jockeys did to the frisky young thorough bred racehorses, *when they were bringing them to heel.* Understandably, the police felt justified in being harsh toward offenders, *but unfortunately,* they could not at all distinguish between a citizen, and some potential offender.

Nor did they like any free loaders getting too competitive on their patch, *or should I say;* on their watch.

I, *personally of course,* having remained unbroken, had then willfully believed that if they could do such cold obnoxious bullying callous things to strangers? *Then, so could I,* and my being placed in a remand section was a lot like giving me a front row seat in a circus full of clowns.

Sept 22nd 2006. A Public Inquiry discovered that police were proven to be torturing many detained persons, and long serving prisoners. Ch. 7 News. 23rd of July, 2015, Police Officer faces criminal charges for releasing CCTY film of six police who bashed a 20 year old citizen, while another washed the blood away with a bucket.

Unlike the; killers, the rapists, the numerous child molesters, *(and the insane,)* my previous periods of prison detention were a relatively minor stay behind the the walls. I guess it was a *short stay* only long enough for me to gather enough information so as to help me to sell my purloined goods. *Or, secretly putting together one more gang of desperate ram raiding thieves to assist me in my illegal endeavors.*

My reasoning of course, was that because of my previous offensive behavior, the society at large would never allow me to create an honest way of life. So it was that I personally felt I had no other choice at all but to somehow forge ahead with a false, *or an impulsive courage,* whenever the opportunity had so often presented itself.

Being charged with any type of criminal offense, was to be part and parcel of any offender's life, and if one had possessed a whole lot of money, the money hungry legal profession would often find a reasonable, *or lawful excuse,* to have the charges dismissed. *Or at least put on hold for a few years or so until the matter was forgotten by all and sundry.* What I did find, was that most criminals were an uneducated, *and wasteful lot,* and so their having plenty of money for a lawyer, was not something they actually thought about until they too were sitting or squatting in a remand yard without a dollar to their name. *Or a loyal family prepared to accept their ongoing behavior. As well as the social community impact on their good, but suspect, family name.*

In describing remand yard life, I found it was the most hectic part of any prison institution, *and as it was,* the old Boggo Road administration had just finished that new motel like frontal facade. Or some massive brick; *portion,* that was then ordered by our Government. Mainly, *I do believe now,* to give a false facade, *or a view,* to the old eighteenth century prison, which had then stood shamefully in the background, and far away from objective, critical, and or, calculative prying eyes.

I found too, that the new frontal structure itself, was in fact a reasonable replica of the old Wacol Farm type architecture, which, with its hard glaring white type block concrete and steel green painted rails, had totally surrounded the upper second story balcony. Surprisingly, I further discovered that my allotted single cell was also white with green trims, and that the bed itself was of solid steel attached firmly to the wall. It had running water, flush toilet, and a foam mattress that old lifers would have died for. Of course, the then Government of the people, still did not allow sheets to prisoners at that particular time, *but,* the woolly blankets were thick and warm, *and,* for people who had little else, they were considered quite a luxury. The yard outside the cells was like a marked out tennis court, with plenty of walking room to move around in. For me, this had certainly compensated for the lack of home comforts.

This then, was the main layout of the Remand Section, *and,* at a very first sight, it pleasantly appeared to be an old lags dream of a home away from home come true.

'This I could handle.' I thought, as I quickly arranged for a friend to send me over some varied assortment of ancient paperbacks, and a stack of

much darker freshly published biker magazines that had somewhat crudely and rudely portrayed a seriously indecent photographic layout of those tender young teenage girls. Girls who were showing off their youthful nudity. *And of course, phone numbers for indecent liaisons with any gullible, or desperate reader.*

Sadly, what I did not at all know at my first glance, was that the new type of architecture had numerous hidden portals, rooms, toilets, and blind spots that had then allowed violent criminals to unlawfully brutalize and dominate any new first time arrivals. Especially, boys of just seventeen or eighteen.

Younger boys on very serious charges, were at that time held in a protection yard, but they were still, 'got at,' with the aid of certain bisexual screws & prison pets.

Still, there I was, back in the big house with out a worry in the world, except that I weakly licked my dry lips as I'd craved the hot taste of malt whiskey. *Which had, by then, become my favorite liver destroying drink.* I later found it had caused serious levels of bowel cancer for many men in their sixties. *That is in years to come when I had secretly studied the hidden prison files. And had long become a non drinker.*

I was not an alcoholic, by any means, *that is in my opinion,* but for over a week or so I had in fact found that I'd craved alcohol badly, *and,* in turn had used nicotine as an appeasing, if not all that pleasing replacement. I knew too, that my having enough civilian tobacco could eventually cause real headaches for most prisoners, *but,* the men whom I had not forgotten when I was outside of the walls, did not forget me then.

All in all, I soon had supply of hot beverages, tobacco, books, and tinned food, which all arrived by a kitchen courier so as to assist in my new beginning in the world of the major losers. Strangely enough, within a few days I was quite comfortably well off, and had soon put that hectic insane civilian lifestyle almost completely out of my mind. *And my system.*

There were very few genuine type prisoners in the remand yard section, and most were ordinary nobody type people sitting there in a confused sad daze on prison yard stools. Or, they were walking around like lost hungry cattle that were looking for a tasty morsel to eat. They had stared at me with some curiosity as if I was some sort of important person who was well known by both the established prisoners, *and, a uniformed administration alike.* The unknown men often judged, or analysed me, only by that large amount of attention and bartered goods which I had continued to receive. On the other hand, I'd stared quite grimly at them in a discouraging way, if, or when they spoke to me. Or had the audacity to approach me and dare to ask for a handout.

'Who are you? I don't know you, *piss off.*'

There are certain protocols that must be adhered to before an unknown inmate is at all accepted, or assisted, by the majority. This too includes prison workers and officials. On the other hand, a few prisoners who had quite a lot of prisons experience, or who had rap sheets, *or form,* were a close knit group that had taken over a private secluded kitchen type store-room in the corner of that brand new section.

Understandably, I, *as a recognized felon*, was immediately invited over to join the shifty group in their misappropriation of edible government goods. So, my being encouraged by all, I quickly made up a large sandwich and nodded as I ate with a full mouth. Also, *it seemed,* that my being a rec-ognizable face, *and or*, past loyal ally in those long ago days of old, *when one good turn had deserved another,* had stood me in good stead. Especially when a cowardly man was referred to as a police dog behind those filthy old walls of old Brisbane Prison. *No!* Not because such a person was in fact an informer, but because he was not seen as a strong violent **prison aggressor,** by those men who had foolishly thought that less muscled people were very easy targets.'

I for one had, *on numerous occasions,* shown many men the fallacy of such beliefs, and more often than not, *a small bit of skin and hair or blood left on the concrete floor of the toilets,* had soon taught them certain harsh things that modern counseling and human kindness never ever at all appear to achieve.

For me, fitting into a prison was a whole lot easier than trying to be accepted in that wider world of ordinary people who lived high on the hog, *out in the growing suburbs.* So, before long, I had totally forgotten my personal concerns and I became embroiled in the rude gossip and daily occurrences that kept boredom and monotony at bay. Only at night, after the dim, *sight destroying lights were out,* did I then recall my civilian friends and those generous people who had for awhile, considered me their friend. *Or a person whom they'd genuinely liked.*

Again, it was time to forget the *Onions* and my *Redneck friends* and all I had needed to do was front the court, *do my time,* and then have another go in making a life for myself in the suburbs.

Hopefully, in a few years or so.

CHAPTER 2

CRIME AND CRIMINALS

As it was, I had somehow expected about two to three years, for my present charge. Mostly because, I had played a clear inconsequential part in that vagrancy type offense of stealing a set of invaluable refrigeration units. *That is, to exchange for a small bundle of money.* Sneakily, I had sold that scrap under a false name, and, had fairly shared out the cash return into the eager *hands-on* participants. I later, was then expected to wear those charges, like a good criminal should. *And do the time for doing the crime like any old fashioned convict was supposed to back in those days of old.*

The old saying back then, *was that the one who poked his head up was the*; 'Bunny,' and it is fair to say, it was not the first time I had put my head up. That large set-back, *of* course, was the real risk one took when taking and selling other peoples property. *I'd known only too well the cost of any stupid and over thoughtless mistake on my part.* In my particular case, the person or persons who had dealt with the buyer, 'or a fence,' was often the only one picked up by the police after a crime had been committed.

Such persons usually took the knock, unless of course he or she had cowardly informed upon that usual array of sad suspects. *And then,* all tumbled down like a house of flimsy playing cards.

As usual, I was to face the music alone, and I had fully accepted my loss, *and my many mistakes,* as just another professional type hazard. I mean, being as the ball bounces? *what else could I bloody well do.*

The detectives of course had that easy job of arresting me, and the Judges of the District Court had the easier job of sentencing me into prison. So being a firm warning to all other offenders who might think that property crime paid enormous dividends, let it be said; *In for a penny, in for a pounding.*

It was a simple equation of past social mathematics, *to all prisoners,* and as the media often wrote: *'If you can't do the time then don't do the crime.'* In reply to this inane stupid quotation, the younger thieves would suggest quite cheekily. *'Crime might not pay, but the hours are good.'* While the cunning old lags would simply say;

'Humanity is a two way street, old mate', I'll see you around the ridges. '

@ 2 Division, Boggo Road

Many criminals may have been unfairly flippant, *and quite rude to their major critics,* but I well knew of such happy criminals, as quite caring but extremely troubled human beings, and as the long years passed by, I often saw the deep regret in their eyes as they had watched their family leave after a final visit. I knew of them as a *feeling* type of people, and I had also observed many of them wipe away a tear when their old partners had found someone new, *or, their mum or pop had passed away.* These were also the better types of men whom I had shared my wayward life with, in a time when Queensland enforcement authorities felt that they held all the cards. While of course the average prisoner considered that being with your mates was better than being at home alone watching telly. Like most crims, *they'd loved music,* and some had even written beautiful songs, and possibly it was music and a deep felt poetry that quietly belied the harsh label that society had placed upon them. Most in fact were simple property thieves at large, and over the following years, he or she had usually hurt no one but himself, *or herself,* in the roundabout confusion of their disordered lives. More often than not, they had suffered more than those who had taken someone's life, in a crazed moment of loss, or passion.

Because I was the first *self taught* penologist cum Criminologist in the world, *do see my LinkedIn Profile,* I was the first to realise that 'Domestic Violence was seen as the major cause of juvenile offending, I wrote a song, *never published,* that I sang to prisoners while strumming a guitar.

I Truly Do.

I love you, my darling wife.
I really, truly do,
But I cannot find the words...
To say that I love you..
I don't want to hurt you..
I guess its just my way..
Oh, true God Almighty,
Help me find some words to say.

I love you my darling wife..
I really truly do..

But I cannot find the words
To say that I love you.
And even now this morning..
At the breakfast table
I want to say I'm sorry...
But I guess, that I'm not able.

I love you my darling wife,
I really truly do..
But, I cannot find the words,
to say that I ...love you........

I later trained a seventeen year old youth, with a perfect falsetto voice, *over in 2 Division Boggo Road,* to take up the female part of the melody, and come in with;

I love you, my darling man..
I really truly do..

Then to join in a duo, which often caused hardened criminals to shed a bright tear that had dripped on their old and worn denim coats.

' Sing it again Flex.'
'*No way,* you'll fucking well neck yourself. .'

Prisons are full of anguished people that truly hurt, when alone in a cell.

On the other hand, the violent men, *who had deliberately hurt others,* had lived quietly and selectively alone, as if they'd suffered some very rare disease. *Yes,* killers, who may have avoided their punishments by some deceit, or, had intelligently paid others to do their dirty work. Only to have gone upon their merry way without any care in the world. *Unless of course a fate decreed that they were to suffer a belated natural retribution, or an unexpected misfortune on their off day, when a close family member was killed.* Or, their beloved spouse chose a brand new lover to escape the uncertainty of living with a sick and very paranoid partner. Especially the lazy man who obviously could only provide shelter by signing some official agreement with an ignorant, rude, *haughty,* as well as unconcerned clerk in that Department of State Government Public Housing. Whatever the real case, the then natural weakness of man was to take from strangers, what was not his. *Hopefully without his ever being caught,* or to try to make other people submit to much higher prices for much higher profit margins. *That is, for cheap tainted goods that had no real value to them at all in the first place. Habits die hard.*

The more that a culprit was punished, *by the prison system,* the more cunning he had appeared to become, and so the *age old recipe for recidivism* soon becomes clear to us all. In fact, they learned in time, that by their paying a small pittance to the local beginner's, *to do all the dirty work,* had in turn protected them, which was something that most Queensland criminals, and police workers, eventually graduated to.

Later on, the lazy emergence of the housebreaking practices, *as a profession,* along with fraud, or even serious shoplifting offenses and drugs, were to be the main *'crimes of the future.'*

It too would be a time in the future, when *over night property security* became impenetrable in small shop front businesses, *or in modern Supermarkets,* and so drug manufacturing, along with random break in's and armed robberies, were the big money makers. In 1970 the teenagers and the many weekend criminals seriously stuffed it up for a B&E man trying to make a non violent living, and so, prison became a meeting place for the future drug trade. *A trade that came like a monsoon, and never left.* I personally envisioned the day when our stealing cars for ransom, would be excessively popular, especially when the many competing insurance companies went broke, *or into an involuntary receivership.*

I for one had envisioned advertisement sites, so as to reclaim the property, *as well as how personal animals,* would be serious moneymaking schemes under a future guise of a; *Private Detection,* or a *'dirty'* Security group, that profited legally from other people's losses. But in reality, it would be nothing more than a dirty updated protection racket for those many brand new bullies and old time users that were much too *scared*, or too lazy, to take anymore risks.

The early drug trade, *to me*, was obviously the most treacherous trade of all, and so it was I had attempted to be quite original when attempting to make a living out of selling other peoples private property.

Thieves, thieves everywhere, in your house and in your hair.' Was one line of a very stupid rhyme I had at one time written in the old 2 Division. It was a type of poem that I often repeated, so as to keep myself amused. In fact, I believed at the time, that every single person in the world had surely taken clear advantage of someone else. *Whom they did not know at all.*

Young girls do it every day to a new girl at school.

The best cheat, and liar around, *of course,* were the local journalists who, *when amalgamating with a foul Duty solicitor,* had maliciously invented legal plagiarism in the state of Queensland.

So it was, that because I did not have even a bent penny to flip in the air, stolen property, *it self,* had no real value for me at all. It was clear that such personal property never would, *until I had learned to live in my own home with all the necessities of life.* Necessities, so as to feed clothe and educate my own children in that special time when I too had something truly precious to lose.

Strangely enough, it was my children that had eventually taught me that stealing was just a filthy bad habit, *which,* I had needed to put aside if I was to stay with them in our warm home. *Rather than in a cold, bare, and solitary cell.*

Prison too, *is a very bad habit,* and sadly, it is a necessity for some who cannot cope with the many stresses of their mostly lonesome life.

But, as for the Prison remand yard, it was quite an expanse of concrete that was compared to some railway platform, *where a train never arrives,* although, if I could describe it to any interested citizen, I may liken it to *them* sitting in a doctor's surgery on concrete benches, uncomfortably, and patiently waiting for the better-dressed type citizen, *or more influential,* to be attended to first. That is, as they try to blank out the monotony and desolation. *'Or so as to envy those that can pay the piper and hope for a few measly crumbs.'* To be truthful, I for one did not do a hard time, and it was the ordinary husbands, and sons, who walked back and forth who did it seriously hard in a darker time warp of deep morbid depression. They'd often sought out any conversation they could from another person, so as to try to pass the time, and that was, for them, *the real punishment.* These lost men, and young teenagers had suffered a great deal more than all of the sentenced prisoners had ever done, *and still do,* in a maximum-security division. Their greater loss was to be etched very deeply upon their faces in an aggravated stress, and belated regret.

'Are you sorry now that you did not listen?' I imagined their family saying to them in the cramped visiting complex. An area where other knowing visitors and or warders, had looked at the bowed head of a broken man.

As one, such non prison conditioned men and boys had all pined deeply for their family, *and some wept quite openly,* which of course marked them as an easy touch for the prison predators. In turn, they too would quickly find out, that if you could be conned, you could be used for anything that was then so considered a valuable asset, or some needed item, behind prison walls. Yes! *'Love,'* is an asset. *Not a right.*

It always got a lot easier after the third, or fourth time, and if you had the right; *withdrawn and arrogant attitude,* you simply attempted to forget your family, *and or your friends,* and to try to; *accept what it was you could not change.* Or ever hope to change by yourself. *Or again,* without any assistance of others that truly cared enough to try and make it a better world for a loser, such as he. *'Or she.'*

I later explained to curious students *(20 years later)* that up until I had been married, I was an active criminal for a total of two years, *and a prisoner for seventeen years,* which is a way of saying, that criminals are outside the walls, *'and the prisoners are inside them.'* Why I, *or they,* would bother to swap a comfort zone of burgers beer soft drinks, *sweet girls lounge-chair cars motorbikes or watching football,* in exchange for a cold dark cell, had in turn suggested we were either crazy, *or there was something seriously wrong in our private world.* I mean, the remand yard had no television set, and no library, as well as a bare starch diet. There were no weekend visits, or concert groups that put on exceptionally good shows that they had presented for the sentenced prisoners. *Men smelled badly.* They were angry, depressed, as well as sexually ill, and were as hungry as bed bugs looking for blood. The 'day visits,' *during the mid week,* were of a shorter duration, *than given to the sentenced prisoners* and the consistent boredom, and lack of amenities, were a sick punishment in itself.

So, to trade a family life for that, simply had to be quite questionable, as far as policy advisers were concerned. In fact, Policy Advisers are paid 40 million dollars a year, in my State, and that is why they steal good ideas from common criminals.

To mix up the pot in some, *continuous feeling of fear,* and uncertainty, was a full measure of just how our realization, *that,* somewhere along the line we had clearly underestimated a precariousness of our own chances of our ever remaining untouched by all that we had done. *With the many chances that life had already given to us.*

Even the champions, know they cannot always win every single race they enter, so, I somehow determined that none of us valued our lives, *or, our families.*

Those inmates were of course, in prison for social punishment, and certainly not placed there just to be entertained. *Even though some of them may have been genuinely innocent of their original offence.*

I personally felt, I had always been a fairly *easy going and humanistic* type of everyday person, or, was seen as being genuinely compassionate towards others. *Even if I was drunk or disorderly and foolishly liked to impress teenage girls.* But like the rest of the world, I was often manipulative with all persons that I did not know, *or,* did not like. Nor did I wish to become deeply involved in serious, or personal matters, that were not considered my immediate concern. *Or, of any real value to me.* In hindsight I may have made a top of the shelf user, *or Sabo's** with a desk and Biro at hand. That is, had I stuck to my guns and pursued a lazy life as some government worker, when finally leaving school.* (*Self advancement before others.*)

Today, I know exactly why I was a criminal, for a few years of my life, and a lost prisoner in the system of male domination, *for almost twenty*, but I was a virtually a lonely child when I actually began to steal. Only to develop into a very serious man when I found a set of values that eventually allowed me to see that there was a better and more permanent way to get what I wanted. *That is, in the time I had left in the free world.*

But in the year 1969, it all lay, *far far,* ahead of me.

CHAPTER 3

A LACK OF EMPATHY

The fact that I did care, and feel sorry for most ordinary men in jail, could not at all change their own day to day situation, and only those that had shown me any degree of forcefulness, or institution type courage, were at all worth knowing. *This was not my rule, but the rule of survival among men who had long needed friends that would do exactly what they said they would do.*

Hard men were always needed for any future benefits, *or a service,* they may provide for a reasonable fee, *when over in the main prison proper.* That is, much later on when we were all crammed three to a cell in the many dilapidated cell blocks over in old one division. I do feel that my own selfish attitude, obviously stemmed from the fact that the ignorant prison departments, *in Australia,* gave nothing at all for free, and depriving us of those barest of necessities, *even under pants,* had allowed them to spend their Government grants in other areas. *Areas that were most suited to them alone.*

During that time, I saw that one man of a much higher education, *and seemingly well into his fifties,* was more an outcast than the rest, and when one loud foolish warder proclaimed the prisoner had sex with his own daughter; the poor man instantly became a pariah. It was alleged, that the man had confessed to the arresting detectives, that his daughters were; *tighter than a fishes arse,* and that his stupid wife was like a oversized sloppy bowl of runny custard. *It turned out he never said those words at all, but when Queensland detectives told stories, they certainly told; 'Whoppers.'*

I was a little skeptical that the man ever said such things, but he stayed to himself and asked nothing of anybody at all. So it was I did not bother to speak to him, and in time I simply forgot him, *although,* I felt that normal reference of a mongrel and '*Rock Spider,* or *'that Kid Fucker,'* was quite unreasonable. Mostly because, it was at that time, a totally unsubstantiated allegation by some old selfish angry wife. But of course, those rules were the rules, and I too had avoided an accused child sex offender, *like the rest did,* and I ignorantly gave him nothing but his main rations when I was handing them out to men passing the open doorway of the secluded kitchenette.

His shaking hands and a polite *'thank you'* were quite pitiful, and I thought later, in hindsight, that he could easily have been any true loving father placed in an unfair circumstance. *And a good father at that.*

As it was, one morning he had climbed upon the second story landing railing, and he dove headfirst into that concrete yard. That act alone had completely changed my personal views of all other men. *And of course my method of judging any fellow prisoner, whom I did not know.*

I was even more reserved when a belated inquest in the Coroners court *later that year,* determined that the sad lonely man was innocent. The truth was revealed, *it seems,* was when his two sweet daughters' gave sworn evidence which had completely exonerated the poor man. It was in fact a terrible death, and it had left some prison hardened warders in a state of shock. Although one older protected lifer named Tom Venables, had caused a callous type of indecent humor, *or sniggering,* when he had tried to take the dead mans tobacco. An angry warder quickly ordered him away and told him to put the tobacco back beside the dead body, *while,* one prisoner whom I had liked at first sight, *and who had been extradited from Sydney,* had shaken his head in utter disgust.

'You'd think that the fucking old cunt would learn after two life laggings.' said Alan Douglas, as he'd sneered at that old prison thief being ordered away from that bloody dead form on the smooth concrete. What, was more amazing, was that the sad old lifer had morbidly defended his action by spitting rudely upon the bloodied section of concrete.

'Well, he won't need it where he is bloody well going.' he said to us, somewhat indignantly, *while leaning on his carved old teak grained hickory walking stick,* and quivering at the insults.

It had been a terrible scene, and a few prisoners looked on as if they were spectators viewing a car crash at some blind and clearly unmarked intersection. One younger man started crying in shock at the graphic scene, and so another prisoner had consoled him with a pat on the shoulder and led him away to share a cigarette. One more death of thousands was to be recorded that day in the medical journals of the old Boggo Road Prison. *And was quickly forgotten by most prisoners within hours.*

If, 'Life,' was worth anything at all, it was only in the lesson that was learned; although, *the tightly knotted bed sheet* still appeared to be that more better option that was available to the many seriously depressed prisoners. Men and boys who took their life in their hands.

There was one prisoner, *a little younger than myself,* whom I had known a few years before in the old 2 Division. He was one truly depressed young man who was on very serious charges

As it was, he sat alone in a small area under the concrete stairway, and so I had made up my mind to approach him in case his moody thoughts were of topping himself with a bed sheet.

Cuddles' was his Gaol nick name, and he had acquired it back in the early sixties when he was then an inmate of the old Westbrook boy's home.

It was also said, that at just twelve years of age he had sexually submitted to the bigger boys, *not out of threat,* but for a need to be loved, and it was said that he would suck you off. *That is, if you gave him a kiss, or a cuddle.*

Personally, I liked Cuddles for his polite manners, *his kindness to others,* and to me he was a face from the old days when I was not all that much older than he was. It was of course a shock for me to hear that he had killed a woman in a park, and I felt that with his record for impulsive criminal activity, he was looking at, *life without the possibility of parole,* for such an insane, or exceptionally futile crime.

I sat cross-legged on the concrete and talked to him about his pending case, and he quietly told me that he had drunkenly bashed a woman with a stick, and broke her neck. *That is, when she had had called him a girlie girl.* Cuddles apologized to me for his crime, but I told him that what was done was done, and that he had to plan his case before the legal aid worker came to take his deposition.

'Why Flex? It's an open and shut case of murder. Mate, there is nothing to say.'

'Cuddles, there is a lot to say mate, and no matter what you told the coppers, you have to try and lessen the blow. *Fair dinkum mate, you could do forty fucking years if you don't put up a fight.*'

I went over the extremely complex case with him, twice more, and then with autosuggestion I told the young man with peroxide streaks in his brown hair, *the story he needed to tell his court appointed solicitor.* That is, when he eventually saw him.

A crime without a motive allows you to be seen as a walking ; 'Time Bomb.'

'*Now remember,* when in the park, you had fallen asleep after drinking all that beer and scotch, and something woke you up. Then, when you had a good look you saw the woman get up and walk away. Now! When you checked for your wallet, it was gone and you knew for sure that the woman had stolen your last bit of money, and so you went over to where her and her friends were drinking, and you confronted her full on.'

Cuddles looked at me curiously as the scene I'd painted for him began to take form in his lost and defeated mind. It was then, that he had nodded slowly.

'Cuddles, you are going to get life, but it won't be willful murder and if you play your cards right, you will be out in less than fifteen years. Trust me mate, even a lawyer or a judge don't like women who steal from a sleeping man.'

'But she did not..!' he stuttered.

'*Cuddles, she stole your fucking wallet, I can see it in my mind.*' I said urgently, and then all of a sudden Cuddles too could also see it in his mind.

Cuddles in fact did get life, *but with a recommendation for mercy.* So, eleven or twelve years later I ran into friends of his that said he was working full time and was happily living a sober and stable life.

Should I have helped him, or let him rot away for the rest of his life? I really do not know. Whatever the answer, I believe in *'Life,'* where others believe in *'God'* but, if they are one, then I feel I am on the right track.

CHAPTER 5

A BUDDING BOOB LAWYER

It was full mid winter in Boggo Road Gaol, and the biting southerly wind blew terribly for weeks on end, but, on the day of my first trial I woke up to the most perfect weather on record. I had eaten my breakfast in a calm mood and I thought deeply of my big plan to defeat that lying police force at their untruthful, and ridiculous game.

Judge Broad had the honour of the bench, *once again,* and I in the past had read somewhere that he too was a Chairman with the big firm of Evans Deakins/ a then ship builders. It did not at all mean that he was a generally dishonest man, but to me he was moonlighting while sentencing poor men and women into a prison for double dipping social security benefits. These were my views, and while no one in Queensland Law was powerful enough to change them, so it was that when I did see that Jurist in court in person, I was quite surprised that he was so young. He was efficiently polite, and in those opening stanzas he had given me a lot of leeway as I'd stumbled ineptly through that confusing selection process of placing the selected jury members.

I only showed some inner spirit when the police officers described my arrest, and then told the court of how I had sold the truckload of units to a firm called Sims Metal. *That I had given a false name and an address on Kessell's Road Mt. Gravatt.*

Those refrigeration units, *they had stated,* had been stolen from an old shed in some paddock, and a truck similar to one that I then owned had been seen leaving piled high with the heavy items.

The prosecution submitted the payment docket as a genuine form of proof of my intended criminal participation's. It was alleged that I had further stated that a Government *'handwriting witness'* would be called, as well as some minor clerk from a Sims metal branch, that would, *he smirked,* positively identify me.

My alleged confession and unsigned record of interview to the detectives, was simply the icing on the cake.'

The Judge had looked a little disinterested and he may possibly have wondered just why in heavens name I had chosen to take up the time of the court. Secretly, I was in no way bored at all and I had crudely begun to question those dishonest detectives who had falsely accused me of making the incriminating statements. Deposition's that I honestly had not made. My confidence rose quickly as I nervously began to manage the case like an ordinary jail debate. That is, by my recalling all the lessons that a prisoner named Des Sanderson had given to me regarding, manner, presentation, and summary.

To the legal brethren, the court process was a means to test their skill, and was little more than a game of wits and showmanship. I too saw it as a game, and although my hearing was quite poor, I used that defect to win leeway in my favour. The goal was to convince honest men that what the opposition table had suggested, was untrue.

And may the best liar win.

The rude detectives of course had showed their customary manners of reclining in the witness box and arrogantly flipping through their official police notebooks, while casually and disinterestedly reading out their reply as if it was a gospel read straight from some religious Testament.

'That is correct, the name on the docket is of a Barry Conan, and for my own information, it is a false name.' This was that man's arrogant answer to my apparent *'disrespectful'* inquiry that rudely dared to question his official and arrogantly unquestionable opinion?

'Thank you officer,' I'd said facetiously. 'Now are you at all aware that I actually lived on Kessels Road Mount Gravatt, and that I actually had the phone on, under the name of; *Barry Conan?'*

Even the bored Judge and prosecutor came alert at last, and the detective's piggish eyes riveted upon me, as if I had just thrown some large poisonous red bellied black snake at him.

'I was not aware of that.'

'Are you aware then, that I was duly threatened with violence by you in the Woolongabba Police station, *and where you sir,* invited other detectives to join you in a back room for a bit of fun?'

'No, that is not true.'

'Do you recall one officer saying to you; "Don't dirty your hand on the cunt. Just verbal him?"'

'That is preposterous.' replied the detective, who was clearly blushing beetroot red, and moving uncomfortably in his seat.

'Do you recall it?'

'No, it's not true.'

I had *not* heard even one reply, *clearly,* but I had simply read their lips and I'd predicted their answers. So it was that the court trial had slowly continued on I'd then picked up fresh new ways to cross-examine witnesses. It was simply just a case of learn as you go, *or try as you buy,* and, regardless of which outcome was to transpire, that rare *'life experience'* was far from wasted.

The Sims metal man, *thankfully,* spoke loud enough for me to hear, and when he had raised his arm up, he educationally pointed to his wrist and told how I had a tattoo of a heart upon my wrist.

When I had the opportunity of a cross-examination, of *the* police witness, I had politely queried him if he was honestly sure of the tattoo. He explained that he saw the tattoo as I had signed the document, and that the bulky jacket I was wearing had accidentally slipped up my arm to reveal it.

'Thank you sir, I do appreciate your irreproachable honesty.' I replied like a sweet gay man sucking up to the organizer of a 1970's Gay Mardi Gra Parade.

The handwriting witness was sworn in, and he had coldly described to that court that he was officially unable to compare what little writing I had reluctantly submitted to the court, to that of the Sims metal Document.

Judge Broad thanked him and raised an eyebrow at me.

'Campbell?'

'Thank you sir.' *'Now sir,'* I said, turning to the aloof and arrogant witness.

'If I may ask you once again, is the handwriting on the docket really mine?'

'I had said that I was unsure.' He replied frostily, and I quickly bent to write my alias signature of Barry Conan, on a spare piece of paper.

'Now sir, if you could determine if this signature is the same as that on the docket, which you have in your hand.......'

Judge Broad had quickly warned me that I could tend to incriminate myself and he had asked to look at that piece of paper of which I had so willingly offered to the court bailiff.

After perusing the foolscap page that I had scribbled on, the good judge told me to write four more copies and had asked the Jury to *notice* how I had, *in a most confident flourish,* quickly signed that self incriminating signature.

'I do remind the witness that any opinion given would be a personal one outside of his laboratory.' The judge had added wisely. That is, as he looked me over in an amused and somewhat quite sympathetic type of contempt.

I also felt that it was Judge Broads way of having two shillings each way on the final outcome.

'Ho hum.'

At last, that cold arrogant handwriting expert was allowed to view my new example of handwriting, and in barely a single fractious moment, he'd had to agree that the scrawled handwriting now positioned before him on the polished witness rail, *was identical,* to the receipt.

'Thank you.' I had said, and the Jury began to warm toward me, even though they were all an older gentlemen type group of males that detested

anyone who broke the rules of the Queensland Police Force.. Except of course for a younger man, who it had appeared to me, was barely out of some local Brisbane high school.

The then star police witness was young Frank, who gave his address as the Westbrook Boys Reformatory, and, he'd smiled wanly at me as if to say he was sorry. His evidence was slightly involuntary, but he told how he had observed me driving my truck loaded up with the stolen property.

'Thank you witness.' said the Judge. Now Campbell, do you wish to cross examine this witness?' said '*His Honor,*' while watching me with cool disinterest.

'I do your Honor, *if I may.*' I had replied hooding my eyes in mock imitation.

In fact, being a deaf man, I was a student of mannerisms, and behaviour. So it was I had observed that Broad had effeminate mannerisms. I had also considered that he may have been '*gay,*' and in 2013 the Police Commissioner Terry Lewis, *(jailed for corruption,*' hinted in a book that Broad was being blackmailed by the Police 'Rat Pack.'

I had noticed the Judge smile a little, and I knew he was well ahead of the pack of court observers. So, I rudely smirked as I turned to young Frank who was sitting nonchalantly in the witness chair.

'Young Frank, do you have a tattoo on your right wrist in the shape of a heart?'

'Yes.' he replied, quite puzzled at such a strange and seemingly ridiculous question.'

'Could you pull back the sleeve of your sweater and hold your arm up?'

Frank complied, and a murmur went up from the many spectators who had come to see those unusual proceedings. Especially where an ordinary layman, *or an Australian nobody*, had defended himself in a trial against a qualified barrister from the Department of Public Prosecutions. DPP. '*Department of Privileged Perks.*'

Franks mother, as well as a few of my friends, including my last one-night stand girl friend, were sitting there alongside my brother Bruce, who was standing back with my other brother Brian. Brian was by then, a well respected Insurance broker, *but I remembered him as the bully of the family whose brains were in his dick.* Both of them seemed quite sceptical of my professed display of innocence, and in turn, I felt it was to be quite expected under the circumstances. *Considering too, I was a light fingered youth that had returned home from Cunnamulla at fifteen years of age with a very bad habit of taking other peoples property.*

Sadly, Brian suffered from alcoholism which was a habit he could not at all control. It was said he went from bad to worse, as the years went slowly by.

Poor Brian, he had everything to live for, good job, beautiful loyal wife, three young children whom he had unnecessarily put through hell with his uncontrollable urge to pour a alcoholic beverage down his throat. Sadly, Brian did not know that my taking or coveting other peoples *'things'* was a bad habit, which of course soon opened the door to other bad habits. *And into the very strange lives of even more troubled human beings than myself.* Unfortunately for Brian he was an older Campbell during our child hood that was given the job of herding and disciplining the younger children who ran wild with our poor sick mother in hospital, and a father who was withdrawn and suffering night sweats bought on by the Second World War.

Brian being the *'Boss Cocky,'* had turned himself into a terrible disciplinarian and I for one had quickly rebelled against his kicking me in the bottom, and clipping me around the ears for the slightest mischief. Still, he was not a thief like me, and even with his habit he carried himself with dignity and a display of self pride. The sad thing was, like all of the senior members of the family they did not see my habit as, *man made,* and honestly felt I had an evil streak that needed prison guards to deal with it. That is, *without kid gloves,* so as to '*straighten me out once and for all.'*

It was sad to see them there looking to give me family support, but even then I knew that Brian and myself had come to the parting of our ways, and the truth of the matter was, that few of my family members ever knew that I had never ever forgiven Brian for being part of the family conspiracy to reveal the nature of my birth, and in turn, my unholy bastardization. Although he was a learned man and seriously respected in the insurance field, I knew just how hard it was to live inside a house with him, along with his most truly terrible and bullying ways.

Bruce of course had loved and admired Brian Campbell for his decent open display of honesty and shining example to other relatives in our extended family, but I myself saw him as a person who had turned his back on the older family home and had helped himself to many unearned opportunities in life.

Like all the older Campbell's, Brian had soon turned his back on his own father, *in his time of need and lonesomeness,* and although I had never known the reason for such disloyal neglect, I judged him, as he had obviously judged me.

Because of our bad habits, and anger toward each other, we would never speak to each other ever again.

As it was, the trial was becoming quite interesting, especially when Frank had revealed the very same tattoo on his wrist that the Sims metal man had described in giving his evidence in chief. What I in fact had done was actually place a crown witness at the scene where the sale of the stolen goods had been committed, *which in turn indirectly involved the Crown,* and that alone had at last bought a reluctant jury back on side.

The prosecutor spun around in his swivel chair and studied my face, *as if viewing me for the first time.* I smiled at him, and I raised my eyebrows in imitation, as if to say; *'Surprise cunt.'* That lawyer turned quickly away as he'd began to search his bonded law books for any miraculous way out of his unforeseeable and unexpected dilemma.

'And fuck you too you fucking powder puff, get yourself a real job you fucking pounce. Try standing on your soft feet in a factory all day, you lousy fucking maggot.' I'd thought quite disrespectfully, as I had waited for the next witness to be called.

The prosecutor and the Judge decided to talk a bit of law and completely ignored me as they covered all bases, and the Prosecutor closed his case.

There were no more Crown witnesses, and then I had given my evidence like an insulted man that had innocently sold a large truckload of stolen property for a friend, while fully believing it to be a scrap copper. A good man who had honestly given the money to him after having extracted the agreed upon sum of fifty dollars for my trouble and assistance.

'Fifty dollars?' That's a lot of money for selling some property to a metal dealer.' suggested the prosecutor.

'Not to you it isn't.' I recalled replying rudely.

In my Evidence in Chief I'd suggested a young Frank had also assisted me, and then for some silly reason, *because of the criminal charges he was then facing of his own accord,* Frank had decided to assist those good policemen in their endeavors to falsely blame me for the actual theft of the units.

That Judge had interrupted me constantly about my taking liberties with the law, as well as trying his patience, but I had managed to give to the court and spectators the prepared story that I had selfishly wanted them to hear.

I further stated in my sworn testimony in a rush of words;

'*Actually,* I recall I had taken young Franks mother in to the interstate bus station on that morning of the alleged theft, and when that friend, or who I thought was a friend turned up with my truck later on that morning, I had agreed to assist him by selling the scrap for him.'

The prosecutor refused to give in, and, in no way would he have an uneducated piece of criminal scum dare attempt to make fools of his highly respected police officers, *or,* the presentation of his previously one sided most winnable prosecution case.

'*Campbell,* I put to you that when you returned from the bus station on the morning of the break in, you redressed and then went to the shed in question, and therein you had stolen a large quantity of refrigeration units?'

'That is untrue.' I replied nonchalantly, much as the detectives had replied to my previous cross-examination.

'I further put to you that a time span between that bus station and selling the metal was supposedly over a two hour period?'

'I beg your pardon.'

The good man's eyes flashed, and he was forced to repeat the question, and when he did I had quietly explained that I had had breakfast after speaking to my trusted friend who was late for work, and then allegedly drove the loaded truck to the Sims Metal firm.

'You drove to Sims metal, which was, I presume, roughly five or six kilometers from your work friends place of residence? *Now!* Did it take you more than two hours to have breakfast or talk to your so called friend, whom you say was late for work, and then allegedly drive those five or six kilometers?'

'I have a very slow truck.'

'A slow truck; How slow is slow?'

'*Slow enough.*' I replied just as coldly and as arrogantly as I could, as he glared at me in a play acting show of hostility.

Personally, the prosecutor did not give sixpence for how I acted and he was simply putting on a staged show for the benefit of all people that somehow thought that legal people were our leading community representatives. They were *supposedly* quality gentlemen that looked with distaste at blue collar workers, yet I knew they were men who had their pick of females that were willing to do anything sexual at all, so as to have charges of a criminal nature dropped against them; *Possibly some males as well.*

Being a person with a hearing defect was seriously hard enough for anyone, but on top of that, my being a criminal with a hearing loss and being cross examined in front of an audience, was not at all an enviable situation to be in.

I felt that a lesser-experienced or less determined person would have thrown in the towel by then, rather that go through such a degree of humiliation, but I was not that run of the mill person that other men could throw loaded barbs at, contemptuously, *and or,* disrespectfully. In fact I was a 'Campbell' and one thing our lot never did, was to give up without a real ding dong fight.

Judge Broad decided to call a halt to proceedings, and he'd demanded that the police present the old truck to the court fully laden so as to give the jurors a clear view of the situation at hand.'

'Ah! Your Honor, the units have been scrapped,' said the concerned prosecutor, as one of the perjured detectives had scurried forward to whisper urgently into his waxed up ear canal.

'What?' the Judge frowned while leaning back in his chair.

What then, I ask, *are we doing here?*' he added

I only wished that the scribe would have kept writing, but obviously he had known just what to write in shorthand, *and what not to write,* as these lofty gentlemen discussed my case without my input.

The discussion went on without the Jury present, *seeing as I did not offer any objection,* and so I simply took the time to grin at my friends who were out on that old Queenslander style verandah, which was the only place where they were able to view the proceedings, or the expected conviction of a Queensland criminal.

At last they called a halt for the day, and the truck was ordered from the water police yard from where it had been stripped of battery, radiator, and those other usable parts. *Not the police surely?* Eventually the police then had to pay for a transport carrier to bring it to the court, and at days end I tiredly went back to Boggo Road to review my wicked day's handiwork.

Back at the prison I changed into the remand clothing and I waited in the holding pen to be transferred back to my cell.

'How did you go Flex?' asked one prisoner, while giving me a cold meal of stew, gravy, and mashed potato.

'Mate, I am so far up their bums they are starting to think they are having kittens with sharp claws.'

'I'll believe it when I see it old mate.'

'Watch and fucking-well believe.' I had grinned, and that night I had hardly slept a wink with the excitement and prospect of going home.

'*Home,*' I thought, '*where the fuck is home now?*'

The following morning, I was once more legally sworn in and then we all traipsed down into the car park to see that old truck looking much the worse for wear, and obviously not worth the six hundred dollars I had paid for it. *In today's money it was possibly worth $3000.* I had stood near that Judge without handcuffs on my wrists, and he had said some mumbled indistinguishable words to me, that I could not hear, but which sounded as if; '*The penalty was not worth the time and effort of the court.*'

I realize now that the good Judge, was in fact, *judging by his manner and action,* advising me to seek a dismissal from him, but unfortunately I was much too inexperienced to see or to fully understand exactly what he was wordlessly suggesting, or exactly what he was then hinting at. I of course had said nothing, and while the good Jury looked over the truck, I myself had wondered just how it had ever made it to the metal merchants, let alone how it had supposedly taken two damned hours to get there.

I later called a witness named Wally Semyraha to explain my unexpected win at the local Rocklea trotting track. *That is, on that Saturday prior to my arrest,* and strangely enough, the younger man was giving truthful evidence and could not be shaken one bit by the angry and disgusted prosecutor.

Another younger man, named Alan Kelly, told of my previous meeting with my associate, *Tom,* who he then confirmed had asked to borrow my work truck that evening prior to the offense. Alan later explained under cross-examination that he was much too busy ogling schoolgirls on the railway platform to notice the full content of the conversation. *Possibly, so as to avoid any later malicious charge of willful perjury'*

The prosecution declined to give a summary, *due to ethical reasons,* and I had rudely smiled as contemptuously as I could, while I thought the rudest of slurs as he threw me one more look of disdain at my own lack of ethics.

*'Ethics you cunt, you go and sit on your arse all day and then go onto a male brothel to get fingered, and then you dare to decline to have a say because of ethics? You fucking lazy twit '*I'd thought as I had stared disrespectfully back in return.

I could not have told him, *even if I had wanted to,* that if the police had played fair and honestly, *or had they had allowed me bail,* I would possibly have been long sentenced on an agreed guilty plea, while serving my three or four years in the old 2 division of Boggo Road.

I smiled at him graciously, and then I explained to the Jury that I had sold the metal in good faith. Furthermore, that I had used that false name of *Conan,* because of a family reason, and that I was as innocent as the day was long. *This was years before Conan the Barbarian was invented, and I would be called worse than a barbarian by the time the courts had finished with me.*

The Jurymen had all watched me quite impassively, and I had further noticed that the older men looked away disinterested while I'd somehow felt they were those older time citizens of a foregone era who had great respect for the poor old hard working police officers. Indeed the upstanding stalwart police detectives that they suggested did not rape young girls in watch houses, beat up teenagers in a gang bashing in police stations, or take bribes from SP Bookmakers and Brisbane Brothels?

Possibly, those naïve Jurymen in turn saw me as a wastrel, but so were the haughty overpaid legal eagles and their bullying police officers. Users who had always felt that the Brisbane courts and Lennon's Plaza hotel was their own private domain to do just as they *'damn well'* pleased. Such men were fleecing every racket that could be fleeced, and skeptical observers would call it *'Pots and Kettles'* if I were to ever say anything publicly of their day to day shenanigans. Police did not call it; *'corruption or stealing;* they referred to it as skimming a little cream from the top of the cake.

In his summary, Judge Broad appeared fair and straight to the point, as if he'd sensed that I might well have only been the sales man and not the perpetrator. *To be truthful,* he was not all that far wrong.

What discredited the Judiciary, of that era, was that they accepted an unsigned statement as positive proof that a suspect was guilty. What the court did not realise, was that they were hypocrites for saying that those; 'arraigned suspects' had a 'right to silence' when being questioned by police, but in the court could not accept that an unsigned statement, or police notebook, was proof that they were not agreeable to being questioned.

The twelve-man Jury filed out to consider a verdict, *according to the evidence,* and, I hopefully thought, *the clarity of it.* I'd watched the Judge thoughtfully gather up his legal books and head for his chambers, while I had coldly considered him the sort of person who had always believed that only two types of people really counted in a modern society. They, of course, were those people of Australia who'd possessed *'Old money.'* and the persons who wielded enforced authority under a *'Book of Laws'* passed down from his British peers.

It seemed to me that Judge Broad, *and those good legal people who were much similar to him,* had long believed that the rest of the world was to be divided up between those two types of people whom I facetiously describe. Such as, those snobbish social parasites that were forever seeking to gain giant monopolies on a wide array of property holdings. Land holdings that uneducated stupid people like me could only dare hope to dream of. *Including access to old peoples secret trust accounts, which is something I would not do anyway.*

To the pompous legal fraternity the working people were of no consequence, and had meant nothing to them, for they were simply there to pay their taxes so that *they,* the self promoting legal fraternity, could go on doing exactly what they had been doing for a thousand years of more.

Judge Broad, I felt, *without being too critical,* considered himself as belonging to the former farsighted eagles who did exactly what they had needed to do to; *'feather their own nest by double dipping as a Chairmen' of Evans Deakin Shipbuilders,* while, using their sharp talon like words to shred the opposite members of the bar.

I'd felt that he, Judge Broad, could easily have afforded to be charitable, or even a little magnanimous to the common fool, *or,* the occasional stupid felon that dared to plead not guilty and contest their rule of law. But, deep down I felt his charitable philanthropic alms giving was to make himself feel so much more superior, and in my own opinion, he may truly have felt that the fact that he as a learned man, *which he appeared to be,* was never ever wrong.

The prison warder, who was escorting me on that day, was named Jack, and it had then seemed that I was going to be in Jacks experienced care until I was either convicted or released back onto the streets. We, *Jack and I,* had been getting on quite well together, and he had given me a wink as if to say that I had put up a very good fight *under those uneven circumstances.*

Jack the prison warder, truly good man that he was, had also allowed me to mix with my closest friends and I spoke to my brothers while I had that needed cigarette to settle my nerves, knowing full well that the callous and insensitive prosecution would seek seven years, were I to be convicted

My two older brothers were seriously unsure of my guilt or innocence but I had found later that my brother Brian had carelessly spoken to the detectives and mentioned that if it were a case of persecution, *or of harass-ment,* then further legal proceedings would soon occur.

If I could have spoken to Brian outside of the court precincts and warned him, *I would have,* because it was obvious to me that a beaten police force would have no other choice but to forge ahead strenuously, *and even illegally,* with all other related false pretenses charges. Or in turn be sued for damages in the civil court. *'Never tell the pig that that he is pork chops, or he will squeal on you.'*

My senior brother Brian obviously did not know that it's all a big game in the emotionally insensitive, or obtuse legal world, and that I was only simply trying to kick a penalty field goal in a reserve grade competition.

Sadly, my older brother Brian and I would never ever speak to each other ever again, for he could only see my faults, *and not his own,* which I believe only his good and loyal wife and children would or could give a clearer and more positive description of, *especially after living with a man suf-fering alcoholism.* Although, *that aside,* he tried to be a good father and never lost sight of the need to provide for his long suffering young family. I may add; Brian Campbell died a millionaire, so at least his young ones that had long despised him, got to follow their dreams. Brian's dream was to have more money than any one else in the family, but it all came too late when he won the Lotto six months before he died from prostate cancer.

Being who, and what I was, I was unable to see that Brian was present at those legal proceeding genuinely looking for a way to assist me, or to forgive me for not living up the expectations of the good woman who had raised us. In hindsight, I would one day regret my lack of foresight and morals, but more than that, I would regret that he went to his grave without us ever settling our differences.

It took hours, but the Jury eventually came back with the teenager as the elected Foreman, and of course with the sad older men following while all were looking on a little shamefaced under the dark stern stares of the tall prosecutor. *Women at that time were not considered intelligent enough to serve on a jury in 1969, or to give an unbiased verdict.*

Possibly the legal eagles had long considered that females were inadequate in a courtroom because they had no balls, not knowing of course that any woman ever born had more balls than they did. I in turn would agree with the good women of Queensland and question the supposition that a woman's place was in the kitchen. Strangely, I believe, that if any man or woman of substance has never protested against an insensitive law, *at least once in their life,* they really do not have any gumption, or *'balls.'*

Eventually, the jurymen had given the District court the agreed verdict, *with some degree of reluctance;* that is, except the teenager whom it appeared had looked quite confident and pleased after being selected as the duty foreman by those sad old gutless men who were obviously intimidated by the legal eagles.

'Not guilty.' Said that brave young man who was obviously a part of the new breed of citizen in Queensland who was in a full readiness for the day when Police corruption would be exposed in the Sunshine State. Or, as many of those weak cowardly media reporters eventually suggested on

their bandwagon, in later years, the *Moon Light State*, or the *Porn State* of Australia down under;

A Personal View

'It is my view, that such inadequate pen pushers once stated such utter nonsense in a belated defense of their untruthful and plagiarist type of profession. People that, still rudely sell or 'pimp' genitalia in their personal columns.' Even worse, these gutter scribes can write books of criminals of lower class 'Families of Crime,' that tend to promote the idea that people who break the law are 'Men of Honor' or individuals to be envied. The truth is, criminals are simply the poorly educated ignoramuses that seldom know a vagina from an anus. In other words, even if they make a lot of money, they eventually die as a vagrant.

While their children have drug or morality problems, as well as bad habits.

The real heroes are people that make our world a better place to live in, set records and invent items, and or medical cures, that save lives. Why these editors or scribblers want to glorify a man with no ears, tattoo's and lacking humanity, is far beyond my full understanding of society. If that is cruel 'criticism,' it is well deserved, for the men I have seen suffer in a prison named Boggo Road Gaol, certainly deserve a much better under-standing of their situation in life. Personally, I would rather read a book of a 'Smith Family' kid who got through university and made a difference in the world;' namely a kid like my youngest son; Josh.

I had maliciously smiled at the somewhat expected courtroom verdict, and, the police ran for the prosecution to push for that minor outstanding charge of *False Pretenses*. The cheers of my friends, and of the legal people in dark gowns who had come to view a very rare verdict by a felon, *who had dared to defend himself,* had drowned out the Judge for a moment as he loudly called for order. Judge Broad being a sore loser, had commented that; *a felon, who defends himself, has a fool for a client. A quote invented over a hundred years before that time in 1969.*

I was quite unconcerned by the learned man's snooty comment and I had truly believed that much like the common prostitute, he and his cronies had sold their time for more than it was worth. Also, that when all is said and done, I'd felt I would rather be a fool than some filthy legal *'whore.'*

If, Judge Broad had known exactly what I was thinking of him, he would most certainly have run to the closest bathroom to brush his perfect teeth with a harsh soap, and with a follow up cleansing of cattle trough disinfectant, or phenol, so as to get rid of the bad taste of semen.

'Board Chairman, my arse!' I thought with utter contempt.

'In the matter of the belated charge of False Pretenses, Mr. Prosecutor?' said that lofty effeminate judge with his bright eyes looking me over, *a little more seriously than they had before,* and with not as much leeway or any charitable benevolence, as he had so foolishly done previously.

'*Ah!* Yes your Honor, I would like to bring to your notice this related case of a False Pretenses.' replied the very eager and revengeful prosecutor. A spoiled brat who seemed to be quite stunned by it all.

I was officially charged with false pretenses, and I begged for self-bail, seeing as my wallet was being held as evidence by the police. As it stood, I could not reasonably have any ready funds to pay the court bail. Funds that a court usually demanded as an surety to cover the cost of; hunting the perpetrator. *That is, should he dare to abscond to another State!*

The good Judge then considered my life of theft, car stealing, and break-ins. He'd unfairly required a financial surety of bond; *Unfair in the sense that he knew the case was quite shaky.* Also, that the police, *under any honest government,* could be by rights joining me in the Boggo Road. Remand yard on a charge of willful perjury. *With a maximum sentence of 14 yrs H.L.*

I'd known then, that without a house or land portfolio, I would be kept in prison indefinitely, and, although I disagreed, *to no avail,* I was contemptuously remanded into custody pending a surety or financial cash bond. They could, *under our still present Queensland law,* keep standing the matter over for up to twelve months or more. Had I of screamed foul their bully boys with size twelve boots, working out at the Gaol, would soon have sorted me out. But of course, I being a docile easy going sort of fellow with a great sense of humor, I would soon find ways to amuse myself in one of the oldest prisons in the State of Queensland.

My few friends *of course* had nothing at all, and, my brother Brian turned away from my most respectful undeserving request. Bruce too denied me that chance to be free so that I could urgently salvage what I could of my personal items, *or stolen property*. In a way, it was a personal property I'd needed to keep some semblance of self-sufficiency, so that I would not need to replenish it by a foolishly planned break and enter. *Whenever I was released on my first night out.*

Brian Campbell, I felt, had never been a real brother to me, seeing as he was really my uncle. In reality, I actually saw him as just some old family spectator from my early childhood that liked to pose as an honest man. My loyal, *fitter and turner brother,* Bruce, observed his brother Brian, as educated, and well read, while I saw him as a snob, a social drinker, and a person of little substance or loyalty. In fact I saw him as a self absorbed and unconcerned person that never had a cause in his life. Further, had our Clan been raised in Scotland, I felt he would have swapped sides to polish the garters of the English Lords. But *then*, I was taking orders from the uniformed Lords of Boggo Road Gaol, *which did not say much for my own view of the Black Watch.*

As mentioned, I condemned Brian for not seeing life as clearly as all men from poorer beginnings, when I myself could not see that real; *'Life,'* in turn, *has impossible repercussions for all of us,* that will not take serious heed of what we do, *and what we say.* With, or without the help of my family, to gain my freedom, I still would have needed a job and accommodation, which they could not, or would not, provide. In my view of things, helping oneself was the only real alternative that I could see, and my stealing cars and objects appeared the only possible alternative for someone left on a city street corner at four O'clock in the afternoon. *Especially, in the middle of winter.*

An overcrowded, Salvation Army Hostel, was of course a possibility for *some* men, but a *'prisoner'* would be scoffed at by his peers. That is, were he to ask for, or accept assistance from such an organization that charitably assisted the lost, the beaten, and the forlorn Freedom for me to re-offend, *was not to be,* and so I was then put back on the Black Maria for that lonely and familiar journey back to those ancient red brick walls of old Boggo Road Gaol. *As well as the new white monstrosity they referred to as; the H Wing Remand Section.*

CHAPTER 6

THE LAW FIGHTS BACK

Although I was a little disheartened by it all, I had soon perked up a bit when finding that Deputy Super, Jack 'Bumper' Farrell, was now to be, *officially,* the new acting superintendent, of Boggo Road Prison.

Superintendent Jack Farrell had been the Boss of Numinbah state Prison farm when I was a young man of nineteen, *and,* of whom I held in the highest esteem for his good open and humane management of convicted persons.

'You little fucking beauty,' I said when the momentous news had reached me. I had quickly forgotten all of my own silly worries so as to join in the quickly spreading gossip in our rejoicing. *Of the new historical political appointment.*

No greater or fairer person, *or should I say, decent official,* was ever a major part of that mismanaged prison administration, and although Jack was not a pushover, Jack Farrell had always demanded a fairer, and of course decent treatment for all. He'd bravely closed down those horrific punishment cells that were underneath the earth, and then he had arranged the transfer of all emotionally troubled or insane lock down prisoners. *Out to the State asylum.*

Jack was not an easy man to contact in the hustle and bustle of his days, but I somehow managed to run into him when I was returning from sick call to see the visiting doctor. Almost, four days after requiring medical attention.

'Good day Mr. Farrell, how are you going?' I asked with a cheeky self serving wide grin.

'All right young Larry; I hear you're a bit of a Perry Mason now?'

'Getting there, and by the way boss, what chance have we got of starting up a library room over in the remand section? Fair dinkum Boss there is nothing to read at all in the remand yard, that is, except that old Woman's Weekly advertising ladies underclothes?'

His eyes closed for a moment, as if attempting to work out my angle, if any, and then he'd decided to give me a few passes to set up an empty cell and to hopefully fill it up with books that were long disused, *and or,* abused by the mainstream prisoners.

As mentioned, the Remand section was not any concern for the *'in city'* prison administration, being as the reason was that we were *police prisoners* who were in turn then supposed to look after our day to day needs. They, *the police*, of course gave the jail warders a legal right to discipline us and feed us non working' rations. There were no normal prison rations, *such as fresh boiled eggs, cheese, spreads, toothbrushes, toothpaste or civilian soap.*

That was Jack's day to day lifestyle; *Stop listen think,* then give out a quick decision and just as quickly run before some other beggar asked the impossible. Jack had his few problems, and I had mine, but I rubbed my hands in glee as I set about planning my next move. My on the spot request had been quite genuinely intended, but I had too also needed to get access to both the prison libraries, 1&2, so as to search for any or all of those Legal type of books dealing with Criminal False Pretenses. Or in legal literary term; *Fraud and Misappropriation.*

I had gotten my precious pass, *and,* along with a few wide eyed helpers I set off to bargain and barter with the librarian, *who,* was as charitable as a lowland Scotsman, and was a man who did not like change to take place in his secret domain. I somehow charmed and coerced him into allowing us to fill up a few old wooden pallets with a great variety of books, while at the same time I'd searched for a special rare legal writing so as to assist in my somewhat fledgling, *but,* quite interesting legal career.

The only book on law was a small tattered comedy of errors that had apparently been written a long time before I was actually born, and so I had claimed it on the small hope, *or unrealistic premise,* that it could help to give me some insight into the offense of false pretenses.

'How to Win a Trial' was the old English version of a sick raucous comedy loaded with callous English quips that a learned historical type of gentlemen attempted to humor their bewigged fraternity with. Mostly to show *'old time felons'* how to be the hopeless ignorant fools that they were then facetiously portrayed in an *'olde English'* culture.

In my very first reading of that seriously defamatory work, I had thrown it onto my rickety old desk in my cell, while considering it a completely useless writing. For I contemptuously felt that it leaned a little toward snobbery. *As well as a rude literary work of humiliating arrogance toward the dominated underclass.*

Two days later I was again called to the special interview room, where I was confronted by two well fed Inala Branch police detectives, who'd wanted to question me on numerous other criminal matters committed by various other offenders from Coopers Plains. *Offenders whom I casually knew as house thieves, and losers who had only got a rare win in a random chook raffle.*

'What other fucking matters?' I had sneered with great contempt at their show of pretended gentlemen like self importance, and *'officialdom.'*

'That young Frank has told us that you had committed a number of break and enters in his company, and also, that you destroyed a large two way radio by hiding it in long grass near his home.'

'What is this shit? you fucking scum bags! *Mate,* I do my own jobs, not run around with all the silly fucking kids in the area who are in and out of building like Jack in the Boxes.'

'We have clear reason to believe that you do.' Replied the leading detective, *officially.* 'And furthermore Larry, Frank has at this time made certain written statements, and he is quite prepared to testify in a court of law.'

'*Oh, get fucked will you.* What are you going to do now, play good cop and bad cop?' I had jeered at them knowing quite well that I had nothing at all to do with Frank and his thieving bunch of younger uncontrollable friends. *'Although, unofficially,* I had sold many expensive items for them at different times for a ten percent sales commission.'

'I must warn you at this moment, that anything you say will be taken down and used in evidence in a court of law.' said the police officer, who was in fact smarting at my rudeness and my complete lack of compliance.

'Really, well you can take this down, you mug cunts, I think that you and your other fucking bum buddies from Woolongabba are actually setting me up because I was smart enough to beat that fucking Sims metal blue, *Aye?'*

Few knew that up close the acoustics allowed me to hear quite well, but from a distance I relied on guess, gesture, and the general reading of lips.

I got up abruptly and I quickly walked from the room before the warder could stop me. I fact, I refused to obey him as I went to that main door of the remand yard. The escorting warder was not all that too happy with my indecent obvious show of insubordination. *But, he did not threaten to charge me with my breaking a lawful command. In fact,* charging me was something I knew that he could easily have done, for the State prisons system was at that time run under military law. Along with a military rule for saluting and a complete an utter demand for a strict obedience at all times. *To refuse an order twice, quickly bought about a charge of mutiny.*

In truth, any refusal to obey a lawful given order could be met with up to seven or more weeks in their dark and airless lock up in an a musty underground cell ' *on bread and water.'* 'Although, *to the insane,* it was not an ordeal but a welcome refuge for such sick and unsociable men.' On the same token, administrators like Jack Farrell seldom locked men down for long periods, *and,* used a firm persuasion and common sense in their attempt to reach a reasonable compromise.

Normally, *of course,* for serious troublemakers, one was simply confined to his cell on half rations, and or, on a full allowance of water. So it was that the tougher and emotion draining discipline, *once in the lock up area,* was a much worse penalty than the Australian Army handed out.

If a prisoner had needed any *physical restraining,* those large hard-soled boots of the warders would quickly be used to restrain him in ways not at all suggested in their rule books.

The method of attack that was then used, was to get a mattress from some other cell and use it as a battering ram to hold the prisoner down while he was kicked. *Or even injected with a stupefying drug,* The average warder was also under a very strict method of discipline that was then officially set down in the Prison rule books, and, *if trained well,* they always obeyed this set of rules at all times. 'Especially under Jack Farrell, as this good man made it quite clear that he would brook no unnecessary or unlawful harassment of prisoners.; *'Nor any ill or unlawful treatment without due provocation.'*

'What are you doing Larry? My orders were to allow the police to speak with you?"

Turn it up Ron, the weak cunts were going to fucking verbal me, *mate,* and you fucking bloody well know it, *mate?'*

I had paced up and down the Remand yard in my barely hidden fury, while fully believing that the rotten corrupt police force had demanded permission from those legal eagles to get me at any cost. Those colder eyed legal men were posturing and warbling their big words, while at the same time attempting to rake in a fortune from the gullible and paying public. I for one, had known just what was going to happen to me, just as it happened to any other Queenslander that dared to beat them at their own silly game of amateur play acting. *And or, their legal manipulations.*

I was pleased that I had that quick sense to walk out of that interview room, but I knew quite well *from a vast experience* that they would be there waiting for me in the car park the very moment that I was released. I'd felt that the prosecution department really had to be furious at me, because normally, *the detectives had to answer to someone a lot higher up,* and those higher up officials even a lot higher up again, until the order was officially returned to cut the trouble maker down to size.

I was not to know, at that time, that the police witness, *young Frank,* was still in the old Westbrook Boys Reformatory, and, after his having been pack raped, he had agreed with the police to assist them, *and to lie for them* in return for a protection by reformatory staff. *And a possible parole if I was convicted.* It must be realized, that *police, political, and legal corruption,* would not be revealed for another twenty-seven years, *that is,* when a shocked Fitzgerald and Kennedy inquiries revealed a small part of how truly rotten that those in power really were. There was in fact no restrictions to what employed public servants could do to anyone held in their clutches, *at that time,* and I honestly believed it was not law, but was in fact *illegal* to allow a public servant to do as he *or she* wished. I knew also, that legal perjury in Queensland was a genuine fact, as sure as I knew that savage dogs ate meat, *and* child brothels were operating on Wickham Terrace, Spring Hill.

Thinking back, I recalled the time I had grabbed the sixteen year old Frank by the neck when he had taken my sedan to do a break in on a shopping center. So it was, I knew by the quick police visit, that it was now past time for Frank's, *payback.*

I felt the ire of the court creeping ever closer to contain me. I smelled their revenge as I recalled my show of arrogance in front of Judge Broad and his weak limp wrested prosecutor, *which had meant,* if it was so, that their presumption came true, then I was dead set going to be a dog's breakfast. As far as I knew, the only real true blue solicitors, with any gumption to even think of taking on their Government in their own game, was a law firm run by an older man named Max Gore. Max of course, liked his pay up front, *as well as his bottle of whiskey a day*, and even then there was no guarantee that he would turn up sober, *or,* even be able to stand up on his feet. I also felt that if Max did fire up, the crooked police would run like rabbits because it was said that Max Gore had enough notebook-holders filled up with some very revealing criminal information that could then sink Police headquarters.

'*As well as a Queen and Adelaide streets,*' added one older prisoner of a long standing. He gave out the legal information when he was making his very critical and informative comment of a common Queensland police procedure. *As well as the unofficial and unlawful methods of revenge.*

As it was, I had a sum of roughly nine hundred dollars or so, at the line, or money that was held by police, *seen as in 2010 values*, and I'd wondered if Max Gore would take it as a lien on the promise of future payment. *That is, had we won.*

Incidentally, poor old Max borrowed a policeman's service revolver some years later, *prior to the Fitzgerald Inquiry*, and it was so alleged that poor Max committed suicide.

Of course, Justice improved for many destitute people when a Civil Liberties and Legal a Aid department was given a funding under a Federal Labor Government. *Supposedly for their not seeking to pursue Max's demise too diligently.* Nothing at all can harm a Government more than when matters of legality are revealed to a placid voting public. *That arrogantly puts ordinary greedy men in a situation of untold wealth and power.*

Like prisoners always said; *Shit always rises to the top of the sewer.*

CHAPTER 7

UNSEEN REPERCUSSIONS

Eventually, these now historically forgotten matters *pertaining to the political interference,* were soon brushed from my mind, seeing as one of the many younger men from that local Coopers Plains area, *who had recently arrived in the remand yard,* had an angry violent bloody altercation with a hard bigger brown muscled man. This was a man who had decided to install himself as the remand yard librarian, *without at all consulting me,* and, he was a Long Bay bully who had bodily thrown the young lad from the makeshift library.

'What the fuck do you think you're doing cunt?' I had said in the manner and jargon of the long established prisoner.

'I'm taking over the fucking library, what's it to you?' He glared hatefully at me.

'No, you're fucking not!' I'd said aggressively, hoping to make the well-muscled darker skinned man back down from a confrontation.

The aggressive man, *who was roughly my age and weight,* had then decided to assert himself physically, seeing as he obviously had served a lot of hard time in southern prisons. He knew that by making a solid stand, he could quickly improve his standard of living in the old Boggo Road House of Fame.

If, I had not of been so angry with the filthy police detectives, I may well have attempted a fair settlement, or, to even back down and let him have the new library. Mainly because, I myself had taken over the make shift remand yard kitchen area. *I mean; fairs fair!*

The younger frightened man, whom the southerner had bullied, *and violently threatened,* was named Michael Semyraha, and was a friend of a friend who had previously made me welcome out in that Sunny Bank and old Coopers Plains areas. We had in fact shared a ton of alcohol, and also many a sweet willing young female girls that liked offenders who gave them oral sex. As it was, I had found that Mick was a very loyal, as well as a sharing and caring human being.

Sadly poor Mick would later be shot and killed by a younger relative over a minor drug debt at Sunnybank, roughly twenty years later.

Still, I had given Mick Semyraha the position of librarian, and it was now up to me to enforce it. *'Or, to lie down and cop it sweet.'* This of course was not an enviable position for a man who was then living on a good name. As well as a much tougher reputation with the real or perceived possibility of being belted senseless by a brown man. *With a hot sick hatred in his eyes.*

The end result was that I then invited the stand over man into the secluded kitchenette, but, when we got to the door we discovered that a jolly warder named *Bugs'* Casey, was counting the knives drawer. *Mainly to make sure none was missing.* We had turned back toward a top landing stairway so as to go up to an upper level storeroom, when the now nervous brown man said something that I did not hear all that correctly. I turned and punched him hard in the face. *I later found he had told me to stick the library fair up my skinny arse.*

We punched and we grappled for some minutes, while hidden by the concrete stairway. *A winding stairway, which was out of vision of the big over-head guard tower.* I had to admit he was a fair to even street brawler and he had, in a sudden and unexpected move, attempted to grab a vicious hold on my scrotum. So it was I quickly spun him into a headlock and used my free hand to grasp tightly upon his exposed windpipe. Breathing heavily, I hung on like a bull terrier and the more he had struggled, the more I brutally tightened my grip.

Men who were doing life in prison, *and who had defeated other human being in close-quarter fighting,* knew a whole lot more than the average guy on the street, on exactly how to bring an ordinary person to heel. Those males and arrogant females out in the outside world, *who'd thought they were tough with experience,* had no real idea at all what they were doing. That is, when they'd stupidly attempted to intimidate a stranger in a suburban hotel, *or on a city street.* Armed forces personnel, *or police and warders, in the prison, and the hospital environments,* knew quite well the art of immobilizing an angry aggressive human being, and so did a long-term prisoner. *As well as a sick stuffed up caged up' alleged' scum maggot crazy psychopath looking for any trouble that came his way.*

There are hundreds of rude people buried in Australian bush land because they were once rude to sick and dangerous people. Sick people who were chewing on an old matchstick. Men. who possessed a mind that actually gave me the willies.

With what I had known then, I could have gone into almost any of those corner businesses, or, *any private home,* and cowed the occupants. That, *of course,* meant ten or more years to life in jail, when the real purpose was simply to steal their money or their personal property, without harming them. *Which, I can assure you, professionals crooks never chose to do.*

Why offenders stole, related either to the home they lived in, or their treatment by people who had power over them in their child hood. Why they took it out on all the innocent tax payers, was that tax payers treated the police as their heroes when homeless prisoners were beaten, and locked up for years in Boggo Road Prison.

This was admittedly an illogical reason or the type of common sense that poorer teenagers or angry thieves had chosen when break and entering or pilfering a citizen's personal property. Not realizing, that the end result was an unavoidable confrontation with a life long sociopath in a state prison.

In a sense, many such young men believed that the expected sentence for taking other peoples property, was to be short, *or hopefully a bearable one,* especially if no one was home. But unfortunately, there came a time when someone really was at home in a bedroom, and many young thieves were beaten and choked for almost nothing, *Or at best, suffered for a television set, or child's moneybox. '*

In some terrible cases, a young good looking teenage burglar was often sexually assaulted, while some boys were even kept for a period of days by people who were a hell of a lot worse than they themselves were. Indeed, one particular father and son were charged with the unlawful detention of children when putting nooses around the necks of trespassing thieves, and keeping them for a period of days. The need to learn a self-defence, was quite seriously important for the many young lost and homeless persons. *Especially if one had chosen to be a property thief.* For it had soon become obvious, that no mercy was usually given to any young criminal who was caught on private premises. In fact some property owners shot them, knifed them, choked them and beat them endlessly. *Even if he or she was only fifteen years of age, or less, when caught in the house of land owners.*

So it was realized, that the younger criminals eventually became those violent armed robbers, of a future time, especially after finding out just how cruel those honest upstanding citizens could really be. That is, when it came to their private property, and personal possessions. Or, how absolutely cruel any detective could be when sending a bullet flying past ones head, and only miss killing him by barely a millimeter. *Bloody violence begets bloody violence, and guns beget guns, while hatred, is the root of all evil.*

As it was, the man I was then fighting, was no better or worse than I was, but, he had foolishly gone low, and I'd automatically went for the throat area. He continued to grapple at my soft genitals, as I in defence had squirmed about. It was then I found his exposed wind pipe, and I applied enough pressure to make him surrender.

Unfortunately for the poor man, *he did not surrender immediately,* and he'd callously tried to punch at my scrotum in one last effort to win the fight. It was not to be, and so it was I methodically dug deeper and vindictively cut off his air. *Under the unwritten law of survival; it was him or me'.*

The Warder, *Bugs Casey,* came out of the Kitchenette, and seeing what was happening, had quickly rushed over and he'd broken my murderous choke hold. It was then, my now limp opponent had fallen to the ground in some serious distress.

The prisoner was close to passing out, and Bugs had knelt to make sure he could breathe correctly, before he turned angrily toward me.

'You could damnwell kill someone like that, Campbell, you just bloody well watch yourself.' He said with deep concern that a death of a prisoner could in reality have taken place on his watch.

The fact that I'd helped the other man on to his feet and told Bugs that I would look after him, had made the large warder give us a chance to redeem ourselves. *Fortunately for us both, the good man took the matter no further.* I did not feel sympathy for the beaten man, mainly because I knew he would have kicked me into Kingdom Come had he of gotten the best over me. But, as it stood, I had showed compassion instead, and I took him over to the corner Kitchenette where I'd got him two cups of iced milk for his throat, *which my group had bartered for.* To be honest, we were both shaking like leaves on a gum tree. I had stayed with my victim until he had completely recovered, and then I'd sent the worried man back to his side of the tennis court type yard to contemplate his mistake in violently confronting other human beings. *Or to possibly think of his ultimate, or belated bloody revenge.*

To my quiet relief, there was no back up after a week, and so Mick had happily handed out library books knowing, or believing, he was as safe as houses. I from long experience knew quite different, and had long realized that a pencil or Biro could end your sight, *or your life,* while an unexpected blow to the back of your neck could paralyze you, and break your heart in two. *As you eventually learned to maneuver a wheel chair.*

It seemed to me then, that the prison security clamp down on razor blades, glass, hobby tools and other less damaging objects was a complete farce. If the truth was ever to be told, a lead pencil or a leather shoelace could be more lethal than such useful hobby type things, and when a sharp pencil tore out a wind pipe, it was all over red rover. In fact it was not at all a fear of the consequences, that prevented this unholy and ultimate crime, but it was that love of, or the need to see ones sweetheart, or even a close and supportive family, that had prevented such a deed. *'Or again of course, the thought of actually being free to feel human again.'*

Without a doubt, prison gave all men a sense of family loyalty, first, *attitude second,* and if others had misjudged me as some serious violent offender, they were so very wrong, for I would rather save a life, than take one. The truth of the matter is, that numerous warders were the first to stand by each other in prison altercations, *although there are those that will run at the first sign of open rebellion.* It takes a lot of insult and torment to make

the varied mix of prisoners stand as one, and as for the prisoner popula-
tion who are willing to die for each other? *It is a total fallacy.*

At times, prison warders may not at all have liked each other, and at
other times some of them had seriously hated each of their fellow officers
in authority above them. But they were quite loyal to a man, mostly, *or mainly,*
because their jobs had depended on it. The inmates, on the other hand, were
seriously loyal to each of his fellows, *only* if it had benefited him or made him
look good in the eyes of other inmates. Daily survival, or any *edible creature
comforts* were the only real reason to get involved in something that did not
at all concern you. It was a very rare type of person that ever remembered
who you were. *That is, once they were outside of those unfeeling brick and mortar walls.*

Obviously, a free life had awaited the obedient inmate, much sooner
than the non compliant prisoner who refused to conform, *while clearly,* each
incident put them a lot further from their goal. This was the attitude of
the family man, the average man, the normal man, but mixed in with them
were all of those men who had grown up in State orphanages, boy's prisons, reformatories. *Or those mental assessment centers.*

Most all of those orphanage based men, *and boys,* had a crude type of institutional understanding toward each other, and in their sad way were much like
true brothers and cousins from an earlier life. Places where they were once
raised to be aggressive and very cunning predators. From this group came the
ageless criminal that either lived in Gaol far into his old age, or he found a
racket that suited his or her way of life, *or nefarious behavior.* To the boys home
victim, the rare act of loyalty had a price of subservience, *and without a sexual
relationship,* there was no need at all to keep the relationship going. Sadly, walls
held secrets, and boys who had graduated to prison were black mailed to do
what they had done as a little boy in the; *reformatory dormitory.* So it was, that all
such people simply faded away and were never remembered at all, except by
the old pedophile that always recalled the children's pain in the long ago world
of conditional love and future expectation. All the boys ever recalled was
the sudden pressure and sharp pain, the muffled cry, and then the promise
of love and loyalty for a boy or girl that never knew a real parent or the true
meaning of love. It would not be until the 21st Century, that Australians were

given a small look into the world of all the pain and suffering that small boys and girls had suffered at the hands of those cruel and corrupt managerial sex offenders in the State run holding areas.

Only then, did those investigations reveal a small extent of that damage, not only to a young innocent child, but also to the helpless elderly who it was alleged were encouraged to die quickly in nursing homes. *Hopefully so, as to make the management a much higher annual turnover.*

Many years later in the old city of Townsville North Queensland, the authorities and the editors of the local daily newspapers had sat cowardly upon their thumbs. That is, while the horrific stories poured out about the terrible treatment of mental patients and troubled young children in local rehabilitation centres. This, had continued on for many years by word of mouth, *only*, or it was so mainly because, Townsville was predominately a public service town of Armed forces, Prisons, and large community of police force personnel. Certain public service workers actually had a strangle hold on the local politics, as well as the media outlets, *and as usual,* stuck together like warders under siege. Eventually Ward 15 fell to a large inquiry, as did that old Cootheringa Orphanage for the abused crippled children. *Not discounting the renowned Kirwan Woman's Hospital.*

In the ignored case of the Kirwan Women's Hospital, my future wife and I bought legal suit against the then discreet northern Health Authority, for neglect, and incompetence. The action was successful, and my wife had settled out of court for a large sum at the urging of inadequate lawyers. As it was, only a sneaky Stuart Creek prison had closed its doors to a public scrutiny, but, the rest had soon come falling down like a stacked deck of shaky cards when the Government had eventually changed hands. Still, it was an excellent town to raise young children in, as long, as your kids did not show their friendship and loyalty to those welfare dependent children at their local school; ' *Hey, His fathers an ex convict.* '

The public service was known to be, *and still is,* loyal to a man, and they now run a very tight ship, but a good ship, as long as you do not object too strongly to their accountancy, or, of their five yearly financial print-outs. That is, of the yearly Federal funding that is commonly referred to as; *'The Bucket'*. Such monies are considered a form of administrative used *cash type incentive sweeteners* for those close mouthed groups and associated departments. *To promote the popularity of all concerned.* If after five years the *'bucket'* accountancy is requested in Canberra, the books are switched and to date 2015, no Federal government, *with an associate State government,* has ever questioned such anomalies that often crop up in out of date costs and figures. That is why Government expenditure, is insured. *As for the public, it is none of their business.*

When I did retire from *purloining*, the local police force felt that they could still knock my front door down and pick through my scattered property in a rough futile search for evidence. That is, while I in turn picked on the State government who paid the wages of their bully boy goons. *Thieving from snobby thieves, felt really good.*

Before the 1980's, human rights was ignored for convicts and indigenous peoples, and the reason the police hated me was I used a poisoned pen instead of physical resistance. The repercussions of their *ramping* me, were that a barrage of letters were sent to local newspapers, government offices and even Churches and community groups. Some, were so revealing that I actually got answers back, and the Townsville Bulletin did a full page layout of my views that made the authorities back off. *It will be donated to the Museum Boggo Road.*

If such people say my later criticism was unfair to them, then their *only* purpose in life is *'self advancement before others,' Sabo's,* and they are too stupid to know, *that nobody gets a free ride through life.* Also, their dues will be paid, whether they like it or not. Those who do not heed my words will outlive their children and they will remember their lack of humanity when they were young. *They will also know why it is that they suffer in old age.*

My later expose on local matters sent to the JCU, *told, among other things,* of the blatant stealing of building supplies and state government furniture. This included new silverware being taken home by all the public servants who had answered to no one at all for their thievery.

The exposure had soon caused a shake up of gigantic proportions, and eventually, *in the end,* the piggish people left me alone. *And I left them alone.*

CHAPTER 8

LOVE & SEX, ARE JUST WORDS

Back in that old Boggo Road, of the 20th Century, *as mentioned,* there was a world of men where only a certain kind of rewarding loyalty had flourished between those basically, *schoolroom uneducated inmates.* Loyalty, which I had then believed, was an emotion based on sexual motives. Those boys, or angry younger men from those youth institutions, unrealistically believed they needed both a crude satisfying sex and an emotional fulfillment, just like anyone else, and some kissed and made secret furtive acts of love, and or endearments, so as to ward off a sad cruel pain of being nothing, and of having nothing. *The secrecy made it even more intense, as well as erotic.*

It seemed to me, that most sensible minded warders and prisoners, who having been raised quite decently, *but obviously lacking any higher education,* had looked on with a rancid distaste at the lascivious queasy male relationships that popped up randomly for other to observe. *Or to criticize.* The disgust was evident, at first, but even good decent men had soon become quite desensitized to an obscene *'open display'* of rude men *and or boys* tongue kissing a more youthful male, in exchange for tobacco, food, or, even a well proven prison protection; *Some too for temporary and totally wasted friendships.'*

At close quarters, the random good-looking girlish teenagers made a lot of men question their personal sexuality, *but,* those previously abused and or many sexually contaminated young boys that were then known as *'Rough Trade' or,* institutionalized *'Cats,* had little qualms about moving in quickly and hopefully claiming a new but mostly rare fresh faced first timer. Those *naïve* inexperienced car thieves, and or weekend criminals who had arrived at the prison daily, were quite gullible in the main, and being young they did not know *what if anything at all,* that they could do to repel a rude situation when a friendly brown tattooed man stepped into a divided shower recess area and had erotically began to soap him up in an inappropriate way.

If the boy had involuntarily erected, the man would slip to his knees and begin sucking the young mans hardened penis until he ejaculated into the warm and eager mouth; *often referred to as tongue rape.* The lead bull would then go back to the yard and nod to the observers who would be pleased that another youth had accepted the ways of the prison culture. As in most cases, it was always a gentle penetration that would follow the oral type pleasurable type of manipulation to continue. *So,* before a coerced youth had known it, he was of an involuntary bisexual leaning inside the walls, and a tough brutal or dominant angry heterosexual outside of them.

Understandably, if he did not make any lawful complaint concerning the unwanted tongue rape, *that is,* the first time around, then there was very little chance he would ever complain to the authorities. So it was that certain different types of men took what they wanted, individually, *or in time,* as a team of four. Oral sex had almost always opened the door to penetration, and it was not all that long before group sex took place with the young man who was the latest center of attention, On the up side, if the youth had become a sentenced prisoner, his rude and indecent behavior preceded him. Prisoners, one and all, would refer to him as a *'Cat.'* Or, if he informed on those men who had indecent relations with him, he would be referred to as a 'Dog.' *Similar methods were used on young girls in the woman's prison, orphanages boarding schools and reformatories.*

The trouble with any seductive form of *'forbidden sex'* was that it soon became a habit, *or a need,* and like a youth who smoked marijuana for the first time, they could soon find themselves seriously addicted to such things. They say in newspapers today, that each person is responsible for what they are, and what they do, but I somehow doubt that the scribes even know what they are talking about.

That method of manipulated intercourse *or tongue rape* seldom failed the experienced long term criminal, and so the aggressive rape, or a forced sodomy of young men, was not a real issue, *at that particular time,* except of course for those many fine defaulters who were placed in the dormitory.

That of course was mainly to let other men know the enormous penalty for not paying their traffic fines, or for being young and defenseless. Although, in my view, it happened a lot less after Jack Farrell took a personal charge of the night rosters. It was not really a personal assault, but was mostly expedient, in that greater sense, that those old dormitories could not be overseen in any other way to save the bed space and money. Paying off fines, *or the posting of bail,* was a young mans way out, but I found that a forced sexual intercourse was not a big issue or as common as one may well believe. Pressure, blackmail, or bribery and of course any rude sexual conversation was the normal way to deprave some youth, and then in the 1980's I judged that thirty percent of warders were of bisexual leaning, and a youth in Boggo Road prison soon found that *surrender* was his best form of day to day survival, rather than a king hit on his jawbone; *Or, locked in a solitary protection cell for months at a time.*

In fact a brutal hit to the bone just between the ear and the jaw is quite devastating, *even for grown men,* and if a younger man is not at all intimidated after seeing, *or experiencing that brutal act,* he is by all right considered, *'unapproachable;'* Especially if he promises a revenge and or uses weapons to retaliate against unwanted attention.

The warders of course seldom know in advance that someone is targeted, mainly because of, *or,* by the rule of silence that adheres to both prisoners and warders. Containing any group of human beings, *en masse'* always causes problems, and allowing men *more space* can often alleviate future social problems for society in general. Few citizens ever realized, that ignoring the needs of prisoners, and not giving a tugboat hoot about humanizing or counseling men after a lengthy stay in prison, was in fact inviting the very same type of habits to be introduced into our cities towns and suburbs. Young men do in time of loneliness, rudely inflict what they learn, on much younger men and girls out on the street. *So it is that the level of violence rises.* This is much the same as when brutal unprovoked violence was introduced by returned soldiers from international wars. That is, when they too were not at all debriefed. *Or humanized and assisted Housed or employed. The Outreach type of program is the best and fairest way to assist displaced persons that are not violently predisposed to hurt others. My project in my writing; The Boggo Road Connection.' outlines a new system that stops the rot setting into young minds.*

Even modern intellectuals, *say to me*, that it is not our problem and that jail appears the best place for such degraded or brutalized victims. Mainly, so that our own children will not be contaminated by that past disgusting lifestyle of; *tit for tat.* When I explain to them that there is an underbelly of dark underground literature and films already poisoning their children, they in turn suggest that; *If their own children need to be put in Gaol for a wake up call: So be it.*

In prison, *to avoid,* the above mentioned intrusive sexual treatment, *or any unwanted attention,* all that one then had to do was take a violent physical thrashing. Possibly bring about charges, or in the extreme go to the hospital with a broken jaw. That is, if some mentally ill or violent psychopathic type person like Bill Taylor, *had decided to place you in his sights.* If Bill, or his jail bred types were paranoid, it did not take a youth very long to be paranoid also, and seriously jumpy after his having been bowled over, simply for just looking back quizzically at a man that was looking at them.

So it was, that the Remand yard, *and 1. Division,* became an informal classification area. *Where the wheat was separated from the chaff, and the 'Dogs from the Cats.'*

Incidentally, in one particular year alone I had witnessed fourteen such brutal occurrences of sudden stand over violence where young men had their jaws wired up, *and,* were forced on liquid diets.

I might add, that certain warders and managers, used the hardest of crims to belt the living daylights out of rebellious young crims with a big mouth.

In explanation, a fractured or broken jaw was usually caused by the aforementioned *king hit* on the younger men who had rejected intimate friendships of rude highly sexed men. Men who had spent a fair amount of their wasted time building up a personal relationship with them. I had even witnessed some youth being struck with a leather belt by their *man'* for talking to other prisoners in an unacceptable affectionate manner. General complaints to those mostly disinterested newspapers, *or even the police,* were always met with a request for eyewitnesses, *and or,* to at least show a positive proof that the alleged event had ever really happened at all.

Once seduced, or 'Broken in,' the youth was fair game, and although a critic might say he should have taken a bashing, the mindset is that young men believe the courts will release them for being young. So it is that they allow man after man mount them, while believing they will soon be home with their family, and no one will ever know what happened.

Without eyewitnesses, *or a medical diagnosis,* the victim usually went out into the larger world a more alert person, as well as a very angry and seriously sick paranoid type of younger man. *The Courts did not support untested complaints.* Decades later, that same released young molested person would prey on the vulnerable, the weak and the innocent, while higher levels of sex orientated child abductions would be shown in news report headlines, *allegedly by strangers.* Or, it was eventually noticed that a number of unsuccessful attempted child abductions on young boys began to take place in the State of Queensland. *'Tit for tat, butter for fat, you dirty rat, don't worry we'll get you back;'* was the view of the authorities; *As well as those damaged felons.*

Similar things happened in the prison cells, *and* because of the many informers in the cells, the security warders had known exactly what had happened, *and of where the shenanigans had happened.* So together as a team a certain group of Union warders would become the judge juries and the executioner.

Quickly, the Boys Home toughs would be verbalized, isolated, and deprived of rations until they too were forced to beg and scrounge for tobacco, *or,* do a requested sexual favor for other older men in the cells. Official, or humane classification, *separations*, or a true counseling, did not take place in those earlier years, and so it was that a youth was told to either toughen up, or, *'Cop it Sweet.'*

Later, some lifer or kitchen cook would quickly move in to tuck the Boys Home youth under his wing, while eventually allowing an adult type relationship to spring from the dying embers. In time, that young *so called wasteful young career criminal* would be taught how to be a real criminal in the big world of shakers and movers. 'Such instruction would usually be in the area of drug production, intimidation, prostitution and fraud.' The basic cost to the damaged young man was little more than what he had already been rudely taught to do to another young or naïve teenager, months, or even years before in a Boggo Road cell. *With the criminal education came instructions on how to corrupt and to train younger girls and boys for prostitution. (See my writing 'The Onion Bed,' downloaded free to your Ipad via email.)* As they grew older, some males saw the need to groom children from an early age to do their bidding, and in any new male relationship, *intimacy surfaced,* and so did a life long habit of pedophilia.

The Boggo Road Prison, *at that particular time,* had two systems of observation, and it had often come about by the differing architecture which embraced the old and the new, into one prison system. In the *old* closed off watch house type style of prison, it was clearly open to prying eyes, and most criminals usually resisted the temptation to seen as a tongue *or oral* rapist. Or anal rapist, as anything said or done rudely in the yards was soon relayed to the administration. *(It was then written in ones file.)* The new system, on the other hand, was soon shut off to prying eyes by its closed off kitchenettes, shower rooms, toilets storerooms, stair ways, and the criminal element had this view, *that if there were no prying eyes then the offensive behavior could not be proven,* and therefore it did not happen. The warders knew even less of what was going on in the yards, as the new system had required them to stay outside the cyclone wire, and to only enter when trouble of a violent nature had suddenly erupted because of problems unrelated to the prison.

Sexual predators of males, *came and went,* and at times there were none at all in the remand section, *that were obvious to me,* and then out of the blue would arrive an experienced manipulator who would quickly set about introducing himself to the gullible teenage prisoners that appeared pliable, *and or,* lacking a prison experience. This manipulator may only be seventeen or eighteen in his own right, and the longer that he stayed there without bail, or having his case dealt with by the courts, the more young men he corrupted. Few of the manipulators would be imprisoned for long periods when facing the court, and he would happily head back to his old haunts with the names and addresses of young men who he or she believed could further his or her advancement in life.

From boys homes to male prisons, and then back onto the streets, this methodology grew daily, *so as to train young children who would sell their genitals,* while that uneducated but wised up ex prisoner would give the girls golden trinkets, clothes, and modern cosmetics that he stole from shops and houses. The footloose youth, in fact, learned to plan their moves well ahead, while the authorities had sought to contain them according to the rule books.' That is with the aid of the long term crims. *Now,* for the observer, it becomes clear that the more street cultured adult version of that young boy's home tough, could, *or would,* soon be living in your own local area, quietly cultivating gullible teenagers, *much like yours were, or are,* so as to be his friend. The question that is now remaining *is;* are you going to blame my children for your problem, *or,* blame the people you pay a small fortune to, so that they can allegedly find a sensible solution, *and or cure?* Even today, a certain spokesman for the warders union likes to suggest, *to the biased media,* that by the time a youth or young man got to prison, he was well and truly corrupted, and so it was not really the warders fault if others did to that stupid youth what he had probably been doing to others for a long time.

That manipulating statement is seriously, *untrue,* and just because some joy-rider or a graffiti artist is rebellious, it does not mean that he or she seduces children. Or, does violent armed robberies on corner shops. Or even rapes some woman in a shopping center toilet on his first day out of jail.

Such acts of social suicide take a lot of ingrained abuse by those much better off than themselves. *And that is the truth of the matter.*

Repetitiously, such an ancient crude cycle had long continued on from orphanage to prison, *and then onto marriage.* In time the resulting children of an unsuited liaison would normally follow the moves of their ex convict father. In turn, that offspring too would in turn take innocents with them, *until,* by that end of the twentieth century, most ordinary people cried for relief from crime, violence, stupid teenagers, and their children being tongue raped.

The more knowledgeable had often invested all of their *'Life'* saving as well as superannuating finances into their large security share-holdings, and later *a; Privatized Correctional Center Group* that had generously paid huge dividends to those; *in the know* investors, *and of course, politicians.* For, such men and women do indeed know exactly what sort of indecent people are today being created behind Prison and Remand yard walls, *and still,* we see them consulting with biased prison workers for modern day solutions.

On the 16th November, 2009, channel seven news broadcast a message from the Prime Minister of Australia, *Mr. Kevin Rudd,* that a full apology has been made to the children in previous institutions that had been hurt brutalized and sexually assaulted. *It was a memorable day for some.*

But of course, without a decree of human rights, the belated apology has the total weight of feather down from a new born chicken. Boggo Road was not mentioned, and nor was the victims in the outer suburbs who are *today's* victims, only because of such ignorant and uncaring institutions. *And sometimes the inadequate people who arrogantly manage such dour places.*

There I was, stuck there in the remand yard over half a century ago as an involuntary observer, and, all I had wanted to do was be free and to salvage a little of what I had accumulated, *and to make money if I could.* So that I too could someday live honestly and watch over my investments. I never would have believed, that I would learn to be quite sympathetic to those convicted foolish people, *at a great cost to myself,* or would ever dare to keep written records of prison incidents. *In the hope that educators would someday listen to reason.*

The stupid thing, *was,* that I did not know then, that the authorities had already known of the ineptitude. *Also that, what I myself would one day receive, I would receive all for nothing.* I did of course know that the many counselors who were attempting to assist the teenagers in the suburbs, could not at all see behind walls, or get young men to admit their sexual liaisons with a good looking male in a shower recess. *It was then I saw the dire need to enlighten them by keeping records of the methodology of intimidation.*

The new remand yard setting was the beginning of a brand new cycle for Queensland prisoners, and it had so turned out, that my biggest liabilities were those good decent every day manners, and the clean morals that my adopted mother had attempted to instill into all of her children.

Where that weaker compassion for a loser, and an underdog *actually came from*, I did not know for sure, but I simply felt it had to be all of the early literature I had read and pawed over during a past decade of cell block incarceration? The motivation I then believed came from my conscience, for I now know, *that violence,* as well as the deaths that had resulted from all the treatment that was once suffered behind walls, *was in my view,* related to a need to change the policy concerning classification and treatment of all men and women at the mercy of other unconcerned human beings in our remand areas. My many brothers and sisters had appeared to lack that same type of sentiment, *and or softer compassion toward other human beings,* and so to me it was the *literature* that I had accredited that weaker debility in my make up.

Not even my brother Bruce had fought for a social cause, or was ever charitable to strangers. Although he always voted for political parties that helped out the underdog. He actually believed *elected leaders* were beyond reproach, and nothing I could say would change his views of them, *or his children,* who saw the greater benefit of working for public servants.

At that particular time, my consideration of others was without a doubt, a survival aid, *as well as a convenience,* and possibly a genuine boon to me over the many confusing years to come. For what I know now, *I did not know then,* but keeping my criticism for my journals, was a lot smarter, in my opinion, than allowing dissidents to know exactly what I was really thinking.

Being the jovial minded good fellow that encouraged a bit of fair go to the underdog, had disarmed many brutal, or manipulating people that had *never* thought of putting their head on the chopping block of history. That is, with humane ideals, and causes, that was not all that beneficial to them. Even my distant Aunts nephew's niece's cousins inside an extended family, would simply gossip and make their blind judgement of me without ever knowing that my writing of prisons *and later speaking in Universities*, would change many terrible laws. My humanity was mostly beneficial to me, mostly because good men often appreciated a sympathetic ear when a parent died, or a girl friend had found someone else to cohabit with. It was the same instinctive caring type of disposition that would follow me when I eventually left prison for good, but I soon found, that in prison my being a sort of basically compassionate person was seen *officially* as a type of pure *shiftiness*. Especially by military trained warders and numerous aggressive criminals, *As well as men who had no compassion for anyone at all.* It was mostly interpreted then, at that time, as my maliciously trying to politicize the minds of those dumber stupid and immoral inmates, *but*, I genuinely felt sorry for men doing hard time. Some warders actually thought I may be a maggot infested communist that was attempting to recruit foolish people for my own ends, but the truth was, I genuinely felt sorry for people that did not know what a true family really was, *in the sense of the word*. One thing was most certain, there were a lot of warders that hated any prisoner who was popular, and they also felt it was their personal duty to cut that '*smart ass*' offender down to size. *The ratio of good and bad was changing rapidly.*

Institutions have always been a learning facility for men and women looking for fresh recruits to their cause for gay rights. But recruiting a teenage prisoner did their cause more harm than good. Mainly because those men from institutions did not draw the line at age race or religion, and with the lessons on oral rape, anal rape, bullying and or a domination, they corrupted hundreds of thousands of Queensland teenagers that were not at all meant to be a 'Gay' person. The social offshoots were drugs, pornography, divorce in great numbers, stealing, shoplifting and violent behavior, among the ordinary teenagers of the 80's, 90's, and into the 21st Century.

What is worse, there are many hundreds of Queensland Prison warders, 'even today,' who encourage the act of 'Ass Fucking,' as they then called it, behind walls.

Sadly, the people of Queensland demurred on raising a fuss about the boys and young men being sexually abused in Queensland institutions, and it was not until my 'confiscated writing' in 1984 exposed the 'goings on,' that a new investigation was reluctantly commenced in Queensland prisons. The inquiry was to be titled; 'The Kennedy Inquiry,' but the incoming Goss government put an end to it by closing it down.

I was called to the Aboriginal Deaths in Custody hearings in 1994, and questioned closely on my knowledge of prisons.

Obviously, in the 1970's, no one really wanted to care about those absolutely foolish inmates who were not worth the time or the trouble to *help, assist, counsel, or to educate,* for, that extremely important time in the far flung future. *A time, when they too might have families and live normally among us, or, beside us.*

'Do your own time Lazza. Don't worry about the disgusting scum, and or, those filthy maggot pansies.' Was the usual advice that one got from both prisoners, as well as those tough but aloof warders, who had often or usually only wanted their own shift to pass without any violent, or impulsive trouble. *Or,* of an unwanted drastic physical exertion that obviously leads to mountains of unending paperwork? As well, as their having to give sworn evidence in a court of law. That is, should a prisoner dare deny the charges bought against him. *Or, again, to give such evidence when a 'crim' is accidentally choked to death in a scuffle with prison warders.*

For an observer, people writing of a male sex in prison, does appear to give the idea that all prisoners are involved in sexual shenanigans, *or violence,* and this is where I can assure all decent good people, that such offender's rate a *ratio of just one in ten.* Although, in a *'badly managed' institution,* the ratio is much higher. Such as, in the Woodford Gaol, when a rags to riches warder named Tom King had managed the youth prison during the 1980's, to the 1990's.

The ratio of *'shower'* victims, is even less, in a well run prison, simply because most convicts are not the pretty boys with skin like young girls. I discovered that most men sport tattoos and scarring along with sinewy type muscles and seemingly, the aggressive looks are a means of keeping the wolves at bay. As previously pointed out, the much older boys from a reformatory, orphanage *or in care restrictions* are the main offenders, but overall, most prisoners in the 1970's were just ordinary men and youth from the suburbs. *Males, that had the caring loyal support and love of their families so as to see them through.*

Such proud young Australians, obviously did not at all seek an unwanted type of man on man sex, and, they had forever asked certain men to leave them alone. Of course, if it came to an altercation, a sensible young man would always try and stand up for himself.

To think otherwise, would suggest that every single policeman who puts on a blue uniform, is potentially corrupt, and I for one know this is not true. To me, a decent policeman is worth a ton of gold, but, even they sometime somehow feel that they too would be more suited in a different type of employment.

Unfortunately, illegal drugs bought both money, as well as brutal violence, and the entrenched corrupted illegal investment, So it was that many Queensland jails were filled with naïve teenagers. Meaning, that the tattooed tough men whom they were sharing three to a cell with, had considered them cry babies and *girly boys* who were thrown into their cells willy nilly to be dominated. *Seeing as there was no where else to put them.* From 1978 to 2008, sex inside a Queensland prison had became accepted, as a natural function between isolated men. So it was, that our official representatives made homosexual relationships legally acceptable. It was my then personal view, that Queensland prisons changed for the worse, *from that day forward.*

Prisoners even lobbied for condoms in the late 1990's

On the 17th of April, 2013, the New Zealand Government granted 'Gays' the right to marry. In December 2013, same gender couples were wed in matrimony under the law. The High Court is appealing the right of 'Gays' to Marry, as prisoners are clamouring to marry each other in prison.

In 2015, due to pressure by the world wide Association of Journalists, Ireland voted for gay marriage. A new clothing fashion was immediately launched where all of the female journalists wear Zipper's at the front, while, the male journalists wear the Zipper's at the back of their trousers.

It is now official that the modern *State Corrective Services,* and or, *Queensland Police,* monitor a total of six hundred released sex offenders, each day, *in comparison to thousands of other various offenders who are operating each day in the State of Queensland. Without any observation at all.* It is also official, that most Queensland sex offences happen inside the home, or by good people whom we know well. Which in turn, gives a much more seriously misleading view, that pedophilia is a malicious scaremongering, *and that*, it is in fact, extremely confusing for serious researchers and local historians.

I personally have told my sons, that if they ever have children? And, they have reason to believe I am going senile, *and could at all touch the little ones on their privates*, to brutally smash my eight fingers with a hammer, but to leave my thumb so that I can eat with a spoon. This is mainly to warn their sons and our other relative's children, that when they reach puberty, they should not do anything silly with the little ones. If a man has not learned to control his urges by the age of fifty, it is time for him to go and live in the town of WOOPAWOOP with men like himself. Also, if required, I will give my blueprint for a scheme called Area 27 which will be devoid of children.

Prisons are definitely not for senile old men, or, naïve young boys, *and girls,* and in time, it is said that the people of Queensland will instruct our soft-brained and selfish politicians on how we truly want that type of offender to be dealt with; *Only, because they could be our father, or son, who had once been manipulated as a child.*

While we were totally unaware of it.

Until then, the *hammer,* seems the best option behind closed doors, but, if we at all can prove that the modern authorities are using corporal punishment on young people, *without aforethought,* we need to march as one on the gates of State Parliament and angrily show them that our objection is genuine. *If we choose not to,* then I will look after mine, and you will be seriously invited to look after yours.

Counsel & educate!
Not be idiots enough to make such fools, even worse than they already are.

CHAPTER 9

SKIM SCAM THANK YOU MAAM

Sometimes I had listened to the bullying, and *sometimes,* I'd chosen to help out those younger males, much like Michael Semyrahah, but, at the time, I did not really understand that I was making a name for myself inside of that old prison yard. And or, institution. *While other criminals made a big name in the media, or on the streets.* It was men like Billy Taylor, and or, Bill Stokes, as well as Billy Phillips, *or other silly Billy's and Rotten Johnny's,* that were the so-called, top guns. And possibly, a lot more violent than the roughly trained Army personnel. Tough guys, *who,* were then thought to be the real men in government uniform. *Although it turned out, that they too were buggering their young men, via in house; 'Bastardization.'*

I personally felt, that each of those media-alleged gangster type were as much *'unreliable'* as a shiny two cent watch. I also seriously felt, that they too were only the attention-seeking criminals who were always spoken about because of their meteoric rise into the world of the players. In fact, they were just cruel sad men who could never at all have achieved as much as they had in such a short time of life, *were it not for the crooked police and the prison personnel who usually warned them, or alerted them, of an impending trouble.*

In doing so, they had protected such shit for brains crims, during their short lived, but most highly energetic careers. *That is,* before selling them all out when the net had closed in. *See the Fitzgerald Inquiry.*

To me, the then crooked cop in the old Queensland police force, was usually a friendly and genuinely less cruel type of an interrogator than any of those *'dedicated slap happy type of detectives'* who were forever punishing the so called dumb criminal. *That is while they demanded with threat. As well as the promise of a belting, that he immediately confess to his crime.* The crooked cop, on the other hand, was simply a crooked pseudo type of criminal who had infiltrated the police force, with the one sole ambition of owning shop front real estate, *and having sex with as many young teenage prostitutes, or orphaned girls, as often as they possibly could.*

In their warped view, it was not a crime to be, *ambitious*, or, to run around naked in the unseen brothel premises chasing some small, *'girl's-home; 'prostitot,'* that had needed to be broken in. Especially while all concerned were just a bunch of good ole mates seeking heaps of fun and profit. Later on in life, they would put their honest daughters through University, *who in turn*, would swear that their father was not at all corrupt. *In truth, we were all corrupt, for saying nothing. And doing nothing.*

Some even had brothers in the Black Ulans and Hells Angels, while many others had the audacity to have shares in Night Clubs, and overnight Auto Chop Shops. Included in the general circle of such rude ambitious men, *and women*, were the ex prisoners, as well as young girls and boys from the reform schools who were willing to do that rude foul dirty work that a normally decent type of policeman would never do. *Or, think of doing.* It took prison to show me what happened to a prisoner's motor car, *and personal property,* when he was raided suddenly and angrily dragged off to jail.

That 1960/1970's policeman's wife, *who had handled the budget,* or the grocery list, knew only too well where the extra money came from. So it was that a tasteless web of acceptance had soon broadened into a much bigger world of Private schools and hairdressing salons. There were literally thousands of the debased police sources where any one connected family member could get a favor done, for just under a few hundred dollars. For many worried citizens, *when it came to their children's Judicial health,* a discreet and underhand payment to a local influential *'dirty'* policeman, *or his wife,* a smart citizen could have those charges buried forever, *or,* could even fix some annoying problem in just a few short hours. *It really was a joke.* All in all, it was seen that the Policeman's wives had *'official privileges'* that the ordinary suburban mothers never ever had. Especially in an area of queue jumping *and or* to bypass their waiting in emergency wards as a specialist met them at the door, *while fawning and bowing like a suck-hole drink waiter.* 'Indeed, *fawning* on them while some good and decent woman with four children, was forced to wait until four in the morning to see a night nurse, or a student doctor? While her bitter teenage children coldly observed the unfair injustice of it all.'

Personally, I had nothing at all against such rotten greedier policemen who ran the starting price set ups out in the suburbs, *and of course,* those smaller country towns? *'Or again,'* of the many wives that helped a friend with traffic fines. I mean, they too had families that had needed those normal creature comforts *and,* if young prostitutes gave them money and sexual favors to assist in keeping away the hard stand over predators that had forever treated working girls even rougher than the users did, *then, that was good.* My bigger concerns were those witty smart achievers who were then using their arrogant power to lock up the teenage offender's, while in turn, letting those people who had paid the piper that full freedom of the street.

They were cops who were obviously using the bullying *'Crims,'* and *'Bouncers,'* to do their corrupt dirty work. 'As well as, the freedom to maim and kill other ignorant criminals. *The files are hidden, on exactly how many offenders they killed, or drove to end their own lives.* Many of the dead had turned out to be my friends, and, my closest acquaintances. *Exaggeration?* Not on your sweet Nanny.

Many of the convicts from that old era, were good caring men who were kicked, bludgeoned or sometimes shot to death for mere nickels and dimes, by those so called police protected night club heavies, *bully boy bouncers,* or by a well known group of protected jail house criminals.' *The Clockwork Orange Gang run by Bell & Stokes that bashed who ever the corrupt police hierarchy, had pointed to.* Even more glaring, *or brutally obvious,* was the media that was strangely silent about, *it all,* but, at the same time, most citizens were more than aware, that certain weak journalists, had squirmed with embarrassment as their editors kept them on a very tight leash. Even more, I hated detectives who lied on the stand and or, put the same men away for crimes they never committed. And still, the *Courier Mail* looked the other way when I personally proved beyond any doubt that ongoing legal perjury was being committed in the State of Queensland. *My 14 Acquittals on verbal?*

Even with the utter contempt I have for two faced journalists, I do feel that most fair minded men and women with ink upon their fingers, had literally fumed in anger when a bouncer in a particular invisible brothel had kicked bashed and spat on a twelve year old prostitute on a certain street in the suburb of Breakfast Creek. Unfortunately they were not permitted by their editors to use film of the incident, simply because brothels did not legally exist in the years; 1960, 1970, or 1980. *The child died two weeks later in the Children's Hospital.*

These were the very things that I had; *thought,* about as I had listened to more and more of the foul street gossip passing slowly and lazily through those concrete yards. *Also, of the rumour that NSW police and politicians owned leading nightspots?*

I had long brooded contemptuously, as I quietly added up the information that swirled around like nauseating flatulence, but, I was never, *ever,* tempted to involve myself by doing any dirty work for such people. There was those filthy crazy tales of all those advertised brothels, those gambling nightclubs, along with the hierarchy of a *dirty* crooked police force running everything worth anything in the 20th Century.

There were those extremely sick stories of criminals being murdered, along with those police condoned armed robberies on payroll trucks which had floated into a Boggo Road prison to be so noted down for future reference, *by both those prison warders, as well as the very observant convicts.*

The selling of information to criminals, that resulted in the death of husband and wife drug peddlers, was as low as the users could get. Fortunately for me, I was not any part of it at all, and I had felt I was just another fool who was classed as a penny ante thief that would never want to commit violent crime, or, *to ever show others what I was indeed made of.* I knew of course, that the sick successful criminal type that ran those indecent brothels for the sneaky detectives, had also taken the blame. Especially if the so called Special

Police closed in to quickly shut them down as a warning to oil the palms of the hierarchy.

It was also to be suggested, that the police were honest heroes, and that I was just a *'nobody'* that was slowly getting tough enough to survive inside or outside of a Queensland prison. But, in that real sense, I was then considered by some as *too weak* to possibly survive on the street. Or in the so called; *'Big Time.'* Mainly because I did not want to hurt anyone, *and or do life in prison. Or go for a swim opposite the Hale street entrance late at night.*

The evidence was to be shown in a thousand files, that police were as bad as the crims, *while the Special police said they were unaware of it.* The public too had an ongoing running love affair with the so called honourable and upstanding Queensland Policeman. Worse still, the public had said nothing at all as police openly fabricated evidence and suggested it as quite acceptable to blame others for what they were doing themselves. Ten years later, I almost vomited to see females tongue kissing uniformed bullies in the *'Kiss a cop campaign,'* and, I truly wished a sexual disease on the whole lot of them.

It is hard for serious voters to actually comprehend, that *offensive* teenagers have actually joined the police force, *and excelled in Police Academies.* It is said that they'd joined up, expressly to have sex with teenage girls, knowing it would be their word against the girls when one cried rape. Others too, saw a chance to steal, do deals with known criminals, and drug offenders, while a Union leader would cover up for them when trouble arose. *A Union Boss by the name of Leavers, does today, quite aptly excuse police criminality as; 'Boys will be Boys,'*

The immunity police had held, *from their being so prosecuted, or their being imprisoned,* was the weight on the scales of Justice that said their names had to be suppressed. *Suppressed, so that their careers were not endangered.* Especially when police officers decided to stop at a set of traffic lights in 2010 and take off their clothes and show their anus, penis and faces to shocked onlookers, *including children. It was quickly laughed away as a case of the 'Boys just being boys.'*

I mean, did they not deserve to be ostracized by a News Limited editor? And, did their families not also need to be ridiculed by a general public, when they too committed willful exposure in front of the children who looked on wide eyed, as a bunch of naked SWAT men gamboled in the street. *Much like the same men they would normally shoot in the head?*

When I looked hard enough, I had actually found out their names hidden away in records, and today I wonder if the families of *Mathew Blum, David Swords, Bradley Inskip or Ross Murray, not forgetting the Salmon family,* would like their names emblazoned in the Brisbane Courier Mail?

Just as I had my name, and my family name, printed for all to sneer at for my selling a quantity of scrap copper to Sims Metal Inc. *Of which I was acquitted.*

No citizen, or top line *'criminologist,'* had ever dared to ask why these fortunate bullies, *and trained killers,* would, or could do such a filthy thing in front of schoolgirls, *and pedestrians,* as well as motorists and shocked elderly citizens. There was no media accusations of latent homosexuality, exhibitionism, mental illness, or child abuse, in their upbringing, *but,* I for one had known why they could do, *and did do,* such an unlawful thing.

What the idiots were actually doing, was rudely directing their arrogance and contempt, at the good citizen, who did not have the power, *the courage,* or the lawful knowledge, to at all prevent them doing anything they had wanted to do. They were in a fact, just *'thumbing their bum'* at the nobodies of our world, without at all realizing they were being recorded on their own Council CCTV. *Welcome to candid camera, you #@)%# dick heads.*

In reality, *the big shots were really the police, and the lawyers,* who'd invested their dirty money in hotels, bars, brothels, nightclubs, as well as a myriad of small businesses. While the so called big name criminals served out fifteen to twenty in a concrete container, *lazily regaling pretty young boys of the time when he was a big time player down on the Gold Coast. Or, a well known player down in the 'Valley.'*

Twenty years later, even the *'top off'* media had tentatively referred to the few bad apples in the force, but, only *'multinational television'* had truly referred to it as; *'police corruption.'* While suggesting that Kings Cross was clean as a whistle. From the viewpoint of the average type of prisoner, corruption had portrayed a dominating cancer type of an underhand network, but the average police today, are generally good men with lots of their younger fools, *such as the 'SWAT constables,'* driving new vehicles like Saturday night cowboys. *And showing wide eyed kiddies their testis.* Unequivocally, policemen were not at all cancerous types of men, and I feel none were intentionally *corrupted,* but nearly all of them would take that dollar or two for a favor, t. The *a drink, a meal, a bet, or a roll in the hay, especially if the price was right.* A downside was that the decent police workers copped the public backlash, *when idiots acted like Pigs.'*

If the media had nothing to hide, they would today be reporting that there is an older 'Crim' up at the Boggo Road Markets, who, is today, writing books about wholesale corruption in the BrizVegas State, of good old Queensland?

The real word by word description shown more popular to a criminal player, *out on the streets, in those days,* was whether or not the so called connected felon, *or those undetected police personnel,* were actually *scamming,* or *skimming* the profits? Such as parking meters, traffic fines, SP Bookmakers, Strip Clubs, Topless Bars, Tow Truck bribes, and a whole assortment of rackets from taking purses out of car wrecks? To, their giving false testimony in return for a future favor. *Or even handing out semi trailer licenses for $500 under the dining room table.*

Corruption, is not a word to describe a policeman, for, it is like using that old adage that; *'one rotten apple spoils the barrel.'*

Such are the sad ambiguous words that do not describe *how* policemen raised by their fathers, *who had been to war,* really are, and who had maliciously taught their sons to; *kick a little, touch a little, and pinch a little.* But, to keep your nose clean. *(Sadly, the culture is here to stay.)*

Unfortunately, police can bash any poor citizen that they wish to, and only an official internal inquiry can decide if charges can be laid. In 2013, an accused Police Sergeant, was forced to retire after having taken part in the bashing and bodily harm of a young chef in the underground parking area. No charges were laid for the beating, and today the same cover ups are permitted in the treatment of innocent human beings. {Courier Mail Wednesday11th Dec 2013.} On Dec 17th 2013, police took a drunken teenager up an alley and kicked as well as bashed him. 'Also caught on CCTV.' They are getting a lot more cocky today, under a Tory Government.

The government simply filed such illegal acts away, because they did not have rules that said that; *if you did the wrong thing, you're out.*

Police learned earlier, that policing was all about money, *and,* that if you looked after your mates, *they would look after you.*

They also had learned; *'what exactly, was what,'* by their own Senior officer's behavior, or, that everything in life had its own value, and to be even more descriptive, *a boy's anus cost eighty dollars while the tight teenage vagina went for a hundred.* A favor, *or a traffic fine,* cost two hundred dollars to fix, and it went up in scale until a barrister asked eight hundred dollars an hour to fix a murder offense, or; *Six thousand a day, or up to fifty thousand dollars a week. B&E charges could disappear for approximately $5,000.*

Scamming, was not really a recorded offense under our Queensland laws, and players had long preferred the description as; *a skimming from the top.* Some young officers would even stoop as low as siphoning petrol out of police cars, *into their own private cars.* Others stole full wallets off crash victims, and the higher you went in the police force, *or organization,* the bigger the *'skim.' The only real offense was in their not paying their income taxes.*

This was in fact, why I had continued to be a criminal, *but not why I was a criminal,* and it was a same type of skim that had then attracted me to the world of easy money. I just felt, that deep down in my concrete hardened bones, that there just had to be a *skim scam* out there that I could milk to my hearts content. All I had to do was to listen and learn, as the slightly familiar faces in the Remand Yard had rudely splurged their *street hard earned knowledge,* and somewhat *shaky,* but a reliable gossip.

Faces that had changed at the rate of a dozen a day.

It was said that corrupted money, *or the renowned skim,* was much like the virginal young faced sweet accessible girls, that had attracted all those people without the decent inner strength to ever refuse her highly persuasive temptation. The average detective, *of course,* was that quick minded worker who knew exactly where to draw a line. *And,* if the favor, or that penalty, was not that big, they would simply value a roll of pro-offered money against their privileged employment. *But like most work places, there was, and there always will be, those who succumbed.*

The hypocrisy burst forth when Judge Bill Carter knew what I knew, and he had still sentenced uneducated young men to prison for stealing a pair of thongs from a Woolworth store. District Court Judge William Carter actually organized a condensed law book, that was referred to as '*Carters Law*'. Detectives swore by it. *They also committed protective perjury by it. Carter allegedly, had began his legal career as a 'Defective Detective.'*

Prior unadulterated gossip had long pointed to four or five career law officers that would participate in getting rid of a criminal's dead body, and because of the '*advancement system*' most officers would not say anything if they had happened to know of such a serious criminal act. In fact, to such sick men, a criminals life meant nothing at all; *fucking maggots,' they would say,* and all it took was a quick nod to the *protected* criminals, and they could walk up to any human being in broad daylight and smash them down with a steel bar that was tightly wrapped in the morning newspaper. The description on the nightly news would of course be quite totally different to what any onlookers had recalled witnessing. *'Information was received that criminals had an altercation over drugs;'* would be the official media report. To such pious men on both sides of the fence, I was simply a second rate thief, and a second rate trouble maker, while the so called career criminals, *or prostitute beaters,* had looked upon me as a cowardly loser that would never ever be a big player in Brisbane by night. *'Mostly because I would never do business with them, or choose to help their official allies.*

Nor would I callously strangle or ever shoot down any human being, *simply to escape a prison sentence,* or, to do the bidding of others that had professed to have '*solid*' police connections. In fact, 'Call me a *'Nobody,'* and I will wear the label with pride.' Were I a policeman, *instead of a crim,* I would never, shoot or strangle an offender who was attempting to escape, and nor would I handcuff any young teenager on the main roadway, and stand by watch him be run over by a passing car.

They call it *mistakes,* while I refer to it as a; *callous disregard for a young human life,* and if future historians genuinely care to check how life has treated such uncaring human beings, they will find that those police persons personal family tree, are riddled with pain shame and suffering. *Like me,* they will learn that if you turn your back on life, then *'Life,'* will turn its back on them. *And, their children.*

The saddest thing was, that the Policing authorities were hiring uniformed cowards and weak gutted wimps to carry guns into minor domestic disturbances. They were *scum bag wimps* that would shoot an old woman down in cold blood because she was waving a carving knife in her front yard. Others would shoot a teenager who had threatened them with a knife at a skate park, when I know for a fact, that of all those media kiss-and-tell excusable reports, I could have disarmed the foolish people with a backhander. *Something an old time policeman could have done with ease.* Even worse, they were compensated when they pulled rank on a teenager, *and* when the silly teenager spat on them in retaliation, they claimed a pile of money from the taxpayer. *Yes! $10,000 Criminal Compensation because some fifteen year old girl spat in a wimpy policewoman's face.*

What should I have received for having my face bashed in, and made deaf for the rest of my life?

The then modern police force was indeed filling up with poor badly trained ego maniacs with a brutality fetish. Maniacs who are unforgiving people which I today genuinely try to avoid upsetting, and sensibly call them *'Sir and Madam,* and, *thank you Ma'am.'* They do appear to flush with their deep pride at such respectful accolades, *and yet,* if I had wanted their guns batons capsicum spray and 'Jolt' guns I could take them both in less than a minute; *Even as an older gentleman, but of course I have no need to, and if I did do such things, I feel I would be dead the moment they tracked me down.* As it is, I have nothing to say to the police worker from the past, but I will say this to all police cadets that want to retire someday with a clean conscience, and, to know they did the right thing. *In Prison, when we give up our mates we are called dogs, but in the Police Force when you do not give up officers on any level for committing a crime, you're an even worse dog. Why? because the oath of service says that to lie cheat and steal in a uniform, is the worse dishonor you can do to the Force, to your family, your honor, and your support. As well as your life. 'Don't be a crim; you are much too good for that.' I can assure you that your conscience guides the eventual direction that your life will take. As well as that of your future children.*

The people of Queensland have not been made fully aware of just how those government employees, do; *operate and conduct themselves,* but they do believe it is not up to them to criticize police workers who they see as needing to keep a secure law and order in their suburbs. *Peace at any cost,* appears to be the view of good citizens, *that is,* those with a lot of property to lose. But foolishly believing they have to accept theft by *such* employees, as a part of the, *price to pay,* is a weak cop out for the next generation of children. Children who shall get to read history books of our ongoing negligence. *We must remember, there are a lot of good men and women who are the life long unemployed, and we can surely give them a chance to prove themselves as a protector of those who pay their taxes. In my view, no person is indispensable.'* Your local member can also question bad behaviour, *on your behalf,* long before it develops into a problem for your own children, and, if he or she does not fire up, then you know where to vote in the next election. But he or she *must know your views* on such things, or they cannot act at all. For us to pay uniformed people a thousand dollars a week to get in violent road races with virtual children, is not at all normal, *or,* to use their muscle on students or even young girls is an insensitive view on our part. We cannot continue to give out good wages to people who disrespect us, and our children, and such behaviour has to be questioned. A thousand dollars a week is very good money, so a need to seek freebies anywhere from food to sex or money for favours, should mean immediate dismissal. Yet good people say nothing of such men and women who have now become a force within a force.

Or, can kill a young man who called out; *'Who let the dogs out.'*

As for the evaluation of my being a *'nobody,'* it came from many quarters, *even from my own family,* and that had suited me just fine. Because, every time the violent ones finished a ten year stretch, I had been in and out, three or four times, and I had unforgettable holidays down on the Gold Coast. Or, running around like an over grown teenager having a whale of a time. In any prison, men such I was, *back then,* were all as equal as the next man, and it was there that the one eyed man and one eared man, was king of all he surveyed.' *See no Evil and hear no Evil.*

I had given the same respect, *or disrespect,* to another male; that was given to me, and I had returned those quick flurries of punches with the same angry aggression that any inmate had dared to throw at me. *That was, in the ignorant 20th Century.*

In Gaol, *it is a level playing field,* and without their normal back up, or having the threat of extra time added on, they more often than not, *had backed down to me.* Of course, I ran the Remand yard ration set up, *so,* it paid them to be nice to a simple nobody, such as I was. I did believe I was a true blue Aussie that bowed to no man of a **'criminal-intent,'** and that, is a personal view I had of myself, although in time, that streak of stubbornness drew attention to my self, and so it was that I would cruelly pay the price for it.

A price I could not at all afford to pay, and today, I truly regret it for I am alone as any other offender, who had pulled up all too late.

At the end of the day, if you had allowed a criminal, *or a policeman who was skimming or scamming to get under your guard*, they hung around like a bad smell, *and* they contaminated your friend's family and loved ones. It was a situation of gross error on your part, and these leeches also laid with the media tarts and effeminate male journalists, *so that their backs were to be well covered in the event of a Royal Commission.*

There was no way out for me, and this, sadly enough, was to be the rest of my criminal life, *I felt then,* and I saw no real logical way out of such a mess until of course I might later have become some exceedingly successful person in the chosen career of a sneaky house thief, poor vagrant, *or,* some lazy-knockabout-no-hoping-loser; *Maybe a pimp?* Who knows? Maybe a good working husband, and a father?

Today I write history, *as it was,* so that media journalists will not get to swathe themselves as misrepresenting *do gooders,* that told the truth, *as it wasn't.* They can if they wish, continue to be weak hypocrites, and urge the fools to be violent, sick, and depraved, **for sole the purpose of selling their newspapers,** *but,* there will be two versions of what happened in 1970's, Queensland, and one of them will be mine. So, if justice prevails, then people in the 22nd century, will know the truth. *And that was, that good men and women, cowardly said nothing, and in turn lost the respect of future generations of Queensland teenagers.*

In the 20th Century, the history of Queensland would in time be so buried under mountains of a media type of salesmanship, which had included word-manipulation. There were pathological liars in many fields that had long studied literature like word addicts, and no future student would or could know the difference between fiction and historical data. When future trusting students read inadequate media files in search of what had happened in a certain era in Queensland, the contradictions confused them until older eyewitnesses explained the real facts to them. *Such as ongoing child abuse in the Catholic Church.*

The whole idea now, is to ridicule the views of the victim, *as well as the offender,* and hope that eyewitnesses die out quickly, so that the only version left will be that of the Justice Department Archives, and News Ltd. *Just as it happened, and was done in the year of 1870.*

In Queensland politics, a future state parliament, would in turn whitewash an old Queensland Premier, Sir Joh Bejielke Peterson. *A cunning old man who went on living into his nineties.* But fortunately, there were good men in our society who said he was a dirty corrupt old man that had made his fortune out of selling Uranium to the Chinese, *while growing Peanuts then contaminated by rat droppings.* A man they considered giving a State Funeral to, instead of being buried in a Wheely Bin. *Which he richly deserved.*

I had seriously thought of that old Peanut Farmer, *some thirty odd years later,* and I wondered if his arthritis was as bad as some said it was? Or, if it got even worse before his death. I do feel that *'Life'* will one day determine what all of us truly deserve. *And, give us what we should so receive.*

I conclude, that to stop alcohol fuelled violence, and sexual assaults, we first have to prevent such public servants from getting away with thievery, *brutally,* and an ongoing indecent treatment of men women and children. As well as troubled citizens who are locked up in old fashioned government buildings.

To do this, there is needed 250,000 Queenslanders to donate a Five Dollar Bill to a respectable local and selected Law Firm, so as to start a fighting fund that can bring suit against any Public Servant, *or Union,* that beats up, *or ill treats,* any Queensland citizen.

Otherwise, sit back and wait for your kids and your loved ones to be picked off; *One by one.*

But, to deter *'Alcohol fuelled Violent Offenders,'* needs the genuine input of men and women who understand the system of treatment from the inside.

This, is why I seek to introduce a system that is foolproof.

A system I have outlined in my writing; *'The Book of Projects.'*

CHAPTER 10

YARD TIME AND POLICE VERBAL

In 1969 & 1970, I became the longest resident in the remand section, *at that particular time,* mainly because the old law courts were all too busy granting a belated reprieve to those fortunate few. Or for many others, a self bail bond to those who had obediently pleaded guilty to something that the courts could not prove as; *'Criminally Intentional.'*

As time passed by, I had become a novelty for my having defended myself in a Queensland District Court of law, *and actually won.* No one could at all remember the last person to do so, and most people had considered that without any formal education *or,* the top-flight barrister to assist you, *that such a task was almost impossible.*

I do know personally the prisoner who was once falsely named *'Legs Diamond' Nee Gallagher,* who had two serious charges dismissed against him, due to his knowledge of Law. His case was an exception, until I threw a spanner in the works and had connected the then Courts with *enabling* police perjury to continue without legal prevention. *In the year 2010, a survey found the DPP won 99% of all trials, and Police Officers were acquitted 99% of the time for killing a citizen. Or a member of their own family.*

I did not mind the nodding attention I was getting at that time, *and,* the majority of the jail warders, either had a verbal go at me, or joked with me in that crude friendly jocular way that the many incarcerated, 20th Century Australians had used. *As both a defensive weapon, and a left handed compliment.*

'How much do you charge for traffic offenses Campbell?'

'Just a quick suck Boss, but don't tell anyone, or they will think I am gay.'

'*Your* a filthy animal Campbell, you should be locked up in the four yard cages.'

'Any time Boss, as long as you want to share it with me! *Hey? How about a ride there for a ride back?*' I would caxkle rudely, but with a bigger grin to soften the crude insult.

'*Fucking deaf cunt, I'd like to break his fucking legs.*' Were the words I had read, when his lips moved to shape non audible words? *But then again, he may have been suggesting I was a nice and caring person?*

Many of those new *clean-skin* prisoners would look at me in sheer amazement, *especially*, at that daring act of familiarity with the warders. *But as I saw it, it was that crude type prison humor that they could not at all understand.*

Although, *in time,* they too would learn such sick crude and very language.

Especially, when they were sent to the main prison.

A few years before the year, *1970,* those same harder & *stern* looking warders, *who'd hid behind their uniform,* would have thrown the book at me for such dour filth. *Or improper insolence.* At the same time, such dour words do not at all mean that I had condoned, or even accepted the indecent obscene way of the poor unfortunate humans who had the misfortune of being in a position to be classified as a homosexual citizen. But, the rude pretentious type of teasing, had by then become a crude means of our warding off total indecency. That is, by our ridiculing a unacceptable '*homosexuality,*' Or by our seeing a man on boy sexuality, as clearly, a negatively weak type of act, *or, by our accepting* such verbal *obscenity, as being normal,* was our way of becoming desensitized to insult. *Strange as it may seem to those who are ignorant of prison yard terminology, or behavior, it is a defensive mechanism that has survived the test of time.*

'For every lad that succumbs, three are usually saved.'

Racism? Or such in house Homophobia? *It is not.* For it is simply a *'Culturism'* '*(my own word)* that emphatically suggests, that a male human species; *may,* if they so wish, reject homosexuality, *or bisexuality,* as a necessary function in their life.

~~~

My bail did not arrive, *of course,* but one special young girl named Adele Punton, *from Coopers plains,* had arrived at the old prison with the necessary funds to release me, *but,* was quickly turned away by Alex Lobban. *Mainly because Adele was under twenty-one years of age.* Two staunch good hearted biker associates, also tried to bail me, but again, could not then prove that the money was of honest acquisition. So it was that they too, *were also turned away.* I somehow detected a conspiracy to hold me in the *'Dream breaker,'* for the rest of my life?

The paid up house certificates, *and the land bonds,* were that sure fire way of our achieving an immediate release, but, it was a rare type of a criminal, *or teenager,* who had usually owned such properties. So, *without the deeds*, any mere prison official was permitted to decide, or to adjudicate, just who stayed, and who was to be released.

I was myself of course, quite unaffected by this somewhat minor set back, and I'd happily slept like a newborn baby until those bullying detectives arrived with their special warrant to take me onto the Inala Police Station. *So as to allegedly question me on very serious criminal matters.*

I had no other choice, *but to comply with the served warrant,* and I was forcefully escorted from inside of the prison compound by a car load of large over weight detectives. Thick headed bullies who had cracked a lot of rude jokes all the way to the Inala C.I. B. *One weighty broken-nosed-bully had called to me from the front seat.*

'Hey, what did you just say Stal? You jimmied the window?'

'Really, is that how you got in? *Through the window.'* laughed a big detective sitting beside me.

'No!' said another. 'The cunt just said he jimmied the fucking front door.'

'Hang on, I'll just write that down in my note book.' said Kenneth Cambridge Morris. *Dick head supreme, on a thin crust.*

I'd said nothing in reply to them, mainly because I was in their jurisdictions, and as it was they clearly had that unreserved power over me. Which included slapping, hair pulling, *and generally,* a rough type of treatment.

It was not my being at the Police station that had ever at all worried me over the many years that I had been a cheeky mischievous offender, but it certainly had lot to do with my then getting to the police station unhurt. That alone was my biggest concern. *In Western Australia. A prisoner was found dead in a Paddy Wagon after a five hundred kilometer trip. Without a drink of water in the mid-summer-heat.*

I need not have worried, because all except one of the Jacks were real amateurs, and the serious one had spoken politely to me. He gave me a friendly wink, and I of course had relaxed. He knew it was a; *put on verbal,* and so did I, but it did not stop him getting me a big hot mug of coffee while the rest of the warbler's took to their new typewriters to make up the very untrue false Record of Interviews. As it was, they had decided to start off with just five B & E's. This, was so that each one could lazily take up a particular case file, as the long day of a slow and inept typing, had began.

I saw them note the date, as well as the time, and my listening to the loud noises of their inept typing, was the one sound that stood out from all others. In fact I had guessed correctly, that each man used the same time of day for each lying record of interview, which in turn, had meant, that I could not have been having three or more alleged interviews at the same time. I'd kept my face blank, as a frozen ventriloquist, while one friendly detective and I had a very serious conversation about the Saturday races, which at the time had featured a magnificent stallion named; *Black Onyx.* A big giant champion stallion that was then post a current favourite in the Doomben Ten Thousand.

'What do you reckon Larry, do you think the big black horse will win?' The detective had said to me as we both studied the weights and the allotted barrier draws.

'I'll tell you what Boss, if I had a house I'd put the fucking lot on him to win by two lengths.'

The other detectives were not so friendly, and one had jeered loudly.

'Hey, cunts like you don't own houses; you break into the fucking things.'

'What do you care? You don't fucking own the fucking things either.' I jeered back

'What I do own, is paid for *honestly.*' sniffed the lanky policeman, who glared coldly at me with a false show of personal morality.

'*Yeah*, so you say, you lying cunt.' I had snorted at him with a exorbitant show of contempt.

'*Is typing up that shit something you call honest?*' I had laughed at him for trying to suggest that he was really a good man? While in fact he was sitting there participating in a conspiratorial act of criminal perjury.

The detective then flushed at this, and the best thing was, that if they had at all spoken normally, I could not have heard them clearly, *at all,* and it was only the loud raucous talk and laughter that I'd ever retorted to. By not letting them know I was partially deaf, they in turn, were not able to write of it, *or to mention such a thing in the Record of Interviews.* So it was, that I had made the prosecutors job all that much harder, *in the final analysis.*

Returned that afternoon to the prison confine, I'd urgently tried to get to see the superintendent, *Jack Farrell,* so as to make a statutory declaration that I had been set up and verbalized by those detectives. *But,* he avoided me, *or he was conveniently unavailable.*

I went to my cell, and in just a matter of minutes, I was asleep, while knowing full well that there was nothing at all that I could do about it. In fact a day out in the police station and of my then being made to participate in all those Magistrate court proceedings, was the most mind exhausting thing that can happen to any prisoner, and so, when people complain about a lawyers exorbitant fees, they are so, truly wrong.

As it was, the magistrate had accepted the false charges, and then duly refused any bail to me, and so there was really not anything to worry about until I could get to court so as to clear my slate of the trumped up incorrect allegations. Strangely enough, not one legal person had ever queried why those detectives had charged me, especially after the fact that I had been legally acquitted of a previous serious charge in the District Court of Queensland. *One bright remand prisoner had suggested it could be 'revenge?'*

But then, *who else would give a damn, except me?* Of course, one thing was certain, and that was that any human being at all could be taken from their place of residence, and made to look guilty of a crime. *And there was not a thing they could do about it.* That is until many years later when DNA distinctly made positive liars out of certain detectives. I also found, that none were ever charged with the act of perjury, *or*, of conspiracy to commit a criminal offence.

Those legal people seemed to be in a world of their own, and many had often used some secret type of language of their very own. A language, that had appeared to humiliate ordinary felons, while making them cringe in shame, and self-doubt.

The flowery sentences, or tarty cold insults to a man much bigger and stronger than they were, had usually gone unpunished. Or, received very little criticism back in return. Insults such as; ' *A filthy flotsam finds its own levels, and you have certainly found yours, prisoner! 'Ha ha ha ha!* They would laugh uproariously.

In the courtroom, prisoners and citizens were clearly out of their league.

Little did the bullies know, that *flotsam* was three levels above legal shark shit, as well as the filthy dirty parasites that fed off the body that they were spawned from. But of course, without any vitriolic fire power, an ordinary man was always considered that never ending roll of used up toilet paper, *in their world of greater privilege?* The educated type witticism, was renowned in the upper levels of Government, *and,* one allegation was, that one foolish pompous legal gentleman had boasted that; *'even'*, God had to *make an appointment to see him.*

It was further reported in the newspapers, that the idiotic man died soon after in a horrific car crash, and it was duly noted, that he was called to answer the stupid and blasphemous statement that he had allegedly made in his Court. *In front of a newspaper journalist.*

Worse still, his innocent teenage daughter died in the car beside him.

'Karma.' said one older prisoner. *'You can't beat it, and you can't escape it.'*

Personally, I'd called it the *'Dissertation of Life,'* , for if *'Life'* turned its back on any man woman or child, they were clearly finished in their world of prosperity.

Strangely enough, I wrote to editor David Fagin of the courier mail *almost forty odd years later,* and I had explained that there was a intelligent way for the *'Mail'* to make a lot more money, *and to attract,* a lot more paying customers. I explained the urgent need for different cultures to have their say, *and furthermore,* that I would work for free to describe the hidden world of prisons. Which I would title; *'Grapevine Gossip.'* I further explained, that even the *'Silks'* liked to hear about their goings on, and that alone would, *or should,* attract a wider audience.

Fagin wrote back, and he said he would seriously; *'think about it,'* and then created *'Earsay'* which I believe had boosted sales. He did not contact me again, and there was no section to describe the day to day goings on in our dark and gloomy institutions.

CHAPTER 11

LOTS OF GOSSIP FROM MAD BILLY

In 1969, remand life had continued on as usual, and numerous men came and went at such a rate, that I had honestly thought there may have been a larger crime-wave taking place, than was reported on the radio. When an offender was released, *or was sentenced,* I fortunately was given their ration bags to hold, and better still, *if,* they had escaped their due penalty of prison, I by right of possession had gotten to keep the largesse to myself. I also was the bookmaker for betting food or tobacco, and so it was that the special cupboard in the kitchen, had soon become quite full.

The younger paupers would hang about those kitchen areas *begging hand-outs,* and the well-known recidivists would growl at them to move *the fuck* away, or to get a punch in the *'fucking'* head. Fortunately for some, I was a little more generous and so I gave out sandwiches and cups of tea to those boys at risk. While the men at my side would shake their heads quite critically.

'Give the cunts nothing, *Flex,* or they will just hang around like dirty stray cats if you fucking feed them! And anyway, those mongrel arse's have got their rations just like every body else.' said a man named Fred Wise, with complete and utter contempt for any man that had the audacity to beg for a handout.

'I just feel a bit sorry for them Fred, and anyway, the dirty hocks will get them if they can't get a smoke.'

'That's their fucking problem, *not ours.* Fuck them off mate they are all fucking dogs anyway.'

I knew that Fred was correct in his view, and seemingly, a prison life was for a punishment, not a children's nursery. But I was also one of those older lags of twenty-six who'd long believed, that today's telegram boy, could possibly be tomorrow's Post Master General.

I had also suspected that I was going to be inside the prison for a very long time to come, *if those detectives had any say in the matter*, and I had also considered wisely, that a friend in need, was a future friend indeed.

Strangely enough, the seventeen year old teenagers could not at all vote drink or even serve on a jury. Nor could they go to war, *yet,* they were put in a maximum security prison with a full knowledge of the authorities. '*That they were at risk of male rapists, and mentally ill perverts.*

Over the following weeks, and or months, I had helped to start up a Manila card game with some big roly poly Greek man, *and,* for awhile this caused a lot of friendly banter and general excitement. That is, until he later got his bail. From this game I met a lot of the southern men who were quite unfriendly to the average Queenslander, but, because I myself had once lived over at North Bondi, *a New South Wales coastal area,* I was quickly accepted as an expatriate crim from New South Wales. *'Probably out of convenience'* I had later contemplated.

This group was soon part of the kitchen set up, but they clearly knew that what I said, *went,* and so for a little while I became that big fish in a little pond. I would have no bar of an escape attempt, from inside that secluded kitchen area, *as,* this would be certain to ruin a very good thing for us all.

I also warned those New South Wales Welshmen, that underneath that kitchen area, there were the numerous garage bays for the prison officials, and that if they so chose, the officials could easily hear all of the private or secret things being said by any of us who were not as discreet as we should be. Especially when prison officials were parking, or leaving their cars beneath our very privileged domain. These Sydney men took no notice, and a few weeks later when I was in court for a hearing, they soon began to talk out of school. Some of the crude things they discussed were not officially appropriate. That is, for the ears that listened from beneath their feet.

Jack Farrell had indeed been listening in, and so Jack had come storming into the kitchen area and he cleaned them out like a smoking hornet's nest. Jack sent a lot of them to the old cell blocks, *to remain there until their court appearances*, and so like many other fools, they soon found a situation much worse than the spotless Remand Section. I'd realized that they had said some very *foolish things*, but I also found they had the audacity to suggest that the untrustworthy Queenslanders had informed upon them. *Not forgetting that they joked about Jack Farrell having no fingers on his right hand.*

I knew quite well of course, they had given themselves up, *as cold as maggot stew,* and that the stupid idiotic rivalry between all those Australian States, had simply divided the foolish men into the weaker, *and easily,* those more pliable, or should I say, very negative groups.

In reality, we all needed to stick together like shit to a blanket, especially when the later bully boy tactics by warders had exploded into our lives. Especially when that cruel and arrogant administrator, *named J.R. Stevenson,* had later arrived to take over the running of the old Boggo Road Gaol complex.

Billy Taylor (*Billy Neilson*)and another truly violent tough man had then arrived unexpectedly in the remand yard, *and,* they were pleasantly surprised to find me in a position of leadership. I'd fed them up and I gave them a start, but of course they did not expect to stay long, and in the time they were there, they had taken physically to a lot of inmates who had allegedly assisted the dirty police in the past. Bill gave a vicious beating to a big Hungarian man, *with a steel metal ladling spoon wrapped up in a cloth towel,* and we physically had to drag him from the corner kitchenette and place that dented bruised and bloodied man in a less conspicuous area.

'Fuck you Bill; you will bloody-well kill some poor cunt some day.'

'You don't know the half of it Flex.' He sniggered in his insane way.

Bill had changed from that softer suburban kid into a prison crazy man, and his blue eyes were glazed with that crazy insane look of the multiple killer. His cheeks and forehead were scarred badly but fortunately for him he had all his teeth and he looked in fairly good shape to me; *Tough as Teak, is a much more apt description.*

The creeping up of *'insanity'* apparently happened to most of the men that had carried around with them that hard paranoid look of the sick psychopath. Men whom I'd strongly believed had earlier been created and nurtured in a rough house prison environment. *Or a boys reformatory.* Totally beyond help of hospitals, or, even qualified psychiatrists that could help the less troubled men when they moved slowly through our uninstructed uncaring society, *and,* those Australian prisons like wily jungle predators. Mathematically, even Attorney Generals do not at all see two or three thousand psychopaths spread out all over Australia as a major problem? Simply because they deal in statistics? But, in that Remand yard, they stood out like a big red boil on a Prime Ministers nose.

I could still, in my own way, manage to reach Bill with that basic prison logic, *mainly because I was a person from the past that he could trust a little more than other offenders.* Of course, other males of a tougher nature, were not given that rare latitude that he had offered to me, *although,* he had watched me warily as I used the carving knife to cut up the bread rations.

I remembered *well* his best friend in Two Division, named Kevin Rodwell, *who had been released with him,* and Bill told me that he had killed his old friend in a mad drunken fight. That is, while traveling across the Nullabor Plains to Western Australia. *The person he spoke of was in the old 2 Division in 1964, and his family never stopped searching for him.*

'I loved the poor guy, but he was dead when I later woke up, and so I fucking-well buried him in the sand.' He had said, with eyes that were dull and smoky, while appearing to have lost all their human sparkle as well as that inner love of everyday life, and of people.

Bill told me how his friend's death haunted him for years, until he'd imagined a ghost was following him around. This apparition was suggesting crazy things to him. *While also allegedly telling him to kill other men and women.*

'Don't ever kill anyone Flex, *they don't fucking well suffer,* it is the fucking living bastards who really suffer the most'

I knew that Bill was totally beyond any help, at all. I personally felt that he would most probably create a lot of collateral damage before those hard line police had either killed him, *or,* locked him away for life.

Strangely enough, he left more quickly than I'd expected. That is, when one younger man whom he had punched in the face crept sneakily up behind him and smashed a heavy china mug into the top of Bills head. Apparently, it left him prostrate and bleeding helplessly, on the filthy toilet floor, as his legs jerked uncontrollably, and not one remand inmate was at all sorry it had happened to him; *Including me,* mainly because I knew he would turn on me at the drop of a hat. With men like Bill, you went for broke with knife boot object or a Biro in the eye. *There was nothing worse than having a silly Billy breathing down your neck.* As for the lad who had hit him, he went on to marry and settle down, but, Bill told me four years later that he was passing a hotel and he thought he recognized him and he quickly king hit him. Only to find out it was the wrong guy.

But at the time, *of Bill's head banging,* the ambulance had rushed Bill for an immediate urgent surgery, and he was eventually allowed self-bail, *when as expected,* he again had began to do violent armed holdup raids on hotel management offices. His apparent method, was to bash up and force them to open up their safe with a brutal frenzied violence. *Until of course a police task force was set up to track him down.* Bill was obviously crazy as a fox, and he was flirting with death in such a way that only a walking dead man acted. *Or could act.*

Bill was simply another half smart criminal that spent his entire life in and out of our hard penal institutions, all over Australia, and he would, *I felt,* probably die by his own hand. *Unless of course whiskey or drugs had finished him off first.*

To be truthful, I was in no way in his league, *or that of Billy Stokes,* but I had been pleased as punch as he had described in detail the violent beating Bill Stokes had received. *As well as his being left for dead in a back alley, in Fortitude the Valley.*

There was no way to stop Stokes, *either,* and the latest street gossip had been that certain police in the armed robbery squad, were allowing Stokes, *and a bully of an informant named John Bell,* to run rampant in the metropolitan area holding up local Supermarkets. Bill described that Chermside Plaza, as a very brazen robbery, *and hold up,* where Stokes had used a big sledgehammer to break the glass doors in. Actually, it seemed, *or was alleged by a friend of mine,* that Stokes had gotten a very good piece of information by helpful security men, *that is,* to smash the glass just as the office staff and security men were opening up the floor safe in full view of waiting customers. My friend drove the car and went and got his hair curled immediately after the robbery. Seeing as, two children had stared at him as he was illegally waiting in the parking bay for disabled people.

It was scary to think, that criminals had by then, wielded such amazing power, and that all of those *'Valley'* prostitutes, which Stokes had a firm strong grip on, were allegedly giving him a very serious information about a whole lot of those powerful Queenslanders. Wealthy men, who allegedly had indecent sexual liaisons with the male prostitutes. *'Stephan who?* In retrospect, or looking back at that era, I'd known quite well, that my own life would have been as worthless as an unsigned cheque. That is, had I ever attempted to operate in the special Red light area that was literally referred to as the *'Brisbane Valley by night.'*

In a way, I was quite pleased, *that when I was free,* I'd at least gotten enough common sense to stay well out in the outer expansive suburbs, and, to secretly live the semi vagrant blue collar life style of those *average* prison rejects. Had the belabored *special police,* known even just half of what I knew of those whorehouse crimes, that were then happening in dozens of City and suburban areas, they would have cleaned up that inner Valley, *or at least,* violently destroyed the child prostitution and drug networks within a matter of just a few weeks? I later found that the *'Special Police'* were the ones who were running the girls in Brisbane, and when they told a girl to jump. *They jumped.* What I had known of police corruption, then, *in 1970,* was all just a garbled hearsay, *and,* not worth as much as a suspended sentence. But I did know one thing for certain, and that was, that if I myself was privy to such information, it was reasonable to believe that the Queensland police force had the same information. I knew also, that if Stokes and his many hangers on felt they were safe from, *eventual retribution,* then, they had another feel coming.

CHAPTER 12

IT'S WHO YOU KNOW THAT COUNTS

B eing a small time criminal, was fine with me, and I could well afford to laugh and joke with all types of prisoners as they arrived or left in passing. Just occasionally, I would get attached to one or two people who made me feel good. In fact, a youth of eighteen had arrived in the twin remand yards, and in days he had quickly singled me out for attention. Foolishly, my ego got a lift when the young lad said I was a well-known *'Big shot,'* in his local area.

'You have to be joking; I have never even been there, mate.' I replied with some amusement.

That youth who was named Christopher Towns, had in turn mentioned people I had known quite well, *and,* were men who had told him to look me up if he'd ever landed in prison. Very soon I had this young car thief following me around like a loyal puppy, and no matter how hard I tried to shake him, he was always there with a fresh hot cup of tea for me. That is, after conning his way into my quite suspicious, and very wary crew of sad sick offenders. *Regulation wise, beverages were only permitted with meals. While, meals were only permitted with beverages. But, those in the know, knew.*

I never at that time thought that anything, *smart arse* I'd had to say to Chris, would at all influence him to be a persistent, and well-known criminal inside prisons. *It turned out, he had wasted that greater part of his life living behind walls.* Our, being *'regretful after the damage was done'* was in no way any answer to another person's problem, but, the lesson to be learned at that time, was not to teach the gullible those impulsive precarious ways to at all solve their day to day financial problems.

'But then, what were financial counselors for?' I today muse to myself as I lazily consider both sides of that dirty old proverbial; *'bent penny'*

I myself was certainly *not,* a correct type role model for any youth who was then starting out in a life of crime, *although,* I had on occasions warned him against gender bender sex, as well as the harder drugs that were quite rampant in certain areas of Brisbane, *at that time.* Of course I was not as well informed as I thought I was, and I would later find out that Chris had been having a *street sex* for more than five years or so. Obviously, with all manner of filthy established men and women. As well as swallowing drugs almost every day that he could find or afford them. *Or, suck men off for them.*

The fact that Chris was eighteen years old, had told me that he was headed for a big wake up call. Especially when he would learn, that once he was an adult, he would automatically be rejected by the users. Variably, he would in time need to either learn a new trade quickly, *or he would be just another bisexual prisoner for the rest of his life.* Later, he would tell me of the professional couples who'd made him the, *'onion in the sandwich,'* and took hundreds of photos of him in sexual acts when he was just; *'Knee high to a grasshopper.'* The confession, was to make me feel sorry for him?

At that later time, I was of course more curious than shocked because that filthy kiddie pornography, *that I had so observed in the prison proper,* would have, I felt at the time, put Chris's social and sexual manipulators to shame. Every man, *and his dog,* had dirty pictures back in those days. *Seeing as the then renowned Land Camera had surfaced with a gusto,* and every twelve year old girl, and her rag doll, wanted to be a part time model.

I'd began to have my court hearings on the verbal, *or concocted charges,* that is, over those following months, and I then noticed that the lofty rude magistrate did the police bidding, He'd also had duly refused me any bail, *against my angry objections.'*

I had called for the matter of the Sims Metal Merchants, *charges,* to be fully finalised and was then ignored by the prosecution, that had smirked like a rich bitch's schoolboy *'shiny shoes'* son. Instead, they had put in a verbal evidence to the court of my alleged break in of some low class carpet shop.

As the first real test case of their impromptu and mostly untrue fabricated charges. In fact, it would take just over two and a half years to finalise a long avoided scrap metal charge, and to eventually receive back my wallet containing the contested money. That is, without considering the other many falsified charges. Of course, by then I was back on the Merry Go Round, *and,* heading back to Gaol. *On, very serious charges*

'What the fuck would I do with a roll of carpet?' I had thought to myself at the time, and I'd simply shaken my head in a total disgust that some rotten snotty nosed public servant could do anything that he had wanted to. *'I guess I could use a bit of it on the floor of my cell.'* I mused as the recent problem of just how to deal with such a charge had followed, and or plagued me, for many weeks on end.

Boggo Road Gaol did not have one law book, *although Hansard was available,* so, any expert advice on my conducting a trial, was not available. All I really had, was my debating experience, and a *firm* knowledge that I did not at all commit the offense as charged. *I was in fact, an* accessory *after the fact.*

On that night before the trial, I began to leaf through that old dog-eared copy of *'How, To Win A Trial',* and, even though it was meant as a show of wit and humor for the legal half wits, and snobs, I had observed the more sneakier underhand way to maliciously influence a fair minded jury.

I had known that the Judge, *would,* in his high loftier position, be a dead set Government man, and for me to try and play up to him, *or even attempt to convince him of my dead set innocence,* would be totally useless. In fact, I would learn in the many years to come that the police had as many files on the legal profession as the legal profession had on them, and so when either party wanted to achieve their own result, they had simply blackmailed or traded off to each other. If a criminal had access to such files, he would soon have his charges put on hold, or could have them totally disappear. *In law, it is not whom you know, but it's what you know about whom!* In my case, the Jury was my one and only chance of an out and out acquittal, and the cartoons portrayed in the novelette; *'How to Win a Trial.'* had given me a fresh idea that was in a sense, quite a devious move on my part. It was a very cunning move that would influence a lot of later trials that followed, *as well as changing the Queensland law to demand a Notice of Alibi* from any uneducated and ignorant defendants. It was quite easy to formulate a plan of attack, and it soon proved to be, that the false face I had intended to show to those jurymen would not be the person that I really was, *or appeared to be,* but the person they imagined me to be.

Like most of the uneducated people who went before the court, I had pretended to be some person *or some one* who I was not. I also felt that with a little playacting on my part I could quite easily pull off a really big upset. An upset that would show the law society just how blatant was that practice of *'verbalized'* or fabricated evidence in the state of Queensland. *Show it was an authority and policy that did nothing to lower the crime level in society.* What it did reveal to the public, *above all other things,* was that it showed that the court proper itself was part and parcel of that most corrupt and unlawful practice. By their maliciously allowing an official perjury in their courtrooms, it had shown; *collusion between police and the district court,* and that the prosecution wholly decided on the sentence. As it was, the judge simply implemented it with a sharp stroke of his gold fountain pen.

In my uneducated way I had felt then that I was in a really good position to show those lofty arrogant people, *who'd felt that they were above an ordinary citizen,* that two could play their manipulating game. Also, that I for one could attempt to bring them down a peg from their self promoted positions and to show them up for who and what they really were. None yet realized they were *'public servants,'* and needed to answer for the methods they had used to convict civilians, as well as the money they spent freely on brand new cars chauffeur's electronic goods and social grandstanding. *Not discounting expensively furnished chambers.*

By condoning the crime of perjury for their hired underlings, it would one day cut even a then *;Judiciary,'* down to size, in the eyes of the ordinary wage earner, and in turn it had revealed them for what, and who, they really were. *Indeed! Arrogant and selfish grand stander's as well as a fellowship of sneering* *manipulating liars that they really were.* Men and women, who still have that media hobbled with ancient laws but had quickly blamed the then police force, when the ominous odor became unbearable. Strangely enough, a change of Government would one day actually save their bacon, and, the ever gullible, *or disinterested public,* had allowed some very snooty influential lawyers, *as well as Jurists,* to legally breathe a great sigh of relief. As it was, no official body of people was more corrupt than the Queensland Unions, who were at that time much like a thick suffocating spider web that had made the Queensland Law fraternity, look like naughty rude boys who were telling dirty tales out of school.

There were no bigger thieves, than those Australian Unions that rudely spent an ordinary battlers union fees, *like drunken sailors.* Worse still, when they got their heads into State parliament. it was World Trips, High Class Prostitutes, and council built humpies by the sea. *Where they went fishing, drank beer, and told heaps of lies to historians that had interviewed them.*

The average Australian male was worlds away from etiquette, and their wearing thongs shorts and singlets was the national dress. Being *appropriate* never worried them, nor dis-speaking or acting appropriately meant a darn thing to them, and so it was, that the snobbish Law Society and their ilk had a time of it by overcharging, fining, introducing new laws that took their homes and property right from under their feet.

The problem was, later generations of students ran smack bang into a wall of *'Nepotism'* and *'Mateship,'* and although highly educated, they could not get into the higher ranks of; *Politics, Unionism, or Law.* So it was the legal eagles also took the uneducated Australians for every penny they had. That is, by selling bags of *Health, Property, Car and Life Insurance,* and then reneged when a poor yokel sought payment for a car accident, a flooded house, or, a Death in the Family.

Australia always has been a place to rip off anyone that is stupid enough to be ripped off. *Or buy drugs on the black market.* So it was that our modern children; *'Sold goods, stole goods, bashed each other, took drugs, and sought to emulate the generations that had come before them.'*

Amazingly, the biggest rort of all was locking fools up in prison, and it is to be speculated today, that hundreds of millions of Tax Payers money is used up holding uneducated riff raff in our prisons, *'Every single Year.'* In fact, it was inside a prison that you'd learned that if you knew no-one further up the ladder of success, you were simply a *'No-Body.'* For me, I knew prison like the back of my hand, and so it was that everybody in the Remand Yard, wanted to know; *'Me.'*

CHAPTER 13

A VIEW TO CLASSIFICATION

In the remand yard, I myself had long chosen to play the gutter type politics of being a good charitable and friendly type person, that is, while cunningly building up my allies among the unknown, but somewhat familiar confident men who'd respectfully sought start up assistance, and an emotional escape from the monotony of that remand yard type of life.

My portrayed joviality was really a front for my own insecurities and my being friendly, *'once the ice was broken'* was simply my covering up for my inner lonesomeness, and the deep depression of having experienced my many mistakes in my early childhood. I of course continued to ignore the introverts, *or square heads,* as they were an unpredictable and quite unknown consequence. *'Or quantity.'*

Experience of long standing made me paranoid where new faces were concerned, but after a few days their real temperament and attitude would surface, and they would soon be accepted on face value.

Some warders were trained observers, but I knew also from long observations, that they were not at all very good at; *face to face psychology, or, were knowledgeable men,* and they would misjudge me as some shifty type troublemaker who needed to be knocked off his perch. On the other hand, they often smiled at other inmates and had jovially patted men like Billy Taylor on the shoulder, mainly because of his good manners and apparent respect toward all the good and supposedly incorruptible prison staff.

How the many senior officials in Boggo Road had *then* classified, or *declassified* criminals, left me at a great loss, and all I could do was shake my head at a decision made to put killers like Billy in reach of the bread knife. Those incoming prisoners usually observed or had evaluated those prison warders in return, and many were given a nickname that described their personality, or a general appearance.

The reasons for this, was, so that the moment that a morning roster began I and others would then have that special advantage when someone signaled to us that the '*Stranger*' or another warder named;' *Dolly Bliss'* was on a remand yard duty.

'In fact, *Dolly Bliss* was one of the fairest minded of warders that the older prison system ever had, and his being an effeminate homosexual was not a bother to anyone. Other names too, had included '*Grumpy, Sleepy, Dopey, Maggot C, or Nosey,* and of course, *Fairy Ford,*' although the caring more reasonable warders who had long balanced the rules with fairness, *and any sensible laxity*, were given those affectionate names that described their easy going attitude, *and or their latitude*. 'There was also a man named '*Brooksie*, or William Brooks, who to me, was a true blue warder that refused a shiny '*Seniors Pip*' so as to make him an official '*Officer.*'

'*Stick it up your arse; I don't need a piece of tin to make a man out of myself.*' He had bellowed out on the compound in the 1960's, and I'd remembered laughing so hard that I got a blood nose. *Good memories, I am sure we would all go stark raving mad without them*

Depending upon the roster, *or the time of day*, I would know exactly whether to go into a far off corner with a special book, or, cheekily barter a deal with the main kitchen workers for any personal advantage that I could. *Hopefully so for an excellent profit to boot.*

Because classification *and or an instruction*, were topsy-turvy, I'd tried to educate young Chris Towns who was loud boisterous and over confidant. His lock up time in punishment had also quickly deprived him of his tobacco, and normally it would have left a good looking youth like him begging from the masses of men who would want something sexual for rolled up cigarettes, *and or,* any edible privileges.

I believed then that my generosity had kept the lad out of harms way, *or so I thought,* and in many ways it was not a good move to have a pretty faced small boy in your company, mainly because of the foul detrimental judgements that could be made of ones, *well meant intentions.*

Weeks later when I fronted Chris on certain rumors that I had heard, I was to be seriously shocked when the young man rudely confessed his long term bisexuality, and of his earlier week to week street survival living off the administrations of older men and women in well to do inner suburbs of Brisbane in the late 1960's. Chris was, in fact at that particular time, in a three out cell and having full on sex with his rude cell mates. He had also confessed to me that he was actually enjoying every minute of those dangerously indecent liaison while he was allegedly turning the table on his formerly manly lovers. If that was bad, I was to find that I being the idiot type to take people whom I liked, at face value, for I was apparently the only person left in the remand yard that was unaware that Chris had that particular preference to lick a man's rectum filled up with excrement; *Referred to as a Rose-leaf, in prison jargon.* Strangely enough I had previously queried an old friend of why he kept referring to Chris as *'Rosie,'* and when I was told why, I was totally disbelieving that Chris could do such a crude and depraved thing. I had also wondered if familiar official prison personnel were noticing my then present company, or were making incorrect assumptions of my sexual preferences. *Mainly because of that blonde youth, 'who was like my inescapable shadow.'* As it was, I had faced the young lad with the rumors of his supposed crude sexual cell shenanigans. The lads biggest concern was, that I would not consider him my friend, but of course, I'd felt that his being more than loyal to me had negated what others thought of me, *or of him.* As I have explained to others who have asked, most women do not like another woman's personal smell, no matter how attractive their face may be, and I too would have retched to lay with a man for a same reason.

'Or to suck a penis that had been in another mans anus.'

I reasoned with some great concern about what others may now think of me, but today. I do know, *that people think what they like anyway.*

Of course, had I at desired the male form, I felt my opportunities to have sex in prison, may well have been double or actually outnumbered those of my lost opportunities to copulate with receptive females in the outside world. A world, where of course. most sex was all show and no go, *'unless one had generously paid the piper and avoided the teasers.'*

Sex to me, was just a word, but I had wondered at times whether government policy makers were actually encouraging prisoners, *in the sixties,* to have sexual relations with each other? *Mainly so that females out in the real world would not be listed high on their sexual agenda when they were eventually released.*

The fact that Chris's personal habits were not at all mine to judge, condemn, *or agree with,* had still caused myself to be judged by the company of which I had kept, and of course I'd known that all of those wet tongues were wagging incessantly. *Especially among the envious convicts who knew me well enough to rib me.* Chris's later descriptions of one of his tougher tattooed cell-mates had given me that clear insight into the lengths that some criminals would go to for a crude sex with a youth. Also, I'd observed his cell mates worried looks that I may indeed know exactly what he really was underneath his tougher exterior.

'I mean to say Joey; I never thought you were that way?' I said to an old street associate, who in turn had flushed a deep beetroot red. A past or current knowledge is all-powerful, *inside prison,* and I would quietly store away such important information for some future time, especially if I had at all needed it to blackmail a man in a prison altercation, or to control him or her out on the street when some people treacherously spoke out of school. I had long believed that all secret sexual information was most valuable in that greater game of prison politics, that had, *over a period,* separated the big winner from the grinner, or a *groover from a loser.'* Homophobia *even now,* in the year 2014 is still widespread, although alternative lifestyles have blossomed out of control for decades. *Also,* men I have known who were bisexual in prison, still professed to hate with a venom males and females seeking same gender relationships. In the street, in crime, remand yards courts, prisons and criminals lives, and finally, in the area of classification; *denial was the name of the game.*

Nobody presented them selves as they really were, and some youth had pretended to be gangsters, *when they were nothing but frightened soft rabbits.*

The old crim of yesteryear was the most able of all to put the right label on the inmate that walked into a yard with their enamel panniken, toothbrush, and a type of look that that told certain men what type of person he really was.

Normally, I would have picked Chris Towns, *for whom and what he was,* but his brashness and loudness actually disarmed me, for he showed no sign of shame or fear of any nature. To me he had looked like an eager young car thief that had been waiting for many years to get his big chance to see what Boggo Road Gaol was all about. As far as describing his life-style, I do not think that Chris's early life, *or commiserations,* should fit in my reflections of remand yard life, and, more than likely, any true or decent self respecting editor would, *or should,* edit such confessions out. Then again, if such a sad tale only arises after my death, then I will be the least worried about that young man's indecent lifestyle. *A way of life that had once been shamefully reminisced by someone, such as I.*

When looking back on Chris Towns filthy adventures, true or not, *right or wrong,* I find it hard to hate a young man who was so depraved that I feel he was truly trying to corrupt me and to break down my last vestiges of resistant to the world of hedonists. As well as those trained from child-hood type child molesters. *Crudely referred to by myself as; 'Wobbies.'*

It is, *as I loosely recall,* the tale I was told from a blonde youth 1n 1970 that caused me to repeat it in an official writing to the State Government in the year 2009.

'The Crack in the Door' tale that Chris Towns had told me, was the basis for a writing that I sent to the Justice Department Library, titled *Child Exploitation and the Criminal Element in the State of Queensland. 2009.*

The *Office Works* bound copy had actually caused a furore in Government Child Protection circles, including a hurried thirty million dollar influx of funds quickly rushed through by the Bligh Government, *so as to get serious on all child abuse offenders.*

Q Weekend magazine justified the expenditure without any reference to the 'Crack in the Door' although their mention of a man that groomed a young girl next door, *had told me,* they were upset with me for questioning their government methods of dealing with an abusive offender. Unfortunately, today, the Government is spending hundreds of millions more in an online search for predators and Bikers, *instead of preventing the children ever being on a pornographic film in the first place*. The amusing thing was, there was no '*Girl next door*' but the woven tale served its purpose and the authorities spent freely so as to hide their tepid embarrassments.

In hindsight it may well have served me better *not* to have bound up and presented the manuscript at all, (*such as the writing I had sent to the Queensland Justice Department library,*) as it certainly could have caused them to kick my door in and to take my personal computer for their ongoing investigations into pedophile activity.

In a nutshell, I had described in the revealing writing of the then widespread corruption of children by similar children in Brisbane schools. I further explained how boys and girls of eight and nine years of age were being corrupted, *with images and furtive activity in the school toilets,* toward children as young as six years of age.

The Justice Department had eventually released a report to the media taking credit for the discovery of widespread sexual assaults on primary school aged children, *but then,* said no more of the matter and kept up their hunt for old males like '*Dennis Ferguson*' that had once touched children over twenty five years ago. A man who had became the modern day scapegoat for an aggressive public dissent when he searched for somewhere to live. *And to die.*

In fact the Queensland community were looking for an ogre to blame for the widespread acts of child interference, and so it was that they directed their hatred at their new '*Hunchback of Notre Back Yard*' when they should have been protesting newspapers magazines and films '*Pretty Baby*' that portrayed and depicted children as under aged sexual objects.

The sad thing today is, that good people ignored the message that allows such malicious activity to happen among all ages of citizens, and I simply ask them to imagine an old paedophiles brain inside the cranium of an eight year old boy, *or girl;* As well as the damage done to so many innocent little girls and boys that could well have been their own child without the parents ever knowing anything about it. *Parents who are today totally puzzled by the behavioural problems their teenagers are today exhibiting.*

To me, it does not at all matter now, as it will eventually be understood in the future as more and more victims tell their stories of their treatments, but it did appear to me back then, *that child corruption, or grooming,* was like going fishing, and if you did not land a few fresh minnows with the first cast, you simply moved to another spot. I found, *from analyzing hundreds of such men,* that all you had needed to seduce a gullible child, or teenager, *was the fresh bait, a spare lure, and a secret place that was not populated by others.* It was then, that you soon had your catch. *Hook line and sinker.*

Chris told me of other mind corrupting events in his life, but his own introduction into a child pedophilia and pornography *via the crack in the door,* was a familiar story that was told daily in prisons all around the world. Seemingly, the simple act of *exhibitionism and the provision of crude images* was the way to gauge the interest of kiddies, and so, *from that moment on, or of the moment of interest,* it was supposedly an open slather of child sex, photographs, blackmail, child pornographic films. It was then of course, a life of prostitution when an older person becomes aware of their indecent activities. *To be then introduced into an adult relationship.* The function itself, then makes immature desire a; *replacement for a dream,* and when that desire becomes all important, habitual, *or even more important than ones own family,* we then have an offender who will teach others how to offend. *Be it drugs, sex, or other people's private property.*

Should a child counsellor read my writing, they need to raise above all the *hate, spite, revenge, and thirst for blood, especially for their youthful client,* and to explain to them that the act of any sexual touching, licking, digital penetration, rubbing, bribing, looking at pornography; *is not child abuse, where they are concerned.* Nor is the sexual act itself all that wrong or indecent, but the message to get across is, that it is *unlawful* to damage other young people, only because he or she were introduced much too young for such activity. By hitting or beating a child for such behaviour, soon adds violence to the equation. *And so in time we have an eighteen year old violent sexual offender, who later becomes a psychopath.*

Abuse, is an entirely different word, and I find that most children are genuinely confused and puzzled by the phrase *'Child Abuse,'* that is being touted every day and night in their schools and households. A child cannot at all correlate Child abuse, *with pleasure, affection, generosity, gentleness and charity,* for this alone puts a child at odds with those who want to kill their benefactor. Or cripple a nice man or woman who is sometimes their, *'Protector, and provider'*

Child abuse, is clearly a media phrase, *so as to sell newspapers,* and when a counselor can assure the child that he or she was not abused, but that they were simply manipulated, *passively assaulted,* or even deprived of their rights, *as well as their self respect,* including a pursuit of their future dreams. THEN AND ONLY THEN will progress be made by a counselor. *This tack also soon opens up lines of communication.*

In Queensland today, defenseless people of all ages and races are physically abused whipped burnt shot broken drowned and killed, while the media in its gleeful search for higher sales and profits willfully uses *Sex, sex,* and more *sex,* to sell all those daily newspapers. *They are dogs with a bone that need to be chained up legally by the High Court.*

In fact, Counselors have a duty to stop the media urging on *'public opinion'* by their singling out children as tasty sexual objects, and their promoting *'child abuse'* as a popular type of attention getter. There is an urgent need to stop children being so confused about their *view of sex,* and to put grievous bodily harm, *assault, deprivation and cruelty,* in the legal baskets that they properly belong in.

There are hundreds of interpretations of abuse, and another is the abuse of a child's rights to see the truth. To know that although they were often a willing participant to such shenanigans, it must be explained that they did no wrong whatsoever for caring for a sick person, *young or old.* A lonely generous person that had tricked them into being their; *partner..*

It is a truly good thing for us to try and explain to those damaged children, that we are not going to bash torture strangle kick hurt burn or kill that sick man woman, *or child,* who was previously their partner. *But to have them treated by a special doctor in a white coat who will help them get better. And to contain their out of control pedophilia type addiction.*

Unfortunately, even a good and decent family man listens to greedy journalists who continue to parrot the diatribe that the *'Sicko's should be beaten to death,'* although, *inside prison,* I would find that not even dead children were safe, and I would later learn of a Bay Side youth whose wealthy father had once owned and managed a funeral home. A funeral home where the youth and his friends entered at night to rape and molest the deceased bodies of poor child accident victims. *If that is not a sickness, then I don't know what is?* Again, the Justice authorities ignored me, because I was just a common criminal with no PhD. beside my name.

Other than my feeling somewhat shocked by the filthy stories that the handsome youth had told me*, at the time,* Chris had also become my right ear in the other parts of the concrete yard, and he in turn would always confirm something I could not hear, *or,* if I had misunderstood some things he would calmly and patiently explain my mistake *without being at all rude.* He was my message runner and my tea maker, and his boisterous or overly loud Australian sense of humor in the yards was quite infectious. At times I felt his loudness was a sign that his mind was quite fragile, and that he would eventually have a mental breakdown; *or would suicide,* when too old to attract any more partners.

Still, I knew the fable, that if you lay down with dogs, you rise with fleas.

On that note, I will say that citizens do not have any right at all to classify anyone who comes and goes in their communities, *town's suburbs or cities.* Anyone in the world can walk down your street, drink in your local hotel, join a Boy Scout movement, *open a Night Club, or even escort agency* and or, attract your spouse or even your own children to live life for today, *and bugger tomorrow.* This business of beating up an old pedophile, is really quite laughable, for the men and women around you are all leading alternative lifestyles, and even the *Bus driver* who takes your children to school could be a lesbian, a liar, a reformed alcoholic, and you, *would be none the wiser.*

Yes, you can get angry, but legally that is your problem if you do not control that anger. An anger which will rebound on you, or your children, and eventually place you all in jeopardy.

Twenty years later on, certain James Cook University social work students asked me if our society has any *options,* and I assured them they truly did have options. I in fact had explained to them that you must treat *with honest counselling* the ones you can heal, and you must give a separate comfort zone to those you cannot heal. To deny them a comfort zone and treat them maliciously, *and with cruelty,* is the exact treatment they will treat others with when again in control of their lives.

The saying that birds of a feather flock together, *is quite true,* but few of them ever shit in their own nest, and so *where* the concept of Remand Yards failed us, is that we threw finches and swallows as *well as doves,* in with minor birds and hawks to be pecked or eaten. So, without classification and separations we allowed them to shit on each other until the feathers flew in all directions, and all suburbs. In the end, various groups did deals for the good of themselves, and the strong survived. *To again fly free, and hungrily feed off the eggs in your nest.*

The problem began of course, when they were at last set free and did not flock together anymore. For then, they had simply used your back yards to do their business in, while sparrows acted like chicken hawks and turned on smaller species. *When paraphrased in such an example, the term 'Gaol Birds' takes on a new meaning.*

I do today believe, that even small children too can clearly understand the hypothetical parallel I offer, but it clearly appears that learned people, *cannot do so,* and they do continue to talk so much *diatribe* that they talk each other out of remedies that can truly alleviate the problems we have today.

In the old days, I saw what had to be done to lessen the burden on young children who had still possessed the capacity to dream. *Sadly,* no one listened, and all I can do today is prepare a text for those in the future who will one day seek alternative answers to the troubles we all are going to face when we can no longer afford the concrete comfort zone. A comfort zone area for damaged people we refer to as *Remand Yards*. Containment areas, or Prisons, which, I today refer to as, *'Dream Breakers.'*

First view of a new day

BETTER THAN THOU

On many occasions when the police detectives had come into the prison proper, they would arrogantly gather on a wide overhead balcony and happily survey their handiwork, *and then it was,* that young Chris Towns would go into his exaggerated routine of being the *servant boy* to the established criminal element. Out of the kitchenette he would march, while loudly approaching us and taking written orders of tea coffee and sandwiches.

'Yes Sir Mr. Campbell, Thank you Mr. West 'Straight away Mr. Jessop.'

This would annoy those big surly detectives who had appeared to wonder just why they had bothered to put criminals in a prison, if all they were doing was lazing around getting a suntan, *or,* being waited on by young boys who could pass for young girls. *That is, had they been dressed in correctly selected female clothing, such as a pleated high school dress* The loud or makeshift humor was all that we had for an overall entertainment, but the detectives could not of course know that we were just putting on some big act for their benefit. As it was, it all came about to serve our purpose, *and,* to aggravate and tease those verbalizing Criminal Branch Detectives. *Indeed,* to aggravate such men who arrogantly decided which suburban youth, or, felons, *would do time,* and not at all leave it to the Judge or Magistrate. *Who were supposed to do what was ethical and above board. It was said in the 70's, that the Police told certain judges what to do?*

To most citizens, the Queensland detectives were seen as clean cut men who daily caught the bad guys, but once you found out the truth of the matter, you soon learned that even they, *were the bad guys too.* To classify, *or to not classify*, is a very important task in policing, and if we dare to ignore it, then it is the little ones that suffer, *eventually*. That is of course, when corrupted young men like Chris are out and about in the suburbs or are entering children's bedrooms to test their response to an indecent act of masturbation, *or oral touching,* from a midnight to dawn intruder. Young men who have never ever known anything but indecency and neglect, and we in our imagined secure abodes somehow think that we and our children are safe from the decisions and actions of all types of other socially damaged human beings. *Sociology is the study of society, and so far I find that Queensland is far behind the eight ball.*

Nor do most citizens know that 80% of violent Remand prisoners are released by the courts, *either on bail,* or with good behavior bonds. *As well as probation orders.*

It is like walking selected human beings through an infectious area and then allowing them to board a bus to the city without any *fore thought* of what effect they will have on other unwary citizens.

So it is for the much younger police cadets, when corrupt police show them the ropes and allow their moral standards to slip by the wayside. So in the end we cannot at all tell the difference between what is lawfully permissible, and what is unacceptable.

Prisoners knew even then, *from long experience,* that the big suited *so called,* "defective detectives," were no better than we were, *and,* if ever placed in our position, I do feel that they too would probably do the same things as we did. *Mainly because they obviously had that same drive and ambition that the habitual criminal elements possessed.* 'But of course, they had approached their illegal criminal activity, a whole lot differently, and fortunately, *much like most prisoners,* not all were rotten to the core, *but,* they did lie, *they did steal,* and they did do sexual things to strangers that they should not at all have done. Police had long investigated police, and the culture grew bigger as ordinary citizens became truly afraid of such people, seeing as their authority power and influence grew ever stronger. *Based on 'Military lines, Police and Prison Warders were untouched by social criticism.*

The same type of detectives would one day be investigated by a big Queensland Inquiry, *The Fitzgerald Inquiry,* that quickly found just how deep rooted the criminality in the police force really was, *at that long ago time in our now historical past.* The Inquiry showed how they had once fabricated *perjured evidence* that had made their soft jobs even easier for them. Certain high-ranking police officers had tons of Gold coast real estate, hidden bank accounts, *as well as, family photographed or fully documented illegal holidays.* Their children were all university trained well long before Government credit was available to most ordinary families. Their boasts of the good life was *information* that came from their own mouth. That is, when they had exulted on just how smart they were compared to all of those mug losers doing time, *and or, working in dumb ass factories.*

There was not any end to the many unmentioned protection rackets in the then police run State of Queensland, *while a particular politically influential group of wealthy Queensland citizens remained unusually silent.* In time a police ownership of brothels and drug and stolen car networks *'Chop Shops,'* would later be exposed, for the entire world to see. *'Cleaning the books'* made millions of dollars as many high profile child molesters paid to have their filthy charges dropped. One particular detective I had known had retired a millionaire, *simply for looking after the sex industry.*

I for one knew exactly what police and their relatives would do for a dollar, and were Queenslanders who never once considered that they had done anything immoral. *That is, like those filthy criminals in the local Gaol.*

The Queensland newspapers were not at all blameless, and they covered up for the police workers by writing the exposes as if *'Boys will be Boys'* *'and at least they are helping people being robbed by thieves or bag snatchers.'* I laughed at such manipulative deductions that had suggested it was okay to do evil,, as long as it was to people who were labeled as lawbreakers. *It was a deduction that suggested; that if you raped my daughter, I could rape yours! In fact a Boggo Road Prisoner in the 60's got out of Gaol and raped the son of a policemen. The inmates name is in my files.*

Sadly, the 1960's to the 1990's were the real boom years for the conveniently ignorant citizen that had long given the police force *'Carte Blanche'* to do as they wished, and, to lock up as many ignorant criminals as they could possibly do so, *in the shortest possible time*. In reality, the entire world did not give a bloody poker machine damn, *or at least,* they remained abnormally quiet when police and paid criminals abused and damaged a whole array of a future generation of young felons; *And then blamed the young people for a lack of integrity and morals.*

Police personnel were in fact the manipulators, *or the back bone, of Organized Crime,* and seemingly they had, *without any doubt at all,* decided just who could, and who could not steal or operate as a criminal, in the State of Queensland. Strangely enough, the mostly ordinary type of policemen had also believed that it was quite deservedly so, *to pull the strings of society,* especially for all their many broken hours and an allegedly dangerous work. As well as for that open exposure to witness accidental death, *and or,* grisly crime scenes.

'Fuck the Yobbo's, they don't care about us.' Were the usual comments from the off duty police who had drank together in those dark and gaudy night clubs. *While watching big money change hands in the sex trade. That is in the Golden years before Aids came to Brisbane and killed hundreds of young people that never knew what hit them. Today thousands are alive in the State of Queensland living on daily doses of newly invented drugs. Some are still sexually active in the Night Spots in Brisbane.* Expectantly, many of my own estranged relatives had looked down on me and had invited such filthy corrupted police officers to their barbecues so as to share their Prawns and Deep Sea Cod they had caught. *In turn they told me that my nephews and nieces were ashamed to have an Uncle such as I was.* The police workers would even *sound their sirens,* when leaving my relatives homes, so as to give all those socially ignorant family members, *a small thrill.* Maybe I read a lot more into the comments than I should have, but at that time, those words hurt me, *knowing well that the police were as bad as I was. Maybe worse.*

No totally corrupt police force has ever been more exposed any where in the world, than when the Fitzgerald Inquiry had exposed them, some 20 years later.

Nothing at all, *it had then seemed,* could ever stop the police abstaining from their filthy criminal and most arrogant behavior. *Or,* doing exactly what they had wanted to, *when they wanted to.* Until of course the above mentioned, blasé Fitzgerald Inquiry, blew the whistle on them. Which had eventually stopped it ballooning out of control for an obscenely short period of time. *As it has been so noted in our past Queensland history?* Thank God they had News Ltd and the insurance companies on their side, so as to employ the sacked ones, as as in house private investigators.

It was not until the Government had called a halt to the inquiries and in turn saved the careers of hundreds of the highly overpaid, *and or very well dressed men,* whom it was said had milked every dirty illegal enterprise for what it was worth. *Even to stealing from corpses.* Or, that smart police involved in the *Joke* could again openly or brazenly run all the *non existent brothels,'* and gambling clubs, as well as the male and female escort rackets that had turned over more than forty million dollars a year.

Especially those that provided twelve to fourteen year old girls, *and boys,* to men who could provide the *password,* and the right amount of monies to those crude shifty people who had over time provided such corrupted youth for any photography shoots, or sexual penetration. Police had files on men who preferred children, and quickly put them in contact with men and women who could cater to their fixation toward such children. *That is, for a price.* Strangely enough, it would be Queensland's ongoing love affair with the invention of; *Microsoft Computers*, that had eventually exposed dozens of sites in Australia where child pornography was to be created and formatted. Obviously, parliamentary investigators were shocked themselves at the amount of police personnel who were caught up in the dragnets.

Children have always been available for prostitution in Queensland, and it is my personal information that State Historical Societies have well documented instances in numerous Gold Field areas, *as far back as the early 1800's,* where children were sold as prostitutes. The well tried method of their testing any loose mouthed customer of child prostitution, was that a new client had to lay with a *childish* but legal teenager. That is, before having any improper access to the twelve and thirteen year old children. *Children who were then being groomed by the well protected and highly experienced pedophiles.* Today, it is quite an ongoing enterprise that has gone underground, but if I was so inclined, I could still find children for barter and hopefully help them out of the life that will one day destroy them. Today of course, we stupidly ask ourselves why no one trusts or like each other, and also ask, just why our State Governments are building the massive prisons and detention centers to try and control the fluctuating moods of a nation? *As well as the moods of young and disillusioned people?*

Because of illegal drugs, mental health is not a priority, and homelessness on its own, is today becoming a bigger problem than it was in the 1970's. *My own solution is in my* **'Book of Projects.'**

In time, an alternative answer came to me, *for many of our social ills,* but I'd realized, that without my having some input into its architectural planning, the idea would be put to special use for the children of the more privileged. While the children of the blue collar workers would have to shower with damaged men and women. *Or,* be invited to look through a crack in the door by a girl or boy of their own age, and watch real live pornography in the flesh. *Until the door opened and invited them in.* Of course, if I was to ever guarantee my own participation in Community Corrections, *or some fresh juvenile program creation*, I would prefer to be approached by a group of genuine citizens that would demand I be heard. The only way to do that, would be to tell the truth about wasteful; *'Remand Yards, and the Prison Experience in the good state of Queensland.'* Not for money, not for fame, but for the historical value that demands a decree of human rights for those young people held in custody by people that still say they do not have to answer to anyone whatsoever. *And are permitted to stick it, to the conscientious objectors.*

Ordinary citizens, still do not know that *they too* are part of the problem related to *'Recidivism,'* or can acknowledge that men and women going in and out of prison are like reprogrammed puppets on a rubber band.

As I see it, good people are blinded by media *'pro-filers'* that defend military style attacks on poor unarmed citizens. Citizens who are labeled; *criminals,* as well as the scum of the earth.

I mean, few voters understand at all that the pro-military styled government advisers had actually celebrated the many uniformed people who apparently see all our citizens, *as blood and bone collateral,* that are as dispensable as fertilizer, *in societies gutters.* The brotherhood, the Force, *the Allies,* do not do what a citizen directs them to do, and will turn on anyone who disagrees with them. They can stun-gun them, shoot them, hit them with solid steel batons, *and then say that the batons are made of wood.* Gas them choke them kick them, and run over them with a police car. These uniformed people simply do as they wish, *when they wish,* and can deprive people of food, medical attention, light, ventilation, legal support, the right to a speedy trial, *and,* refuse parent's all, *or any access,* to their teenage children until they have finished with them.

Whether such deal makers and *'Dream Breakers,'* like it or not, prisoners really are human beings who do have every right to live in their suburb, *and,* to legally send their poor children to the local school. The whispering, and criticism, that established families speak against any prisoner, *and his family,* simply adds to the wide-ranging social problem, and some stirrers even exaggerate a situation by writing letters to local newspapers suggesting that prisoners *as well as Aboriginal families,* should be housed in separate areas of the State. In fact, criticism is like a social cancer, *and yet,* when they are criticized in return, they call the police and make waves, where of course there does not have to be any waves. Few even realize, that, *if directed,* the military will violently turn on them just as quickly, *if ordered by their superiors.* It may be in bad taste, but most suburban critics are unread, unaware, and have no real idea of what they are talking about. As for *their* views that a prisoner and his wife are immoral and sexually indecent, I know there is not a man or a woman who has not once woken up in the early morning hours and not stroked their engorged genitalia, while thinking of someone else. *Other than their ignorant and sleeping partner.*

I find also, *from reading certain literature,* that every child in past history has touched themselves in a pleasurable way, but if you condemn them and humiliate them for their doing so, you will immediately isolate yourself and your family from them at all ever trusting you. *Or wanting to know you at all.* The media, of course, *deliberately fragments our society,* and their greatest supporters are government and military advertising groups? As well as those erotic sex industry groups that spend millions of dollars every single year in their advertising employment opportunities and vacancies for schoolgirls seeking skimpy modeling work.

The media does not inform the same kids, that all genuine models are imports for the Australian Fashion week. *And that teenagers are wasting their money.*

The community groups that do not have any access at all to the large amounts of money, *are very seldom heard,* and teenagers and indigenous groups are mentioned only as; **'An ongoing problem for established citizens.'**

Obviously, out of the latter groups come the deeply oppressed that rebel against being typecast as the, *lower classes,* and then, the cycle turns and the uniforms are ordered to quell the riff raff from the outer suburbs.

Now, for those who are derided and ostracized,
I will say to them;
No one is perfect.
Australia was built on the back of convicted persons.
Do your time, and go home to your family.
It is the business of no one else what a lawyer has to
say of any convicted defendant, or their children.

Your critics don't know, that, if some criminal was at all going to rob them, hurt them, or rape them, he certainly is not going to tell them he is coming to do it. In fact, this is where we get the saying; *The Devil you know, is better that the Devil you don't.'*

I personally have never been angry with, *or robbed anyone,* that was kind to me, or gave me shelter.

Anyone who criticizes a family, whom they do not know, and passes gossip to others that affect a family trying to pick up the pieces of their lives, does indeed deserve a troubled neighborhood. Including their own children that choose to smoke drugs and to foolishly swallow; *Ecstasy,* behind their parents back.

I do mean, the only real answer is to live with your family in a passive and quiet way, and *time* will reward you, and *'Life' will reward you,* and one day all those critics will see that you are no danger at all, *to them.* It is then they will begin to nod at you on the street, *and eventually,* they will stop to talk to you cordially.

It takes time, but time changes all things, and, I will continue to say to any man or woman with a past; *'It is not about you anymore, it is about your kids, and they do not have to be caught up in the maelstrom of your past mistakes. Or the label that others have placed upon you.*

'All you have to do, is to paddle your own canoe.'

Self harm is not the answer! *Healing takes time,* and the best thing I can say to any person, who has at all been under the thumb of rednecks, *is; 'Don't shit in your own back yard.'* This, not only applies to past offenders, but also to the armed forces personnel, along with ex security men who moved to the outer suburbs to start afresh. All, were previously *unlit fuses* waiting to be lit, and it was only due to their suffering and their many numerous years of well practiced self restraint, *and self discipline,* that they had closed their eyes and allowed the ordinary house husbands to get away with beating up on their intimidated wives and kids.

The 1970's taught me, that the *'Tories'* or the Liberal and National Parties, did not care a hootenanny hoot about human rights, and, that putting the boot into the low class nobodies, was a pastime that they relished. Car thieves, as well as Bikers, were their *'red Herring'* to draw attention away from the fact that they were cutting up large swathes of land, and selling it to *'family companies'* for a song and a dance. Big land developers and Business men of an immigrant based background married their young daughters off to budding politicians, and then, they'd spent a lot of money grooming them into *'High Office.'*

The *'red Herrings'* got worse, and the prison system had soon filled up until a beleaguered tax payer was footing a bill of up to half a billion dollars a year to keep the *'red herrings'* in prison. Then in they created glaring front page headlines, while a new filthy *'Wealthy Class'* put up the rates, the taxes, and the rents.

The result was, that Queensland *'Battlers'* began to get angry, and the *'Pollies'* had to build new jails, as a new generation of angry teenagers angrily put the boot into each other. As well as into the business owners.

That was where I came in.

Stress and a lack of wealth, was the poison that got ordinary people steamed up, and before you knew it, *everyone hated everyone,* and young men and women were bashed and senselessly glassed Both in our pubs, and out on our bloody streets.

The trouble was, that *bullies that bullied,* frequently did not at all keep their anger locked indoors, and sometimes they tested a new neighbor named Larry, and that is when the ambulances and the flashing blue lights were called. I found that without counseling, these men, *even I,* could be pushed to the edge, *and in the ex convicts case,* pushed into the back of a paddy wagon.

In prison, violent hard men rule the roost, while ordinary men and women are turned into punching bags, *passive recipients of sex,* and are men and women that become depraved, cunning, and quite *violent,* themselves.

Understandably, most citizens realise, that indecent things happen to teenagers inside of our prison system. *What,* few ever realise is, that teenagers are released on an average of four out of five times than the adults, when facing a judge. It is then the ordinary citizen is forced to face a young man who has been in a sexual relationship with a bigger and stronger man, and the trouble is, they do not know where or when he will strike back. Or, whose ten year old son, whom he will *'ass-fuck'* in a belated attempt to get even with his most hated society.

So it is, the decent family in the suburbs, become the *'Onions in the Sandwich,'* while the Political Families and Business families, *live high on the hog.* High enough that the stink of the *'Lower Classes'* do not reach them, as they continue to count the weekly income from adding up the rents. Which they take off the *'No Hopers on the 'Merry Go Round.'*

Reading hundreds of books, can of course ease the way for you, and of your family, *or,* if you do truly want peace and reason, in your community, then you must know the back ground of the people you are voting for. If he or she is in private business, *vote them last*. For you must look for someone of higher education, ethics, empathy, and a whole lot of down to earth common sense.

In time, I would find solutions for many social ills, but being classed as the, *bad guy, even still,* it is hard to put such ideas into the public arena. Of course, back in the year 1969, *in the Remand yard,* we the prisoners in our tattered raggedy tagged shorts, and thongs, who sat back sun baking and drinking our coffee, as well as laughing up at the detectives, may well have irked the bullies a little. We possibly had given them that false impression of a comfortable prison life, *but,* that was our secret intention, *and truthfully,* we had both admired and had totally despised them for all of their career privileges. As well as their new cars, guns in shoulder holsters, and a cruel unopposed power to assault maim and or to cripple any incarcerated man or woman that they so chose to. *'Either by their own hand? Or, by having some paid informers, or prison officer's thug, to do it for them.'* One might also add to the equation, of their unfair unlimited access to the beautiful, attractive teen-age prostitutes in the inner city areas.

As well as the bonus envelope every Friday evening.

Better than thou? I don't bloody think so.

I had honestly felt that if we could have had our lost lives all over again, and still wished to be serious criminals, we may well have chosen to be an Australian police detective. *So as to live the life of Riley.*

For crims to be given a gun, and a tin badge, would mean that we could legally flog all of our personal enemies, in a room, *or underground basement garage at police headquarters.* Many of us also felt, that we would have made the type of detectives to equal the very best of the best. Although I feel the many dark cells in the Queensland prison system, may well have been emptied overnight. *With a much longer waiting list steadily lining up at the Toowong cemetery. Or the Jolly Bridge funeral parlor.*

In our view, the killers of little children, *under our imagined systems,* would get the Star Chamber, rather than a fair trial under a prison law.

Thinking as a '*Policeman,* I'd truly believed, that prostitute's children, would be groomed to be like their mothers, so that we would have a continual flow of fresh meat. In fact the example I give now, was actually happening, and the '*Star Chamber*' example, was that the sad evil practice of '*Verbal Evidence;*' had decided a defendants absolute guilt. *In fact,* the younger children of prostitutes, really *were* being groomed by the policeman's pimps, so as to provide future services. *Just like their drugged up and alcohol addicted mothers.*

Fortunately, police did not intentionally kill children, *although some did have sex with them.* But in the main, they'd came down hard on those criminals that did seek to harm small children, *and,* even if it took permissible perjury to convict them, then the police and legal men felt quite justified. **Police did not see teenagers, as children.** *Sadly, police, on surveillance duty, did not interfere when children and teenagers were slapped around by angry parents. Today they spend 500 million dollars a year of tax payers money, simply chasing 'Child Molesters,' using lap top computers.*

I would also find, that most men and women who'd killed, *or molested children,* went on to suffer a living hell for many years, until, they too had blended in with the sickening daunting walls. *Much like the walking dead of science fiction movies.* Mostly, *once inside a prison,* such men were totally useless for anything *but their being an in-house informer for all those Union protected warders.* Warders who'd sometimes charitably threw them non-collectable tidbits of *'Hope or Parole.'* Or, the promise of a low security farm. *Maybe a seventeen year old boys bottom, if they were especially loyal and obedient to their masters.*

It is well known, that life in gaol for child sex killers, means that; **life means life,** and on the 17th April 2010 a child killer named Tony Rawlins eventually died in jail after serving a sentence of 54 years. A life sentence that wound along slowly, from 1956 to 2010. *As for forgiveness, it was not in the vocabulary of a 20th century Queensland Society. Nor it seems, the 21st Century.*

The warders, *as I see it,* were in a higher position to influence the behavior of any stupid teenage prisoner, *with a big chip on his arrogant young shoulders,* They *of course,* had failed dismally, mainly because it was, *much too little,* too late.

Like the police, those warders in turn had pulled rank, while they too decided to inflict their own punishments on inmates, *as our prisons continued to fill up.* Especially while our suburban streets became a very dangerous place to live. That is, when drugs were introduced to teens by certain upper class citizens trained in Universities. *Thirty eight years later after my time in the Boggo Road Remand Yard, I actually went back to Brisbane to track down dozens of past prisoners, and I found that all of them had died relatively young. Close acquaintances had seemingly committed suicide at a very high rate, and although I am not in a position to ascertain the ratio of suicide among past detainees, I feel the percentage is quite high, and wholly related to depression and drugs, and alcohol.*

So it was, that few people could understand that if a good or normal people did not question the *Banks the Media, Police, prison warders, armed forces, legal fraternity, Government's or the church,* the average man on the street would always be even more vulnerable to a manipulation. '*Or would be worse off than if a false pretender had full control of his bank account savings;* 'One thing was certain, the Queensland Police Force had a system to lock away any man woman or child, *they so chose to lock away,* and if that was not a form of a legal backed *Star Chamber,*' then I do not know what is?

In 2013, the Liberal Party politicians acceded to police demands to hold Queensland Bikers with out bail, *as well as lock them in solitary confinement for 24 hours a day.* This then meant that the Police Star Chamber demanded who would be punished, and who would not, and humiliating them by forcing them to wear '*Pink Jumpsuits*' when going for a shower, once every three days, was to provide society with big problems in the years to come. Being aware of the truth, is much better than being right, or of our seeing oneself as loftier than all others who share our world.

But, kicking an Australian male when he is down, is guaranteeing there will be enormous repercussions for society, in the mid 21st century.

For one particular policeman in the mid 1960's, an inmate who had been bashed senseless in a police station, eventually went back and raped the policeman's son in the anus. The inmate got five years for this dark crime and his name is in my private files, should researchers seek to confirm that terrible crime of the long ago.

Repercussions can effect anyone in our society, but it is usually the very young, *or the helplessly aged,* that are attacked by cowardly males.

CHAPTER 15

HOW TO WIN A TRIAL

On the next trial, I was quite prepared to play-act my way through the first day of the legal proceedings, like, the ever loved *'Country Bumpkin.'* I also had thoroughly studied the illegal tricky, or, of those called legal tactics, that were mostly used by the prosecution.

So it was, I had eventually arrived at a wise plan of action.

Sympathy was to be the basis, of my false-acting, inside the district courtroom, and by that time I had arrived at the old Brisbane district court precincts, I had felt that I was as prepared then, *as I would ever be.* The; *'How to win a Trial' novelette, had actually shown me how a fool, could be a fool, so as to fool the fools.*

I had deliberately left my thick warm pullover down in the court cells, and I'd dressed only in my thin freshly ironed *'donated'* short sleeve lime green shirt, and tie. *With a summer weight light brown pair of slacks.* I looked a little sad and sorry for my self. That is, as I was led shivering into that hand polished and ostentatious courtroom to supposedly face my just desserts.

My pretentious presentation, *and,* my planned sneaky act, was to so appear to a waiting jury, as if I was some type of stupid country yokel. A poor yokel with a sad confused, and *'beaten by life'* look upon my pleasant face. *A clean, fresh dial, that most disadvantaged country people could relate to.* All of those men standing at the back of the courtroom had silently watched me enter like a sad lost citizen of the policing system, not at all knowing I was playing for their sympathy. *'Or, how that Country Bumpkin had found his way to town.'*

I also appeared to stupidly gaze up at those impressive hundred thou-sand dollar ornamented plaster ceilings, and to look with monstrous awe at the richly polished teak tables, benches, and carved furnishings, in a simple and impressively curious way. *As if not at all believing that such places had really existed in real life.*

I was giving the impression that I had never at all before been in a court of law.

Jack, *the good prison warder,* had quietly followed me into the courtroom as I had deliberately walked past the dock, *as if not knowing what it was actually for.* Jack had quickly caught my arm and had shown me the dock. He had opened its small door so that I could so enter, and be seated behind a higher placed partition, *that had maliciously suggested I was guilty.* I'd apologised to Jack, and he had nodded a little seriously, as if thinking that I was in shock. *Or was mentally unbalanced.*

It had appeared, *I'd hoped,* that I was a helpless babe in the woods, and so it was I'd felt that I had quickly established that; *I had never ever before been in any court of law. That is, in the eyes of the prospective jury.* I silently sat shivering on that hard wooden seat, much like a poor man who could apparently ill afford any warm clothing, *and,* it had also seemed to me that my stocks had risen as those spectators had frowned in apparent sympathy, at this obviously, *uneven situation.*

The serious looking Judge, then appeared amid all of the usual traditional play-acting, and the main pompous display of their scraping of leather padded chairs. *Then,* an assisting bailiff came into the room loudly calling the court to order. I'd later found that Judge Nicholson, was to be presiding, and, that he was an efficient decent family man of mid fifties. That is, in appearance, and, after his noting me and speaking warmly to the cold prosecutor, he'd explained the formula to me, *of,* just how, to select a Queensland Jury.

I was also soon to learn, that most Judges chose to act much like Inquisitors, rather than the legal adjudicator, *which they were then supposed to be,* and, any person without any learned or an equal type of representation, was like an ingrown toenail in a wooden clog at a bush barn dance.

'Do you understand me, Campbell?' Called out the dignified Judge, immediately stating his personal stance to me, that he was not going to address

me as a citizen, but, as some common ignorant felon being charged with the monotonous crime of breaking and entering.

'I understand what you are saying sir, but I do not hear all that you are saying, simply because I have a serious hearing problem, *and I usually read lips.*' I whispered tentatively, and quite shyly, as if I had mischievously played my deceptive part in that pretentious playacting that was so clearly taking place on that biased courtroom stage. Possibly also, in all the other many courtrooms operating on that particular day, where the university trained warblers stuck it up the common folk. Whatever the case, *in court-room one*, there was one cuckoo that was not coming to their party, and, he was soon going to throw a cat into the birdhouse, so as to disturb the house trained pigeons.

My reference to my hearing caused a stir in the court, and the judge addressed that prosecutor regarding legal aid. It was then the court was informed that I had still owned a truck, and had clearly been arrested with ample funds, so as to hire or pay for representation. I did not argue with such unexplainable statements, *because I in fact did not fully hear him,* and I agreed that I would defend the proceedings by myself.

'That is if, it is agreeable to everyone concerned with these wrongful and unfair allegations.' I'd added facetiously. . .

The good man stared at me, for a long moment, and then he had bent to the task of writing in his legal journal. I felt even then, that in his opinion, *he would have the last say,* no matter the manipulated outcome, had resulted in. *'Guilty, or Not Guilty.'*

I was soon ready for the Jury members, as they were called up one by one, and on the long list that I was handed, there was the occupation and the name and address of each juror. There were a mixture of citizens, *but no females,* and all those men wore a brand new suit for the occasion, and so I quickly realised that discharging any person from that selection process, *by their general appearance,* was not the done thing. So it was that I then began to challenge the snaky looking shopkeepers, and large arrogant business-men, as well as those beady-eyed taxi employees. *The type of workers whom we had often referred to; as, 'Half Pie Policemen.'*

The stylish arrogant and self-absorbed prosecutor in his turn alone, had *rejected* those hard tough looking Waterside workers, *factory workers*, and many of the poorer people from less affluent suburbs. I quickly picked up suit, and I slyly challenged all of the decent people from a Riverview, and snobbish St. Lucia area, especially on the second round of polling. My ears were totally useless, and my eyes that were glued to the tyed written information, had told me everything that I needed to know.

All in all, I did manage to get the more every day type of pleasant jurors, whom I had wanted impanelled, especially by the time I ran out of defence challenges. As it was, I had to do all of this legal manoeuvring, while, appearing to be a dumb yokel, as well as a country style fool of great magnitude. While, in turn, sadly giving a sign of apology to those of whom I had timidly challenged to stand down. It was, *I had felt,* the first inkling that the alert Judge and his prosecutor understood *that,* I was a shifty and very cunning type of person. *A person who may need to be watched carefully.* Both of those pasty faced so called learned men had gazed at me quite curiously, as if they were looking for a good fight before arrogantly putting me in my place. *Which I presumed they felt at the time, was a concrete prison cell in Boggo Road for up to five years or more of my life.*

It was not in my Scorpion, *or Scots type Irish nature,* to ever lie down *and or* to allow a group of arrogant people to have their own unrestricted way with me. *I mean,* if a cunning, or even a perjury, *saved my bacon,* then that is what I felt I would use to defeat all those well-paid conspiring public servants. My view was, that if I was to lie down and allow them to; *verbally rape* me, I would then at least want some form of lubrication in the form of a caring humane leniency. In truth, I had felt justified in my behaviour, especially when the court system condoned similar type methods by police detectives. Bullies, who had appeared to have a bright green light to commit any act of criminal perjury, without any hindrance of enforced legal repercussion.

Regardless, I was not at all finished by a long shot, and I had then deliberately played to the Jury by showing them my apparent ignorance of our biased Queensland court procedure. *Or,* of, by my pretentiously misunderstanding, just *why,* that cold presiding Judge had haughtily criticised me for my speaking rudely when I'd angrily and frustratingly cross examined those Inala Police detectives.

'I am very sorry your Honor, but if I cannot call him, a *bloody liar,* then I do not know exactly how I can show the court that I took no part in his alleged record of interview.'

'Just deal with the specifics of the case.' was the overly loud and tired suggestion of the malicious bench. *As he'd closed his eyes in contemptuous disgust.*

I had thought of more, and even *more* ways to expose such an obvious legal collusion, as I had stared balefully around the courtroom in my pretentious act of perturbed confusion. I also made it appear, I was being treated unjustly by those upper crust power abusers. Verbal abusers, and or, *over paid nincompoops,* who had allowed the legal machinations to slowly evolve like a big Mechano set, *'on the courtroom stage.'* The detectives of course, had their *untruthful* story down pat, and they had told the court of how they'd went up to the old Boggo Road prison to interview me, and that I had tearfully broken down and confessed to a number of break and enters on local businesses. *Including some posh private homes in that Brisbane area.* They suggested, *untruthfully,* that they had warned me of my rights, and that I replied that I had wanted to clear up the past so that I could get on with my life. I did not hear them actually speaking all that clearly, in the expansive court, but I had the *copy* of the low court hearing depositions, which were available to me. It was then I had an idea of exactly what they were saying.' *Or about to say.'*

Due to my inadequacy as a legally trained representative, I could not shake their sworn testimony, but I made them feel quite uncomfortable as I'd reminded them of those prison warders who had been present at the prison, on that day in question. Later during the trial, *when I'd queried the Judge about a subpoena for the warders?* I was coldly refused, and so had reluctantly let it drop. I knew only too well that those idiot prison warders would of course be instructed to agree with the policemen, *in any case,* but the courts most prominent concern was, that those prison warders, might just be scared enough, *under oath,* to actually confess the truth. That Judge, had felt it would not in any way serve a purpose under the then circumstances, *and,* that it was simply a deceitful delaying action on my part, in my stretching out the proceedings.

The owner of the carpet business gave his sworn evidence but he could not at all throw any real light upon the matter. Although he had agreed that I was not one of the suspected persons presented some months before. That is, as one of those investigated participants in the staged police line up. *Neither descriptively, nor photographically.'*

All in all, the police workers had put their reputations as honest policemen on the line, *against a criminal from a prison,* but not at all understanding, that the alert Jury was watching them like attentive parents seeking to determine, *exactly,* which of their suspected children were in fact, telling the truth.

My torn, and dog-eared book of; *judicial English defamation,* had shown quite wittingly, just how those early English Barons had jovially subpoenaed the Crown witnesses, *as their own witnesses.* A legally hired lawyer then smugly sat back and arrogantly waited for the foolish witness to be examined, when in fact, *knowing,* that the *'Baron'* would not call the said witness, which left the crown case floundering. In a sense, I did much the same thing. I subpoenaed all of the known perpetrators, and so, after being cross examined by that angry aggressive prosecutor, I had then abruptly closed my case. Leaving that prosecutor quite disgusted that I had perpetrated a blatant indecent and most serious act of unethical deceit.

Meaning, I had subpoenaed their own witness's while they thought I was dumb enough to call them to be cross examined by the crown prosecutor.

In effect, if the prosecutor could not then convict me of a *B&E,* he could later charge me with receiving the property, *that is,* due to the evidence that may have been elicited from the real perpetrators, during the prior trial. *Double Jeopardy?*

Giving my sworn evidence, I had simply told them the truth of my whereabouts when the crime was committed, *and so,* that decent Jury of citizens was able to observe my honest answers and personal description of evidence in relation to what actually happened in that interview room. *Or in the police station, on the week in question.*

The Judge, in his cold unfair summary, explained that the police had no reason to lie to the gentlemen of the jury, *and that,* such honorable men could in no way gain anything at all from their at all suggesting that; *I, the defendant*, had confessed when I claimed I had not. But on the other hand, *did I,* the defendant, have anything to gain by my lying? *'And, in my wide experience,'* said the Judge. *'I have often found this to be the case.'*

Belatedly, I would have liked to ask the Judge if the courts were there to sort out the evidence at hand, *or,* to examine the personality of the defendant. But I had decided not to push my luck after finding the precise details. *From Jack down in the lock up area.* Back in the cells I'd put on my jumper, for I knew that I could now safely wear it back into court, as all that evidence under examination was now in the Jury room. The Jury had later returned, seeking a legal guidance, and they were apparently quite concerned about the matter dealing with Police evidence, *and,* again they were returned to consider their verdict. *How can words be construed as physical evidence?; Was the supposedly puzzled query.* They of course were given a wonderful expensive evening meal so supplied by one of those leading hotels in town, *and paid for by the Crown Law Office,* while I sat there shivering in my cold container, munching on a dry cheese sandwich, *and my cold cup of water.* Obviously, that, was the way things were, and still are, and I'd known too, that a Jury would be indebted to the court for not only the meal, but also their signed Bank cheque that covered their lost wages and traveling expenses. *It was apparent, of course, that I had given the Jurymen nothing at all except entertainment, and, I'd reasonably expected the verdict of Guilty, beyond a reasonable doubt.*

I was truly shocked when they firmly gave the verdict of; *Not Guilty,* and I sat down in the dock in sheer amazement at what I had accomplished.

'Fuck my bloody dog.' I had whispered to myself, and was genuinely amazed that I had once again won yet another trial inside of the cheating enemy encampment.

The police were shocked, *even more than I was,* and they glowered at me as I called for a bail on the other matters that they had charged me with. The prosecutor also looked seriously angrily at me, and he had objected quite strenuously; *'No nookie tonight cunt.'* I thought with a grin, and then I opened my mouth and widened my eyes so as to torment him further.

That good Judge had duly denied me my self bail, and so it was that I went back into the custody of the prison personnel.

CHAPTER 16

A KISS ON THE LIPS

I was quite elated at my most unexpected victory, *although, it was almost nine o'clock at night by the time that very tiring trial had ended.* Exhausted and hungry I had arrived back at the prison well after a lock down period, and the warder escorting me back into the new remand yard had explained to me that he had allowed that young Chris Towns to stay out, and to wait up for me.

'How so boss?'

'He has been crying uncontrollably, and he apparently thought you had been released after winning the trial.' that good easygoing warder had replied to me, and I had truly begun to wonder just how fast the news traveled between the courts, and the Prison proper. *Or*, if those authorities had believed he was my *'boy'* and or, that I was supposedly sucking his penis. *Or he, mine.*

Chris of course, was waiting at the entry gate to the yard and he had grabbed me up in an emotional bear hug and kissed me full on the mouth, while telling me that he thought I had gone and left him on his own. His eyes were full of tears, and his relief was quite obvious to all, but I had never before experienced such an emotional type of adulation. *And or, an extreme worry*, from any prisoner, prior to that unusual and strangely embarrassing moment.

I quickly struggled from his grasp and attempted to push him away from me. In fact, such behaviour was unheard of, and I calmed him down as I had observed all the interested and leering faces peering from inside their tiny cell windows. I knew quite well they were reading whatever messages they had wanted to of the portrayal of a boy kissing and hugging a man. I had felt at the time, that such a display of emotion could give an incorrect summary of my personal, *sexual morals,* and so it was that I had flushed and frowned at the lad while using a serious tone in my shocked voice

'Chris, for fucks sake, settle down mate, you're in a prison you fucking idiot! It just isn't done mate, believe me.'

'I don't give a flying fuck Larry, you're the best friend that I have ever had, and, I really thought I had lost you forever.' he said as tears of relief coursed down his face.

I'd felt then, that I really was probably his best friend, *possibly because I had not used him or manipulated him into a shower stall.* Or probably because that young man was then searching for a father figure? Or maybe a defacto family? Rather than a dark image of a never forgotten pedophile. *Or rejecting parent?*

In a way, I was secretly pleased to have someone that cared for me, *or had at least pretended to care,* and I never again prejudged those prison friendships that I was to witness, time and time again. That is, over the many years to come. The warder had shrugged at my open palms of denial, and he had allowed me to make my plastic jug of tea to take to bed. I then took the opportunity to assure the poor lad that I was going *no-where* at all, in the next few months, *or years.* It was strange to be hugged, kissed, and feted by another male who was not your brother, *or your family,* and sadly I could not get the kiss out of my mind. *Mainly because it had been no different to kissing a tender woman on the mouth.*

The moment the warder had left the kitchenette to answer the phone, Chris had attempted to hold me again. It was then he had lowered his worn shorts to show me his massive circumcised red erection. It was then I had stood back alarmed at his display of crazy indecency.

'For fucks sake mate, pull up a bit, hey?' I glared at him, and I was seriously concerned that he had not at all washed his mouth out properly. *In fact the vision of him licking a rectum, had actually made me sick to my stomach.*

Later I would study such relationships, *or rude actions,* and I found it was quite common among young people who were isolated or lost in alien territory. *That is, to actually care for a person of the same sex, and to show a natural affection.* In 2001 a television series called; *'Big Brother,'* had confirmed my deductions, and, I knew just how such teary relationships grew strong in any close knit and somewhat deprived fraternity. *Even inside a Maximum-Security prison.* In truth, it was mind boggling to see grown men that had never known each other before, reach out in total desperation, hoping that desire would bind them together as friends. *When, nothing else would.*

Whatever the case, Chris needed help, *and quite soon,* as far as I was then concerned. I also was to discover, *when, later speaking at Universities,* that genuine counselors *and or interested students of penology* were also inclined to ask if I'd personally had intimate relations of a homosexual nature in a cell block during my periods of incarceration.

I would explain, that due to lack of secret, or physical opportunity, I was then unable to consummate the indecent sexual act that held their uppermost interest. Logically, even if I had been a homosexual, it would have been my business, and my personal business alone. *I would add seriously, and a little contemptuously.*

For some unknown reason, sexuality had grabbed the interest of students, whereas the later cruel bullying and medical abuse, of the inmates, *by staff and their pet prisoners,* was not a topic that they had cared to talk about.

Those anthropology students, also felt that the prisoners were, *in their opinion,* inclined to be bestial and indecent. *More so,* than those people in a normal civilized society. *Where of course, their inserting a sex aid into an orifice was an acceptable pastime.* In fact, the truth is known, that in all of our own most unexplained cultures or races, *including the unknown world of prison,* the average males and females of such societies, were judged by the indecent actions of the few minorities that had attempted to take over, *or,* to influence the majority; *'Such as the journalist culture that drank like fish and copulated like fleas.'* In other words, if a few were cannibals, it suggested that the whole tribe were cannibals? Furthermore, suggesting also that the culture of the minority, was the only way to behave, *to act,* or to socialize.' There was also the hypocrisy of the Queensland journalist, that would later demand the police culture be bought to heel, *and,* when they actually *were* investigated, they had then claimed that police were receiving the *Star Chamber treatment,* and that they were not at all receiving a *'fair go.'* CM.*27/02/2010.*

So, when those confusing opinions and brutal regulations *enforced* such views, those ordinary dissenters were soon ostracised by a roomful of legal or educated critics that usually judged the subject as a, *fool.* Or a willing participant for their being seen in the company of the minority. *Which is the usual explanation of how we are judged by the company we keep.*

Not at all making it clear, that prisoners, *or men on remand,* have no choice on who is to be placed in their company. *Or into their concrete cubicle*

CHAPTER 17

LEGAL SHENNANIGANS

The Remand prisoners had congratulated me the following day with pats on the back, *and,* even some of the new warders had eyed me in a new light, as if I was much more educated than I had originally appeared. Of course, winning trials, *especially without the aid of a good Barrister of law,* was a genuine rarity under a system where a false confession was accepted as irrefutable evidence. *In the eyes of the courts.* I found that many of the inmates also wanted to know the smaller intricate details of how I had outwitted the detectives,' *and.* 'How I was able to win two '*verbalized* trials in a row.'

Present criminologist views, do today estimate, that police win 99% of cases prosecuted in a District or Supreme Court in the State of Queensland.' A good fifty percent of decisions are clearly overturned on appeal to the High Court. Meaning that you have to have money, or rat cunning, to get real justice under any British law.

I did not bother to tell the yard crims of that defamatory British book that had explained the courtroom scene, *as a stage,* and I had simply told them that the mug coppers were not convincing enough to fool those very observant and down to earth Jurymen. The truth was, that if you did not playact, frown, and or, look shocked, shake your head while appearing horrified at such outrageous manipulations, *you were gone like flatulence in a thunder storm.*

The courts were a stage for witty pompous men in wigs and gowns, and if you did not learn straight up on how to play the game, you were in a very serious trouble.

Without that Jury system, only the wealthy or the quite influential citizen would not be unfairly verbalised, *or orally whipped,* while obviously, criminals of all or any dubious background, *would be found guilty as charged by an elected panel of Judges;* Especially those offenders with tattoos, scars, a shifty type of demeanour, or someone who smirked and appeared rude and quite contemptuous of the Queensland courts system.

I in fact was really quite exceedingly thankful for the old Jury system, as well as that mischievous small English novelette that had opened up my eyes so as to fully understand just how my betters had seemingly operated. *While looking down their noses at the 'Common Folk.' And, making fun of them.*

Such a system had long pulled the proverbial wool over the eyes of normal trusting and ignorant citizens, who were blindly asked to give an honest and a down to earth verdict. In *my* case, the good Jury was adept enough to know that a hearing affected person could not sit through an hour long record of interview without the examiner knowing that he, *or she,* was deaf as a doornail. In turn it never crossed the mind of one single high placed man on the bench to review the cases pending. Male Adjudicators, who were simply and obviously irritated at my slowing down the court process. *As if the financial expenditure had came out of their own pockets.*

That next trial had gone much the same, *as did the next,* which was noted by that earlier local media, who'd began to follow my many charges. *Sunday Sun, and the Sunday Truth. Certainly not the political biased Polly loving Courier Mail'*

I'd gotten Judge Nicholson in another trial, as he was well aware of my antics by then, and try as he would to bring me to heel, he had only created an aura of sympathy for me. With some serious concerns, *for me,* that lowlife shifty Prosecution Department threw everything at me in the following trials, but still, they'd based their main evidence on the perjured record of interviews. *Interviews that had not only replicated each preceding court case, but gave the same date and time.*

Before Judge Carter, I'd attempted to introduce those many discrepancies into evidence, *but I was denied,* even though I had won the trials that contained the same verbalization, and similar times and calender dates.

'You cannot, introduce an evidence, from any other case into a case now being heard.' He had said calmly to my face, as I'd stood there frustrated at the lack of logic in the rules of our law. I knew of course, that the old Judge had written; *Carters Law* and that he was once a policeman long before becoming a Jurist. So it was that I was left with the hard task of facing charge after fabricated charge, while the worried and beleaguered prosecution had desperately prayed for just one guilty verdict.

It was not to be, and again the skeptical Jury acquitted me, and *again,* I was refused bail. To think the judges did not know what was going on, was too much to ask of anyone that sat in a courtroom and listened to their deliberations. The detectives had begun to seriously panic, and they had quickly arranged a warrant to *again* take me out to the suburban Police station at Inala. Once *again* they wrote up their alleged Record of Interviews. This time they had watched the time, and I smiled at them and reminded them of what happens to dirty detectives when put in a prison yard for perjury. *On that occasion, they had noted my hearing loss in the fabricated statement.*

Societies official liars had a new witness who was a friend of mine named Alan Kelly, and Alan, *was to my great surprise,* at the very moment in the cells on various multiple charges of break and enter. *Charges which he was quite prepared to plead guilty to.*

Alan Kelly was offered not only his bail, but he was also guaranteed a probation order if he would willingly put my name in with other charges that he was facing.

'Have you done it yet?' I asked.

'No I haven't mate, but I am gone for years to come if I don't sign up, *and Stal,* I need bail badly, or, I'll lose my car.'

'You know I wasn't in on those jobs Alan, so how the fuck can you place me in either place when you know quite well I was in another?'

'Yes Stal, but you sold the stuff later that night.' He replied, feeling that a personal freedom was worth more to him than a false loyalty to a non-family member. *Or to be so charged with perjury, attempting to save some other minor criminal of no consequence, whatsoever.* The temptation of an immediate bail, was always a larger incentive than being respected by criminals, but I also knew that Alan was intelligent enough to know that he would not dare to derail me inside of a public courtroom. *Not with his best mates watching from a spectator balcony in the District Court.*

Alan's intention was to tell them that I sold the property, but was not present at the break in at all. It was because I recalled those electrical items, that Alan and his friends had given to me to sell, that I also remembered just where I was on the night in question. So it was, that I had laughed with a quiet amusement. *My hearing seemed to be better among my fellow offenders, than among my enemies.*

'That was the night I escorted that blonde piece to the debutante's ball, *and,* then later met you at Reds place?'

'That's right, I remember that now.' Replied Alan understanding immediately what I was up to.

'Mate, you have to tell them I was in on the B&E, and then go and tell the truth to the court that I, *was not there,* and that they offered you bail and a bond to say that I was.'

I'd quickly devised a plan where Alan would agree to let them type up and to sign a statement that involved me, *and in return,* he would get bail and or probation on his own under taking. If the police kept their promise, he would allegedly sign more statements down the track. *Or so, they were led to believe.*

'Now you remember, that when you come to court, and they ask you why you made a false statement, you simply tell the court that I'd told you to do it, so you could avoid a longer sentence. That you signed their false papers, *only because you knew I did not do it,* and that you can honestly state that I was not present at, or on the break in. So it is, that you just forget to mention that I had bought the stuff off you.'

'No perjury and no worries.' I assured him.

We talked for some number of minutes on the cyclone wire meshed in verandah partition, and I explained that we would need to put on a very convincing argument. Mainly so that the detectives would genuinely believe we had fallen out. We had raised our voices and argued quite angrily. *I do feel that Alan could well have received the academy award for his most outstanding performance.* Soon those excited detectives and uniformed men came rushing in to break up the apparent conflict. They then led Alan away, and he had shouted back at me.

'Fuck you Campbell, you were there you cunt, and I am not going to cop the blame by my fucking self.'

The detectives were most seriously overjoyed, and they then had immediately consoled Alan and taken him into the C.I.B. Rooms, while I in turn was left to smile to myself, *knowing exactly what would happen in the old courtroom, in front of the 'Bail' magistrate.* Just two hours later, young Alan was taken up to the nearby provincial courthouse and the detectives soon came back without him.

'*Hey?*' I had called out from my mesh enclosure. 'What happened to Kelly?'

'You're the big fucking know all, *you fucking prick,* you tell me?' said the tallest and youngest of the magistrate licking detectives.

'Oh you get fucked you fucking skinny parrot.' I'd called back at him, and a few minutes later they had returned with three hefty uniformed men. They manhandled me into a cell, while tearing the shirt off my back.

I'd continued to shout at them as the steel door was closed, but secretly, I was pleased by their impulsive actions, as it may well show to a future jury that I was not the cowardly pliable and helpful good citizen who made incriminating statements, *for or against my self.*

That is if the next damn Judge on the bench allowed me to introduce those violent police actions to show the court a reasonable cause for the ongoing acts of police perjury.' I naively thought at the time.

Later on, a rotund detective came back to the cells and he spoke jovially to me as he had handed me a tailor made cigarette.

'How's it going Larry?'

'Not bad Sarge.' I grinned. 'How are you going to explain all this fucking blood, and a torn shirt that cost me an arm and a leg?'

'Well Larry the position is this mate, it's my job to charge you with assaulting a Queensland police officer, and I just want to know if you're going to bung on a turn.'

'Turn it up Sarge I'm not that bloody silly.' I had smiled back at his big display of officialdom.

That large detective had walked me up to the courthouse without handcuffs, and I in turn faced the bony old magistrate who had ignored my urgent explanation, while sentencing me to ten days imprisonment for assaulting a police officer of the Crown. He had further dismissed the one solitary case of obscene language, *seeing as the watch house was not a public place.*

Legally, that one single conviction had denied me the right to sue the Queensland Police Force for my ongoing victimization, and because of my being inexperienced, *I did not appeal the ten days, soon enough,* and so I did my time in the lower yards.

I was returned back to Boggo Road with mild bruising, *and minus my torn shirt,* which gave me the big chance to charge the police with assault and battery. Including the wilful damage to my private property.

This time Jack Farrell intervened, mainly because he had enough of prisoners arriving back from watch houses hurt bloody and bruised, and he had quickly asked me if I preferred charges. I of course said I did, and so the next day an official complaint was made to the higher authorities.

The men languishing in the remand yard had come and gone and young Chris Towns asked me to write a letter to the sentencing Judge. My having some idea of the lofty attitude of Judges had alerted me to the fact that the servile attitude *of acquiescence* was what Judges wanted to hear. So it was, I wrote a long pre sentence letter to the arrogant Judge who was to hear Chris's plea for leniency.

Gossip had it, that the Judge in question was once a country boy who had bettered himself to his high position in that old District Court of Queensland. *'Armed with this knowledge,'* I'd seriously stated that Chris's Uncle and Aunt, who had allegedly owned a pig and poultry farm outside Toowoomba, were willing to take the young man into their care, and to give him a well meaning chance in life.

It was a total untruth, and I knew also that if Chris were released he would be virtually homeless and probably use his knowledge of an anal male intercourse to make money in the homosexual clubs and the pubs of

Brisbane by night. I saw nothing untoward in his morals, mainly because he apparently had been introduced to such behaviour at an age when an ordinary child was climbing a tree, or building a canoe. *That is, if one totally believed his tales of corruption and adult injustice.*

Chris of course had tried his indecent bag of tricks on me on a number of occasions but I would quickly discourage him with some serious examples of male relationships. I'd sensitively explained to Chris that I once had a old Great Grandfather who was alleged to be a very sick sexual deviate, and who was referred to by my natural mother, *Shirley,* as a very *'Dirty and disgusting old man.'* An old man, who it was alleged to have given her money to let him digitally penetrate her and her younger sister.

'I just don't want to be some dirty old bugger someday, Chris. I really don't care what others in the jail do, and as far as I'm concerned, if they get caught or diseased, they just have to pay the penalty. *Not me.'*

'Do you think I am really wrong for doing what I am doing?' Chris had asked quietly, as if I was prejudging him for what he was.

'How can it be wrong if you like chocolate, or Cocoa Cola? You didn't invent it and you certainly are quite old enough to choose what you want to do, *or swallow.'* I had teased a little, as he flushed and then playfully attempted to tag me.

I hated having to explain myself, especially when I myself had often questioned my own sexuality in the hot throes of a self manipulated orgasm. As far as I was concerned, a person could mate with animals, or even loaves of bread, and if she or he could live with it, then so be it. A different stroke for different folks was one of the old rude prison sayings, of the time, *and of course,* it was the usual excuses given for an unacceptable behavior behind prison walls. *Because of pornography in jail, I preferred 'female teenagers, and, had corrupted many such gullible girls in my later years.'*

Chris actually got probation, even when even his legal aid worker had thought he would get at least four to five years.

Of course the very next day it was truly strange, and somehow quiet in the old concrete remand yard. That is, without his happy and smiling face. *And it rained, to boot, which I had long called; 'Heavens Tears.*

The bisexuals, *I felt back then,* were luckier than most prisoners were; mostly because they could easily move in even greater social circles than just the plain old homosexual, *or, the lonely heterosexual,* who obviously had a very limited choice of partner. *And or, employment opportunities.*

My own personal piece of philosophy is, that do not do something you cannot tell your own children about. Or, grandchildren, for that matter.

As it were, I had long promised myself, that when the soft emotional movie, or book, did not make me weepy any more, I would disregard my previous Methodist upbringing, and join in the masses. Until then, I would hold out a uncertain hope for a wife and kids, or some big roll of money waiting for me inside of a rich man's safe. Still, the making of friends, *even on a desert island,* had hit ones emotions when they were lost by fates? Or, by any legal, *or higher decree,* far removed from our personal control.

Incidentally, I got the rich man's safe and I also got married with children and it was time to pull my horns in and do something decent with my life. But of course another decade was to pass before I held my son in my arms and learned to trust in 'Life' once more, in a life riddled with stupid and wasteful mistakes.

A few days later, I knew I just had to get busy and to ignore those few inmates who had asked me;

'Where's your boy Flex, did he do a runner?' and I would rudely reply with venom.

'Yeah, that's right Terry, only I thought he was your boy in the shower room the day before he went?'

'I wish!'

'I'll bet you fucking do.'

This type of banter had got us through the days when spring arrived with only a slight improvement to the cold weather. And with the change of seasons, came the expectation of a future hope. .

OUT OF THE BLUE

The administration invited me to some impromptu, *official meeting*, with some big Police Inspector. An arrogant man who had wanted to have a quiet chat with me about my alleged allegations of common assault by his respected police officers.

I told him of my having to accept a conviction of assault, without any trial, and how I was attacked by police officers in the Inala Police station. He had told me to my face, that he did not believe my version of events, and that his police officers did not tell lies.

I had quickly got to my feet and I had glared at him.

'You! You're just like the rest! One of the boys, and I'm wasting my bloody fucking time talking to you.'

The big boned man in his gold braided uniform had flushed red, and he was not used to having mere prisoners speaking to him in such a manner. His mouth opened and closed, and then with one last glare I had walked out of that interview and never saw him again. *Until of course he appeared on Television in the Fitzgerald Inquiry Trials where he was being interviewed over very serious acts of ongoing police corruption. That was twenty five years later, but the pleasure of seeing his worried face made me laugh until I got a stitch. My confiscated writings named him, so I can only hope that he squirmed like a worm when threatened with perjury.*

This treatment by officials and the department of prosecutions only made me a lot more determined to make big waves for the police, and their methods, but, with a six grade education I knew the best I could ever do would be to slightly embarrass them. Strangely enough, the shifty cunning Department of Prosecutions decided to do the last charges first, because with Alan Kelly's statements they clearly had an in house corroboration to the perjured fabrication and verbalization by the police.

The average view was that the plains clothed police were hard working stressed out detectives who were only doing their job under a great pressure. A daily stress that an ordinary people in the suburbs knew nothing about and were simple family men who were considered the real type victims in this ongoing war against crime. In reality, many were rotten liar's bludgers bullies and rapists, then in very cushy jobs that the Queensland taxpayers had paid for, *while such good citizens pleaded for financial and property protection from the teenage criminals running rampant in their streets and schools.* The sad part was, that the genuinely honest policeman and their families had truly suffered from above, *and below,* as they were shunned by their social associates, *as well as by the ordinary citizens,* for their being part and parcel of an unbending and corruptible force. Frustration for the good, *and the good times for the sneaky ones,* was the only way to explain the situation that was then facing the decent police, or innocent men and women under interrogation by the '*Jacks.*' In fact the majority of policemen and their families were good people, but when they were told to commit perjury, they reluctantly did it. *And some not so reluctantly*, for they knew, that with a legal support being provided by their superiors, there would be no penalty to pay; *The end result being that if it was okay to lie, it was okay to skim whatever could be scammed, and the reality was, that they never got charged for drink driving or paid any parking or speed fines.*

Determinedly, *on my very next trial,* I did my country boy routine and I had looked quite dumbfounded at the untrue police allegations, as I imaginatively stumbled through my well prepared questioning of the insolent detectives. When Alan took the stand for the prosecution, he'd quickly disagreed with his previous statement and explained that Mr. Campbell had told him to make the statement. Only so that he could gain bail, and get probation.

'*Did you get bail and probation?*' asked the Judge.

'Yes sir.' he replied, and, I got a sweet pleasure of examining the rebellious police witness, who was in fact, *on my side,* and not that of the fuming police officers.

'*Whack that up you.*' Were my thoughts of the matter at hand.

I took Alan through his allegedly honest interview with the police, and I had shown exactly how he had been forced to substitute the name of another youth named Paul, *instead of my name.* Paul in fact was a youth that was; *some years later,* caught up with corrupt police in a stolen car chop shop racket. That is, where a manipulated Main Roads personnel worker had illegally arranged registration, and licensing; *Regina Vs Paul Flynn.*

It was still one of those eras where Juries were made up of old school gentlemen who'd wanted to have faith in that system of policing. The trouble was, that they did not know the difference between the term of a; *Policed State,* and a *Police State.*

The verdict was reluctant, but it came late on that evening, and once again I had given those swivel hipped fat assed stupid detectives, a large aggravating smile. *That is as I squinted up my eyes like a china man.*

The Judge again remanded me in custody, mainly because he was the type of person who'd believed that; where there was smoke, there just had to be fire, *and correctly so.* Or, because there was an ongoing **collusion** between himself, and the corrupt Department of Prosecutions.

Weeks later, the Prosecution made another mistake and had decided to remand all my cases for a stand over until the next District Court sittings. This time I was handcuffed to an array of much older criminals, as we'd all faced the Judge to have our cases remanded for a lengthy period.

One tall red headed prisoner beside me had been recorded as a serious thief since the age of five, and being then in his late thirties he was known on sight to the legal profession. And also to the presiding Judge.

His Honour looked him over with a half smile, and a playful frown.

'Your face looks familiar to me! *Arthur Riley,* if my memory serves me correctly?'

'I feel you have mistaken me for a chap named William Jolly, your Honor. It is he that the police should be dealing with in relation to this matter.' replied Arthur Riley, *without missing a beat.*

It amused the Judge to no end, and it had put him in a good frame of mind as he'd continued to smile widely as the prisoner again bowed slightly as he again spoke respectfully to the district court Judge;

'*Your honor*, if I may bring your attention to the fact that a lot of good men have been locked up in the remand yard without bail over long periods, and this young man next to me has been incarcerated for more than twelve months. Furthermore I do genuinely feel, *your Honor*, that many of us would appreciate self-bail while waiting to prove our innocence on matters now before the court.' He'd suggested softly.

All eyes turned to me and there was little I could really say, as *Blue* had said it all.

I wished at that very moment that I was able to speak like this tall; *good time thief*, and so it was that the Judge had spoken to the prosecutor to confirm that I had indeed been held on property charges, *without one conviction*.

The time limit was a lot closer to well over a year, and the Judge had left me until the very last of our group was dealt with. It was then that he signed all of the necessary documents to have me released on my own recognizance.

I was in total shock, and while waiting down in the cells below, I had thanked the tall red headed man profusely, and with a deep gratitude.

'Thanks a lot Blue, I don't know how I can ever repay you.'

'Just don't get caught next time.' This big hearted Australian grinned. So it was that the truly staunch felon waved goodbye as he was loaded on the Black Maria and taken back to the old Boggo Road Remand Section. So as to await his trial.

Instead of my being released, the Inala detectives arrived at the watch house *en force,* and took me out to the Inala Police Station, where I was again verballed on a charge of break and enter. It was unbelievable that they would spend so much time and money on me, for little, or no return. Later the following month, other remand prisoners, *and myself,* had roughly calculated the cost at over one million taxpayer dollars. Just to try and get me, *alone*, convicted convicted under Queensland Law. *It is said that the Australian dollar has valued ten times over since that time. .*

The magistrate at Inala had again remanded me without any bail at all, and in desperation I spoke up with some determination before he could deliver, *or stamp*, his official verdict.

'*Your worship*, I was given a self-bail by a district court judge on all of the other similar charges this morning, and now these men have added another.'

'Is this true?' the old legal man said looking at the prosecutor in a perturbed manner.

The police prosecutor cleared his throat while glaring at me for daring to open my mouth.

'That appears to be the case, your worship.'

'*I refuse to overrule a colleague. A self recognizance order is issued at two hundred dollars!*' were the words from the bench.

The detectives were spitting chips when I walked from the sheriffs' office with my bail form. It was then I saw that all the cops had only cold dark brooding looks for me, *suggesting a promise of violent retribution.*

That late afternoon weather turned gloomy, and the moment I had stepped on to the stairway, an ear shattering sound of thunder shook that sky. It was then the pouring rain tumbled down in a last attempt to hold me in police captivity, *or in the presence of dogs.*

As it was, I had to hesitate about leaving the shelter of those court precincts, but the looks of the glowering detectives made me step forward into a murky teeming torrent of water, where a lighting flash had heralded my eager departure.

'Nice night for a break-in Stal, *you fucking cunt!*' said one big bellied detective loudly over the sound of the rain.

I was not all that confident enough to retort back with an obscene insult, and so I'd bravely walked away into the drenching rain, *and,* to my most fortunate and unexpected taste of freedom.

I walked to the Inala shopping centre and espied some young Hoons in a red Premier Holden. I informed them I had just got out of the watch house with no cash whatsoever. The teenagers were immediately on my side and they quickly got me safely to a good friend's place that had charitably fed me, and clothed me.

Then it was open slather on any business that was not patrolled by any armed security.

CHAPTER 19

DONE LIKE A DINNER

The police had picked me up at another friend's place, just two days later, and so it was they drove me to court unshaven and quite ill-prepared to conduct a District court trial. Judge Carter, *of all people,* had arrogantly brushed aside my plea for an extension, as he calmly, and arrogantly said;

'You have had an ample time to prepare your case Campbell, and I hereby deny your application for a stay of proceedings.'

I could not of course explain in front of the prospective Jury, of my then sudden dilemma of my being released as homeless as Robinson Crusoe. That is, after a full year on remand. It was because of this sudden move by the detectives and the smarmy Department of Public Prosecutions, I clearly had no suitable clothing. Nor could I introduce my past act of being a simple *'Country Bumpkin,* or, be in a clear state of mind to select a jury of my peers.' I could not even explain to the independent juries that Brisbane Judges appeared to *collude* with the unrestrained DPP, *as well as other Judges on their troubling or difficult cases.* Of course, any such criticism may well have caused them to quickly withdraw to their well furnished chambers. Especially, when any suggestion of impropriety had arisen in the political arena. *But, they were really safe as houses, seeing as our Tory government had long reigned supreme, and, as history shows, they reigned supreme for another twenty or so years. .*

I was found guilty, *as charged,* at nine O'clock that evening, even though, that younger lad named Frank, had stupidly attempted to help me by declaring that he had hated me, *and that his hatred alone was the sole reason he had agreed to help the police to conspire against me,* it was all in vain He did not say that being raped in the Westbrook Boys Home by police informers, had encouraged his perjured participation.

At lunch time, the alert jury, *who were filing out,* actually saw the younger lad shaking hands with me, while giving me a friendly pat on the back. This too had not helped my case one iota. My tearful or emotional plea to view the evidence and release me, was met with hard cold blank stares, along with an intimidating stony silence that reeked of arrogance and total contempt for the obvious riff raff of their society.

I would later attempt to understand my tears of emotion, and could only reason that the stress of a full year of fighting manipulating people, had somehow left me drawn and quartered. I was totally exhausted, beaten down, and still reeling from a hangover. *It was all over, Red Rover.*

Unfortunately, I had come to the end of my run, and I had, it seemed, clearly wasted fourteen months of my life. I knew also that if I had pleaded guilty to the scrap metal charges in the first place, I would be almost halfway through my sentence and planning my next illegal move. Even my older brother Bruce, who had come to view my impossible task, *as a waste of time,* did not return for my sentencing.

The smiling Judge seemed pleased at the outcome, and I angrily denied my guilt in that matter. As it were, I gave up a quickly handwritten sheaf of gibberish that stated my angry and clearly indignant case against false police evidence; *Written gibberish now in a State Archive.*

He, Judge Carter, sentenced me to three years in prison for a crime I would not have committed; even had I'd been paid to do it for over ten thousand dollars. *Simply because it was alleged to have been an empty building.* I was demoralised, and I felt whipped and beaten, as I was then taken back to the prison to serve out my sentence.

I spooned that thin gravy and rice meal, into my mouth, and felt the cruel dark depression of failure negatively close over me.

It was the first night *'blues,* and every man and child who suffered the feeling when going into a sentenced cell, for the first time, had felt what I had felt on that particular night. It was a very serious and depressing time when all guilty prisoners reviewed their early home lives, as well, as their parents and their major mistakes.

Once that first night was over, it would all soon disappear into the land of Nod, *where incidentally Cain lived after he killed Abel, and where Cain found a wife and married. While his children went on to build great cities.* 'Half their bloody luck.'

It was then the convicted persons daily regime and or posturing, would all start once again, *without let up,* until, a day far in the distant future he would be released. A future, when we all are forced to face the lonely and uncaring suburbs. *All, over again.*

As it were, I had spent my two and a half days of unexpected freedom breaking randomly into shop fronts, in my search for ready cash, but nary a penny could I find. I hit delicatessens and grocery shops, and at times ate well as I had searched, *but,* that allusive roll of money, or bag of coins, had always eluded me. How the police found me at my friend's place, *Adele Punton,* on the Monday morning, did not matter now, and I had stared at the curved ceiling of my cell and wondered just what I could have at all done to help myself.

The small cell in the older Division was suffocating, and quite nauseous, that is, after the spotless clean cells on remand, and to be truthful, my emotions took a serious battering. The fleeting memories that were left remaining in my mind, were of being released on bail, and experiencing those few extraordinary days of freedom. As it was, it had been quite hopeless attempting to survive on a lonely dark night in late summer, and only for the charity of old friends in Coopers Plains, *who gave me a roof for the night,* was I able to organise myself.

All in all, the poverty of the released man or woman from any worldly prison, *or the watch house,* was never recognised by society, and the choices were to go help themselves, *or, to sell themselves.* I could do nothing but help my self to what I had needed, and obviously, my trying to start all over again from scratch was one of life's greatest gambles. Especially for a poverty stricken displaced convict, or of some poor homeless indigenous person who had nothing and nobody to give them their early jump-start. *Over the first hurdle. Or, any social obstacle.* In fact the only way that an ordinary citizen could have any idea of the problem was to imagine their eldest child being destitute, stranded, homeless, and without any identification, in some other European country. *Where Australians were despised and ostracised.*

Boggo Road Gaol welcomed me with the sanitary tub, and that steel bed with a compressed sweat stained foam mattress. Anything else of necessity, *that I would in time accumulate,* would be by my bartering, *and,* my habit of gambling in prison.

Fortunately, I awoke in a better frame of mind than I did when I had at last fallen asleep, and so by mid morning I was very determined to at least give those big perjury puckered asshole dog Inala detectives, a massive, *future shock,* by immediately lodging an unexpected Supreme Court appeal. *It was said that hand written appeals by a non represented defendant, were said to be successful in only 1% of Supreme Court lodgement.*

I had heatedly demanded to see an on duty Chief Warder, and after a long delay I was permitted to approach that main Administration, where I had respectfully spoken to a certain senior office clerk. *Who had reluctantly handed me the appeal forms to fill out.*

This clerk, named Alex Lobban, was a very quick-eyed, quick-minded man, who'd seldom ever spoke. He obviously knew me by sight, if not by reputation.

'*Get it back soon if you want it to go with the next court escort.*' He'd advised and shut the grate in the big barred window.

This strange man, *Alex Lobban,* would eventually be the Comptroller General of all the then Queensland Prison service, *and it appeared,* would be the scapegoat for the big legal inquiries that would one day rock Boggo Road Gaol to its old convict built foundations.

I was left with a number of forms of which I could not understand, *let alone fill in,* and, I got permission to go to One Division Library to search for anything at all on appeals. That quiet librarian saw my troubled look and he asked me if he could be of any assistance.

He, *the librarian,* was a clean-cut prisoner who was somewhere into his late twenties. But, what he had lacked in a maturity, he made up for with a much higher education. *And stacks of legal knowledge.*

Strangely, he was at that time referred to as *Legs Diamond,* because he had at one time submitted that name to the court rather than create any embarrassment to his elderly parents. I had a quiet talk to him and I had spoken of my impossible dilemmas, and, he had suggested that I describe in my own personal words the manner in which Judge Carter had handled the trial proceedings. *Legs was patient, and he had seldom interrupted me as I spoke.* He eventually nodded, and then asked if he could fill in my appeal papers.

Of course, I had nothing at all to lose, and so it was that most highly intelligent criminal had efficiently begun to write in swift flourishes and very neat handwriting. Most was in Latin, *and,* he had described to me what *Affuncious Officio* had meant in legal jargon, and said that I *should,* under the law, win my appeal. '*Affuncious Officio means wrong in law.*' In fact, I got Legs to sign it to give the document that legal, or authentic look, *and feel,* and then I again approached that convenient hole in the wall and was received by the same unfriendly clerk.

Lobban glanced at the forms, and then his eyes jolted to a stop as he read and reread it. It was then he had turned around to look at me as if seeing me for the first time.

'Did you write this?'

'Yes sir.'

'*Okay,* that will be all.

Original sign by prisoner. 'Ray *'Rusty'* Holland.
Now owned by the author.
'Bids Welcome.' for charitable purposes to assist
the children of any present day prisoners seeking
counselling by a new batch of counsellors who are
trained by the author; *Of this facetious writing.*

CHAPTER 20

AMONG OLD FRIENDS

With Jack Farrell as a superintendent, I had no trouble transferring to my home away from home preferred type of cell block, over in 2 Division, *and unsurprisingly,* quite a few men were glad to see me and made me very welcome. Roughie Regini, *the main 2 Divisions bookmaker,* had generously helped me out financially, and I had also managed to buy back my old pale blue painted cell. That is, from a decent and friendly lifer who had wanted to live on a higher tier. *So as to view the surrounding sights.*

The library books and women's magazines, grew steadily beside my bed, and I again fell into that old jail house routine of eating, and of sleeping like a baby. It was then, during those early morning hours, I would curl up in a somewhat foetus style, while reading novels by candlelight. *To hide the candles, I would place wax over the wick, and submerge them in my 'Shit Tin.'* If I could have thanked the people of Queensland, it would have been for those many beautiful novels on our past history, *which incidentally, caring citizens were allowed to donate in those historical days of early Brisbane.* Sadly, those charitable practices were to be eventually halted, and destitute prisoners are now supposed to buy their reading material with funds from their personal property. *No mun no fun.*

But back then, the many books that a many good caring people had sent to poor prisoners, had genuinely helped to repel the illness of an institutional insanity, and had allowed people like myself to fully understand writing as a means of communicating effectively. *Literature, is the best medium to challenge any form of ignorance in the human psyche. Although, the Bible is not a good read for mentally ill people. LDC*

Not all of the faces had changed as much, *this time around*, and before I could arrange employment in the sanitary yard,

Roughie informed me quite early during the morning muster, that he had heard a fresh whisper that my Supreme Court appeal was to be heard in less than a week.

His source of information had been spot on, and this time I had found the court had supplied me with Legal Aid, on the strength of my previous applications.

A legal team soon came out to the prison to *view that upstart* who had been such a sharp thorn in the prosecution's shoe. So it was, that the presence of the four legal men in thousand dollar suits, who had met me on the 2 Division compound, *was quite impressive to say the least.*

We shook hands all around, as a highly distinguished Barrister of Law named Mr. Bavington, *who was head of Legal Aid*, politely motioned me to be seated. This good man was a very influential Barrister in his hey day, and he had smiled at me quite warmly, and began to explain the tactics in presenting my case. Deep down, I had a conscious idea that Mr. Bavington had only taken the particular case because of my well-presented appeal application, *and so it was,* I had little choice but to inform him of my very poor primary school education. *As well as the matter of my falsely produced appeal submission.*

The good man was a gentleman, *but not a snob.* He too had quickly under-stood that my past obstinate fight in the courts was against a system of; *verbalization,* and not for my innocence, or for any acquittal that may arise from my attempt at playing at *'Lawyer for a day'* with the big boys.

We shook hands again, and then an hour later I had rolled up my recently acquired contraband inside my flannel blankets, and had headed back to the remand yard, *quite highly pleased with myself.* On the way I had met my friend Slim Halliday, *who had been in the infirmary*, and he told me that he was soon to be released to an old peoples home at Eventide. In one sense, it had been a much wasted life for Slim Halliday, *locked down in Government Institutions, and in Prisons*, but in a way Slim had represented to all of us habitual inmates, that undaunted resilience of the hardy Australian. Especially when ever faced with ongoing cruel cold insensitive hardship, *and serious legal injustice. Today, tour guides have made Slim into a 'Legend' as they take visitors from all over the world to view that old preserved prison, that I find is the subject of much genuine curiosity,*

This resilience, *or determination,* in young people, *was I felt then,* the major reason why so many rebellious young people often pitted themselves against higher authority. Of course, in doing so, had refused to admit the inevitable defeat that always followed. *'That simply had to follow.'*

I shook the old mans hand for the very last time, and later heard that he regained his health and lived on for many years. Also, *that he went gold mining,* although in the end, it was said he could move himself around in an old squeaky wheel chair at the home for the aged, *at Eventide,* while telling all the patients about the Boggo Road warders. *Slim carried a vitriolic prison poem in his head and he always espoused it to all that would listen, or those in it that cared to listen to his rendition of the Boggo Road Screw.*

The Screw

A Boggo Road screw
is a two-legged animal
with a cork screw back
and water logged brain
made out of a combination
of jelly and glue.

When a Boggo Road screw
walks down the street,
decent people turn their backs!
Angels weep tears in heaven!
And the Devil runs and shuts the gates of hell.
To keep the bastards out!

Old Tom Verney had allegedly created this partial verse, so titled.' from a poem titled; '*Lifer!*

CHAPTER 21

A LITTLE FRIEND, AND, STRINGBEAN CHOKES

In just a matter of days, I was once again back in full charge of the remand yard kitchenette, *although,* I had clashed with an old friend of Billy Stokes. A tough rude man who was named, *or referred to,* as; *Tony the Greek.* To be precise, I had butted in *out of sympathy* for a Downs Syndrome youth, *or a disadvantaged young man who Tony was rudely and sexually taking aggressive sexual liberties with.*

It had appeared to me, *that almost very single day,* Tony the Greek would order the little man up into the storage room, *directly above the kitchenette,* and by using the reflection of the glass panel, in that door, the brutal disgusting Greek person could view any one approaching. *Including warders.* One morning, that victim had looked at me, sensing a rare in depth sympathy, *which very few longtime desensitized criminals ever had,* and I quietly wondered *what, or if,* my good and decent caring parents would have thought of my just standing by while such unfair bullying practices were taking place, before my very eyes. *Strangely, the penal authorities suggest a person who goes to prison is a 'Sociopath' but from my later studies, I know that anyone capable of 'Empathy,' is not a sociopath.*

At that particular moment, I had truly then believed, that our possessing a clear conscience, was what had truly separated genuine real Australians, from their cowardly counterparts. So it was, that I had stood up and broken the unwritten law of; *Open slather,* which was then the usual enforced rule of most State institutions.

'Leave him alone Tony, *for fucks sake,* can't you see the poor silly cunt doesn't know whether he is fucking well coming or going, *you dirty fucking prick.'* I said in a critical, but determined voice.

'Why don't you mind your own fucking business, *Campbell?* Tony had snarled back.

I had always been a highly-strung person, with a short fuse, *for most of my life,* and I'd totally deplored any personal insult by such foul arrogant people. People who somehow believed there was no penalty at all for their rude and insulting arrogance. *Emotionally,* I was seriously unfit for a prison, or any of the armed forces, and the one thing that I did not like at all was a prisoner using my surname. *Especially without that respectful correct title.* 'Mr'

Warders could call out '*Campbell,* and those Police and Judges did it also, but this well-known stand over man had just made a very big mistake. I had known Tony out on the streets of selfish old Brisbane, as teenagers. *He had also been present when Bill Stokes had beaten me to a pulp, many years before in 3 yard, 1 Division.*

There was obviously no love lost between us, and physically, he was a whole lot stronger than I was, but at that precise moment, I was a whole lot meaner, *as well as leaner,* and I'd slammed two quick punches into his slit eyes. The Greek grappled at my clothing and he'd pulled me into a tight bear hug, and lifted me off the floor.

'I'll kill you cunt.' He said in his exaggerated gangster voice, and in return I had head butted him, It was then he loosened his grip. I had slammed punch after punch onto the bridge of his long narrow nose. *Or Grecian Bridge?*

It was the torrent of blood, *and not the punches,* that made him back away.

'Fuck you Larry, look at my fucking nose, I have to go to court on Monday. What will my poor fucking family say? Fuck it man, if you had wanted the fucking Strawberry Ripple, you only had to bloody well ask me, *you fucking cunt.'* He said looking at his face in the aluminum mirror.

I did not even bother answering him, and nor did I inform him that my damaged bleeding hand was giving me a great pain. Seeing, as I had once again dislocated two of my main knuckles, and so I said to the poor frightened Downs Syndrome youth, *as kindly as I possibly could.*

'You don't have to do those dirty things anymore.'

It was my way of telling Tony, that I had won the fight, and was in full charge of the kitchenette again. I knew that had he of launched himself at me, I would have been fighting him with only one hand. *But luckily for me, the fight had well and truly gone out of him.*

In hindsight, I do believe it was Tony's vanity, that had beaten him, and rather than be cruel, or arrogantly critical toward him, I had gotten some cleaning cloth, and I had helped him to clean himself up. That is, before those new 2pm. replacement yard warders came into the kitchenette and espied the evidence of our sudden altercation.

It is my own view, that if we fight for the right thing, *we will be okay,* although brutal violence was becoming second nature to me, by that time. I guess that in looking back, I'd long realized that I had honestly hated myself for describing such altercations, *as it seemingly appeared,* I could be regarded as some sort of show off. Indeed, being seen as a; *'showoff,'* or some person who had boasted of a Pyrrhic victory, so as to try and promote oneself, *was seriously frowned upon.*

The only real reason for my describing such angry violent clashes, *that I'd had back then,* was to show clearly the slow or damaging changes of such a serious *mental violentization* that was taking place in my darkening personality. In fact, the man I had later developed into, *prior to my marriage and having my two children,* is not the sort of man I would like to meet today. 'Or, have living in my neighborhood.' *See my later writing; The Boggo Road Connection.' 231 pages.*

That gentle Downs Syndrome youth? soon became my personal tea and coffee maker. *Almost overnight.* In truth, the lad would watch diligently for me to finish my tea or coffee, *so that he could replenish it.* Sometimes I would hide my enamel cup and his bird like movements would make me laugh loud with amusement, as we had both searched for this most important item. Actually, that poor little *man-youth* had gained my respect for a number of reasons, and the most prominent being that he'd had a very artistic handwriting. *While his memory was infallible.*

A church group had later then discovered his presence inside the Boggo Road remand yard, and like hundreds of thousands of various or *so* confused remand yard prisoners, *before him;* he soon disappeared into the mists of my memory.

Downs Syndrome, blind, deaf, retarded, as well as crippled men in wheel chairs, were also put in prison, and it had proved to me, that Queensland citizens, *along with people in higher education,* did not give a half baked damn if our police hierarchy *archaic enemy* openly acted improperly in the placements of remand prisoners.

By law, remand prisoners are still under the care and jurisdiction if the Queensland police department. Such men women and children are not eligible for any privileges that are so endowed on the legally sentenced inmates.

Late one afternoon, I saw the Inala detectives come out on the balcony that had overlooked the main remand yard proper, to survey the human waste. One recently arrived Coopers Plains youth, who was then standing up against the cyclone wire with me, *had said contemptuously,* while nodding at the plain clothed men.

'There's that scum bag that pulled you out of the Oxley Creek the night you ran away from the pigs.'

I quickly looked at this young man in deep surprise, and I had frowned in a puzzled disbelief.

'Don't tell me Stringbean was the uniformed copper who went in and pulled me out of the drink?

I was shocked at the information, and immediately my mind went into over drive.

I quickly recalled that *one stupid night* when I had taken a group of teenagers to the burger bar in Inala. I had also remembered how the bullying gang members set upon me, and surrounded our group in the car park.

At that particular time I had used a steel tyre lever to hold the Inala street bullies at bay. That is, as we quickly decamped with the enemy's cars and motorbikes taking after us in hot pursuit. *Then,* as I approached the Oxley lights intersection I had failed to stop. *Soon we had a patrol car on our tail within a few short seconds.*

I had obediently pulled the car over to the side of the road, and then, when I had remembered I had no driver's license at all, I'd stupidly and impulsively ran toward the scrub at the far side of the road. It was when jumping over, *what I had then thought had been a fence*, I found instead that I had plummeted helplessly down into a deep and marshy cutting.

Going down into the murky darkness, I flailed through empty space where I fell hard onto a water soaked creek embankment of the old Oxley Bridge.

Proof, that if the crocodiles don't get us, the alligators will.

At that time, I was in a semi unconscious state and I felt myself sliding slowly into that foul murky waist deep stagnant water of the Oxley Creek. *I felt as if I was in a similar type dream state, when in a much later period in my life, a kindly nurse had liberally injected me with morphine.*

But, down in that foul cutting, I had experienced a wave of swirling blackness as I slowly submerged into a cold wet oblivion. Any personal fear was the least of my problems, as I'd gratefully welcomed the serene peace of a most possible near death experience. In fact, *in that dream state*, I had vaguely recalled being dragged from the shallows by a uniformed police-man who then began was pressing my chest. Later he carefully helped me back up to the roadway. For some reason the two officers had let us go after they had heard the tale that the two accompanying, *and very frightened girls had told,* of our dangerous and quite harrowing ordeal.

I was confused and suffering serious concussion, but out of the blue a sudden emergency radio call for the police, *elsewhere,* had fortunately allowed me to go free, once again.

At that time, in the remand yard, *during 1970,* I did indeed see clearly how both power and or prestige had changed that tall policeman. It was, *as I'd looked up at that most arrogant young detective who was tapping a Manila folder on the steel Remand Yard railing,* that I impulsively walked over and had called up to him.

'Hey! You don't remember me Stringbean? Do you, *you silly cunt?'*

He and his fellow officers had smirked at each other, as if it was a pleasure to see me in that concrete penned yard, while being dressed as a vagrant, *and suffering a serious dose of sunburn.* So it was that I had continued to smile back, while saying smartly.

'Thanks for pulling me out of the Oxley Creek that night, you silly fucking cunt, *I would have fucking drowned if you hadn't.*' I said as I had twisted my face up into a silly rabbit smile.

The total complete shock on String beans face, was quite genuine, and he had immediately dropped his smile and spoke seriously to the detective next to him, *who grinned back.* It was then that they both laughed out loud as if to dismiss me as a fool.

Exactly three days later, I had faced Stringbean in the District court, and it was seemingly, because of my new appeal then pending, that they wanted to get another conviction up. Just in case I won the next trial and received appeal bail.

This time I was in a bigger quandary than ever, mainly because the very night before, I had been called up to the Chiefs Station and given a late evening phone call from the prosecutor's office.

'We have decided to go ahead with the Two Way Radio charge, *if that's all right with you Larry?'*

'Yeah sure, no worries,' I replied, *feeling then,* that at least one decent sounding lawmaker had probably realized that I was indeed loaded up with the wrong charges.

Seemingly, they were now at long last taking me very seriously.

The man had spoken in an amicable and a cheerful friendly manner, and soon I went back to my concrete container feeling buoyant, *as well as a little egotistical.* I had realized much later, that I should not have been so swell headed, because I had stupidly taken the court file that had contained the two-way radio, into court. *It was then I had found myself up on a charge of a housebreaking that I had honestly known nothing about.*

If it had been a criminal offense that my casual associates had committed. It was certainly one that I personally had not at all received any benefit from, *and then,* my confidence had wavered under the gaze of the room full of men.

The trickery of the prosecution, had really thrown me, and so it was that I had forgotten to do my big country boy act and later in those proceedings I made a whole mess of selecting the Jury. Even my cross-examination of the detectives, was quite below par, and so it was then, that the stress and tension of the past fourteen months flowed over me as I threw caution to the winds. In one last-ditch effort by my using untrue allegations, I accused Stringbean of making it all a personal matter. I reminded him of our differences, especially after a so called previously heated altercation at the Sunny Bank Hotel. *Only just over one year prior to the charges being laid?*

'That is untrue! I never saw you before this matter was earlier bought to the attention of my fellow officers.'

'What about the night you threw me over the railing down at the Oxley Bridge?' I said smoothly.

Stringbean had almost choked in his own spittle, and the tall gangly clown went as red as a boiled beetroot.

'That was clearly an entirely different matter; I *uh huh* mean it is not true.' He spluttered, while looking at the prosecutor in sheer panic, as well as personal anger while motioning at the malicious way I had twisted the situation around to suit myself; *'Much in the same manner of a crown prosecutor ringing me up to tell me a bare faced fucking lie.'*

I quickly cut him off, and I adamantly refused to examine him further. I knew too I had dented the case immensely, but this time the Jury was on a personal mission, and as I saw it, I had made the enormous mistake of allowing the older gentlemen to be the dominant make-up of the overall Jury. So it was, that by lunchtime I was not at all making any real headway. I could feel that deeper down, that I had been set up for a very big fall. My brother Bruce had again taken a time off work to come and listen to the case, although I knew he had considered me the liar, *because of my past behaviour,* and those detectives he had viewed as honest as the day was long, simply had to be telling the truth. In his opinion. .

I did of course feel that this time around, *the legal mulberry bush,* even he could not help but believe beyond any doubt at all, that I was guilty.

That is, because of the well presented case put forward by that prosecutor named Martin. A barrister who had incidentally been invited down from the higher Supreme Court so as to try and convict me in one, *last ditch smash bang,* effort.

I had no witnesses to call, so I decided to speak of my criminal record to prove that I was experienced in the world of prisons, *and Police stations.*

Also, that I would never under the experienced rule of the convicted criminal ever consider, *under any circumstance,* of confessing to a bullying policeman. *Even if I were the guilty party.*

The Judge had tried to warn me against doing such a thing, and as I saw the case slipping away, the choking tears and inner emotion took over and I babbled out a statement from the dock. *Realising much later, that I was not making any real sense at all.*

I knew then, that all was now lost.

I was going down like George Foreman would eventually do in the African city of Zaire, *a few years later.* Mainly because of Karma, and, *my clear inexperience in Queensland Law.*

Somehow the mood quickly passed as the haughty Jury sat stony faced and had stared back at me without sympathy, *without empathy,* and nor were they in any way influenced by my immature, or childish mannered outburst.

With nothing left to lose in the later summary, I took up the stiff stance of the **Masons,** and I spoke that secret word of greeting, that threw a whole new light onto the matter. I then saw at least four of the Jurymen stir, and or move slightly, in a very wary, and most uncomfortable way. *As a young man in the mid 1960's, a prisoner had taught me the secret signs, and language of the 'Masonic Lodge.'*

Even the Judge sat back and wiped his glasses, and he stared at me as if he was actually seeing me for the very first time.

I was quite drained after the Judges summary, *and,* as the Jurymen filed out to consider their verdict, good old Jack the warder, quietly took me out for a cigarette, and in his caring way, he looked a little sad for me. In turn I simply shook my head and shrugged.

'I fucked that one up Jack.' I said, as I flicked the half smoked *darrie* away.

'Not to worry young Larry, you did your best.' replied Jack, who was quite sympathetic to my deeper concern of an impending legal repercussion.

Normally, a non smoker, the stress and pressure of defending the many cases had caused me to take up smoking for a short time.

It took a six-hour jury room deliberation, but the Masons, *who ever they were*, had generously won the day for me. *I was acquitted in an aura of total dumbfounded disbelief.* I also noted that very short in stature, *dumbfounded* prosecutor, had appeared at a total loss on how they could ever at all convict me.

That very experienced lawyer, *Mr. Martin,* had actually died not that long after while quietly jogging on a morning run out at the sprawling and scenic Queensland University. It was reported, that he was barely a twenty-nine year old man in the prime of his life.

'Maybe he was too good for the dirty work that he was doing.' I thought back then. *Which was in his; Aiding and Abetting Corruption in the State of Queensland.*

That evening, I was seriously deflated when I was put back in my cramped cell, and as expected, my brother Bruce had not even stayed to hear the verdict. Which, I of course could not blame him for doing so.. *That is,* when all the signs were that my case was well and truly lost.

So it was, that for just for a while, I had carefully reviewed my attitude toward my life, *and the many people in it.* I had wondered also, if I was just wasting my life trying to be a criminal, when in reality, I was only an above average prison vagrant in a cell, who was obviously never going to change. The truth of the matter was, that I had been nothing but a beggar, **by using the tears and the sign of the Secret Society** to win my case, and so, I then decided, and determined, that a fair degree of control would be in order on my very next trial.

The department of Prosecutions had also cheated, and it was clear to all of those legal eagles, that I had cheated too. But of course I was so totally demoralized by the event that had taken place, and for one night, I had felt like giving in and allowing the detectives to have their way. *Like a virgin that could not fight off an assailant, further.*

It may have seemed stupid to just simply lay down at this late stage of the game, *by my pleading guilty to the few remaining break &Enter charges,* but I was extremely sad and genuinely tired, for I was at that very moment in time, feeling a emotional burden upon my slowly sagging shoulders.

CHAPTER 22

WHY ME

Each morning, I had repetitiously walked the length of the Remand yard, *back and forth, to and fro at a fairly brisk pace,* and, I also considered that the then most common phrase used, *by almost all men,* was; *Why me?* As it were, walking relieved stress, *and helped one to think clearly,* and while doing so, I had pondered their *inane* outspoken question, that was seemingly without any positive answer.

As it was, *at first,* I put their attitude of *'Why me'* down to ingrained selfishness, and had, more often than not, avoided people with such self centered values. Normally, the men I had usually talked to, and walked with in the yard, were always those happy *'Go Lucky'* Australians that had said; *Why not me?*

It would, *as I found out,* take me many more years to understand the *'why me'* people, and then, at last, I began to see my own future more clearly. **To know exactly what I had needed to do with my life.** It was not luck, *or good fortune,* that opened my eyes, but I did later believe it was my basic, or general empathy for the *'Battler'* that bought me into contact with an alcoholic defrocked priest. *Who, was determined to drink his life away.*

At the time, I gave him some money out of pure common kindness, and then on pension day, when it rolled around, he turned up on my door and gave me the same amount back. I then invited the old bloke to stay for awhile, *until he was on his feet.* Now, from this old man I learned all about the *'Why me'* people and why they actually stuff up their lives in the pursuit of *impossible self improvement, at any cost;* 'Or, self advancement before others;' *Sabo's.* A type of people that do believe you have to help yourself first, before you can worry about anybody else. *Something I found was not true, and our stopping to help others, had nothing to do with success, or the lack of it.*

This good man started me thinking, and over time I came to realize, that all the little babies in the world are born with a dream. Including a certain skill that is bred in them from generations of forebears. It turned out, that all of those little people ever needed, was someone to help them *develop* that skill. *And to grow their dreams to fruition.*

Sadly, most lost adults have been; *stilted thwarted degraded desensitized and sexualized, punched in the mouth, bullied and 'owned'* many years before they had even reached sixteen years of age. There were also times when a *grandfather, father, brother, uncle,* or the man or woman next door, rudely rubs the clitoris of their slowly developing daughter, and grand daughter, *or their silly young neighbor, and gives her some gold or silver coins,* which insensitively interrupts her soft developing dream, and stunts her *'skill growth.'* What he or she, in fact does, is to teach the young child to be greedy, *and* to show her, that her experiencing sexual rude pleasure, is better than following a dream. *Or, developing a skill that I do know lies dormant in all of us.*

The truth is, that there is no exception to gender, or age, and when a stepfather breaks a twelve years old child's undeveloped nose with a swift back hander, *it is the last straw,* and the child feels he or she would be better off on the street, than being treated so dismally. Science too tells all children, that their life was given to them *perchance,* and that religion or faith of any kind plays no part in the lives of successful people. Hedonism, self idolization, pleasure, and money, are the real pursuits of many young people, *and atheists,* and most of those type of people can be touched or licked on their genitals for money. *Also an iPod, mobile phone, even relatives houses,* but, once in the long ago, *it was for lollies or milkshakes in the local pictures.*

Each generation passes onto children, and young people, what it is they have learned, *or experienced,* and most of it destroys the *'Dreams,'* the *'Skills,'* and the self esteem of our gullible young. *For many, I have known in my life, there was suicide to ease the pain of being nothing, and of having nothing at all, that, you had once believed in.* For myself, I had been living my life on; *'instinct,'* ever since my teenage years, but in my case, I had a Grandmother and a *few* brothers and sisters that instilled in me, *a belief in myself,* while all around me were hurtful, self indolent, self centered people that wanted to taint my dream. *As well as stilt my skills until the world that I once saw through a child's eyes, 'had no longer remained.'*

Sadly with that decent and wonderful woman passing on into the world beyond, *My Grandmother,* I got hurt damaged and sexualized, *and as expected,* I went to prison for a few decades or so. The old priest of course, opened up my eyes, and virtually told me that the *'Dream was dead;' only, if I stopped believing in it,* and, that *personal skills,* can be developed at any age. *That is of course, if you can separate the bad from the good.*

I don't mean to say that I simply up and changed my life in a split instance, as it was not at all true, for I still stole cheated and bribed young girls to lay in my bed. *Yes,* I did to those younger greedy teenagers, what was once done to me. *Yes!* I too had my habits, and I needed to change my old way of life, *urgently,* but in the quiet times my dream emerged stronger and stronger. So, one day I simply went to a library and found some amazing books that had titles; *'Writing for Beginners,'* as well as; *'New Effective Communication,' &* of course, *'Don't Sweat the Small Stuff.'*

Immediately, my mind settled, and I quickly involved myself into developing my personal natural skills from an interrupted primary school education, *and in time,* a most funny exciting but amateurish tale was told of a young man running amok in the big and spread out city of Brisbane, *Australia.*

I destroyed the finished writing of my youth, *one sad day, in a fit of anger,* but I had that; *'Special'* dream back, and because I saw that life had a purpose for me, I again tried to write more positive material that somehow grew and grew into a mountain of old unedited memories. More than anything, I had discovered, that the atheists were wrong, *and so it was,* because *'Life* had no use for them, *or they for Life,* it had simply turned its back on them when they asked mere mortals; *'Why me?'*

In the year 1970, I did not know the answers, but I knew for sure that flies were caught with honey, and young girls could be kissed for money, *and,* way back then, my skills were directed into obtaining *either* pleasure, in any order that was then available to me. The one thing I had sensed, even then, was that '*Life was an entity*' and that if you destroyed life in any form, *for no real reason at all,* you were done like a dinner, *forgotten, never to be wanted,* and you could ask the reason *why* until you were blue in the face. You would never know that it started the first time someone, *relative or not,* had taken you into the shower recess and had soaped you up. Or your dad flogged your bare bottom in front of your siblings, and you, *found,* that then it was, *that your dreams were tarnished.* The truth of it is, that sex is not a dream, *it is a function,* and when one has reached a climax, *it is not at all that important anymore.* No matter what skills your partner has in their bag of tricks, sex is not more important than food when your starving? Or cool water when your dying of thirst? Anyone at all can achieve a function, but to develop a skill right up to its full potential, is the most amazing thing you will ever experience in your lifetime. Your skill can show all who ever doubted you, that you are better than the person you once were, *and will be.* Even better, as you age and assist your own children. Maybe, one or two others will also listen to you and to truly follow their own dream, as you, *at long last,* have followed yours. But never *ever* forget, that *Bullies,* as well as damaged, *Pedophiles, and Puppeteers,* do destroy young peoples dreams. *Why did such young people lose their dream?* Well it is because their dreams were once tarnished in the long ago when they had felt ashamed for doing *something* they had no possible control over.

But, you can, *like all youth,* revive and live the dreams again, as you go on with your life, and totally refuse to pass on the poisonous chain letter type of behavior that the cruel '*Dream Breakers*' still pass maliciously on to small, and gullible children.

To get a second chance, you simply have to nurture your dream. Have your own children, and treat them the way you wished you had been treated during all those many long years ago.

Belief, ... not sex, ...is the energy fuel, that makes your dream come true.

CHAPTER 23

THE GODFATHER IDENTITY

*I*had another trial the following Monday before Judge Broad.
Mainly, because it was not my important appeal case, *on that day,* I was to
be underrepresented with only my own wits, as an ally, *or guide,* so as to keep
the wolves at bay. I had no memory of the major details, seeing as I had lost
a lot of paper work during those few days of precious freedom, and so, I
fell into my old wily routine of simply acting like some sad, shocked, and
fascinated curious innocent person from the rural back blocks of southern
Queensland. In fact, the only thing missing, was a straw hat and a twig in
my mouth. *Much like a hillbilly, who is too far away from home, and much too stupid
to get out of my own foolish way.*

The prosecution, *of course,* had this last chance to convict me before
Legal Aid officially took over my remaining charges. Malicious charges that
the legally branded *fresh faced prosecutor* had then looked at me with disdain,
as he ran his eyes over me from head to foot. I in turn had pretended to
look quite shocked and allowed my mouth to drop open in askance. I came
to the conclusion, that I may as well have some real down to earth fun, seeing as they were going to skin me alive, one way or another.

The selected Jury, was a make-up of modern businessmen, *mostly
because that was all there was to choose from.* I'd smelled a rat, but, there was very
little I could do about it, *and so,* I had began my play-acting as Judge Broad
spoke to me in half smile contemptuous disdain. *As if he was genuinely going
to relish every single moment of my impending downfall.*

A fast moving legal man in a faded white wig and a dark silk shiny black
gown hurriedly entering into the court proper. His sudden appearance had

then diverted my attention as he respectfully faced the Judge. I was a little shocked to find out that he was there to represent me, *and,* by the look on the good prosecutors face, he was also appeared a little fazed by the unexpected intrusion.

I could never at any time in my whole life recall when I had taken in a whole courtroom scene, as an observer, *that is,* in one *'express'* moment, and I had quickly observed those expressions change on quite a few faces, as if, a dark shadow had fallen over the court. It had seemed then, *at that time,* as if the silly fun and games were now over. *Also,* that an obviously bigger new kid was now on the block, and willing to put an immediate stop to the shenanigans. The newcomer was about to change all the rules of a game of indoor cricket. *Where I had been considered the the red ball so as to bash me around the ball park, at will.*

In my belated recollections, I can today suggest, that the good man had actually looked the exact image of Al Pacino, in the Godfather 2; *bias aside.* Of course the book, *or movie of the Godfather,* had never been invented, *at that time,* and I observed a man who was neither fazed nor concerned by anyone. Later, he would speak to me in a hallway and rather than seek my opinion, he quietly told me what we were actually going to do to deal with the problem at hand. *I nodded in full agreement at his every suggestion, as if he was a surgeon with a scalpel.*

His appearance or aura was quite powerful, and the good Judge Broad sat up as if he had been bitten by a bull ant. *Seeing as his face went blank with frozen alarm.* I also saw that the side view of the skinny pimple faced prosecutor, had shown his complete and utter surprise, as if some bigger bully boy had unfairly arrived to rudely interfere with his dirty little game; *'Of his fingering the prisoner.'* The jury had too appeared just a little curious at what was actually happening, and many of them had looked around a little confused by this impromptu halt in the proceedings.

The good man had introduced himself as Mr. Barbeller, who was known to be a private barrister from a large Brisbane law firm. The good man, had authoritatively explained to Judge Broad, that he had been retained as counsel for the defence. He had turned to me in the dock, *as if seeking confirmation,* and I had quickly nodded in deep confounded gratitude *With an acceptance of his most generous offer.* Mr. Barbeller, *it seemed,* was one of the rising stars of the Queensland legal scene, and he was also what many '*Romance authors*' would describe as, quite handsome, with dark attractive looks along with his dark or Mediterranean coloring. His obviously excellent manners, and his extraordinary word power, had made him more attractive as a lawyer, *than as a character,* but this did not deter him from being blunt and quite straight to the point. In truth, this excellent barrister soon had the Judge agreeing to every sensible thing he suggested, and soon I was out in a small internal corridor, *agreeing with him myself,* as he had then quickly consulted with me on how the case would be fought, and won.

What later took place, was to be without the presence of the Jury, '*Vi-ore Dior' I believe,* and Mr. Barbeller, who was as sincerely polite, as a fresh bucket of frozen ice cream, had soon given all of those legal men, *who were present,* a thoroughly harsher lesson on law than they had never at all before experienced. *Or had probably never forgotten, during the rest of their legal careers.*

Even the arrogant Broad had a stunned look of complete respect, *and attention,* and without my at all having understood one word spoken, *the case in a nutshell,* was quickly dismissed from a lack of constructive evidence. *Or balance.*

I was quite dumbfounded, and I sincerely thanked the clean-cut man profusely, but before I knew it, he was gone as fast as he had arrived. Jack the warder gave me a wink, as if to say that I would be fine now, *and he, Jack, being my only ally in my long ordeal,* had smiled at me gently, and with a deep and personal satisfaction.

Judge Broad in his most facetious and prudish condescending manner, had been cautioned by his own brethren, and he had clearly lost his effeminate-smile.

'*Who's got a fool for a client now, you Cunt?*' I thought as only a prisoner or criminal can think or speak of when he is involved in such one sided legal situations.

I was to later find, that an older retired Barrister named Colin Bennett, had read of my most extraordinary situation in the old Sunday newspapers. *One fine Sunday morning.* 'When the '*Sun*' was published. Apparently, the minor segment in "*This Week in Court,*" had risen up his well published; '*Ire.*'

This magnificent man among men, *Sir Colin Bennett,* had, it appeared, used his personal funds to pay for my defense. Or indeed, that good kindly man may have used his well-appreciated legal influence to have Mr. Barbeller represent me on a good will alone? *Another thought was, that the 'Masons' may have supported me, believing I was one of the brethren?* I was never at all informed on how, *or at what financial cost,* my good fortune had come about. I dared to think positive in a pessimistic way, and I was again quite grateful that some decent and unrelated legal men, had agreed to act independently of their legal standing.

The word of mouth information, *that was relayed throughout the court system, and inside the prison,* was not always that accurate, but a great deal of it could be believed, and I for one had felt just a little humbled by these exceptionally decent, and well educated extraordinary men.

It was a time in my early life, when I'd first believed that the higher that the education one had achieved, the more ethical they had become, and I had personally regretted, not having had the past opportunity to rise above the life of a thief, *and a prisoner.* It was a waste: A sad and sorry waste of this only life cycle I had been given for free, *and which,* I then knew would never turn like a big wheel for me, ever again.

I had no family, no support, and no children, *nor any normal love,* and it was clear to me, *even then,* that it was all just a futile game, and a total waste of a quickly evaporating individual life.

I'd felt even at that relatively early stage of my life, that I had now lost any chance to be normal, but of course, I never really understood the true meaning of; *What goes round,* could actually work in my favor.

I would, *eventually,* find later on in life, that what I held in my bare hands was far more important to me, than what I did not actually have. So, in some strange and roundabout way, I had eventually learned to chew what I had in my mouth, rather than look at what was on the other persons plate. *Or in other people's houses.* I further learned, that only young people had ever felt that; *Envy, was the same as 'Need.'*

Such young people, were so very wrong, and they stole cars and cheap property while using the cost of their life, *as gambling chips,* hoping to be a big time player. No one had ever sat down and actually told them that the deck was rigged in favor of the police personnel, and that, their life would never be their own again. *All because of a pedophile, or a homegrown bully, that had degraded them in the long, long ago.*

If teenager's felt a human life was so valued at the equal of a speeding car, then someone had a dire duty to explain, that *when,* they crashed at an intersection, *not if they crashed,* then they not only crippled themselves, *but their whole family, or best friends.* Possibly it was Mr. Barbeller who had motivated me to think in this strange way, *(actions speak louder than words)* and it was the first time I had understood just what I had repaid the Campbell family, *for their taking in a newborn infant that wasn't theirs.* I'd thought even back then, of trying to write a novel for young teenagers, so as to show them the real genuine cost of their using ones life's blood as collateral in a weird game, where the other side always won. *At the end of the day.*

The legal people and the police, *won hands down,* because they played by a set of rules, *as well as developed skills,* and we as idiotic fools, did not. But of course, when they cheated too, we felt more than justified in sticking it up them.

The Author, with an undercover police informer.

CHAPTER 24

THE CRIMINAL CASE WORKER

Back at the old Prison, the latest news had soon spread of my eleventh acquittal, *against verbalized evidence,* and this in turn gave a lot of men hope that they too could beat their flimsy cases. Charges, that were then based on similar or a clearly fabricated evidence; *(Most admitted doing the crime to me, but not to the police detectives.)*

Few offenders ever believed, *for even a single moment,* that my charges were totally false, which were somehow incorrectly submitted under the wrong headings, *or,* that some stupid or proud arrogant men, would never, *if ever,* admit their defeat.

It was of course very little use my explaining to my remand yard associates, *or prison based enemies,* that *any* street smart lawyer could instinctively read between the lines, and so, I had simply shrugged and had reluctantly agreed to look at their pile of transcripts. Just to see if they had even the remotest chance of gaining an acquittal. It was quite plain to me, *when reading the legal Depositions,* that they were genuinely involved in their crimes by some concrete set of circumstantial evidence, *or,* that the verbalization in the low court transcripts had simply blended the more obvious facts of the cases together. Prior to Genetic Identification, *DNA,* verbal, was the only method the policemen had to fight serious crimes with. But, because of that particular verbal weapon being abused so freely, it was apparent that an innocent man, *if he were at all an innocent man,* was sure to be convicted, *and or,* wrongly incarcerated.

In one case, of *Regina v Greaves,* a first timer *square head* had accidentally shot his father in a very serious family dispute. When he waved the gun at his violent parent.

The lazy detectives simply added the words;
'I was planning it for some time.'
Which showed legally, a serious intent to willfully murder his father.

'Without intent, there is no charge, except unlawfully discharging a firearm.
Or, an unlawful killing.

The man named Greaves, had gotten willful murder, instead of *Unlawful or Accidental killing,* but thankfully, those Legal men who were on the job, were not so lazy, *or so easily taken in,* and arrived at unlawful killing, after hours of negotiations.

Among those other lesser hopefuls, in that remand yard, were the career crims with their arrogance, *and the overall shiftiness of Judge Bill Carter.* When looking at their Depositions, it seemed clear to me to be an open and shut case of guilt, but they still continued to plague me for my view, or some sly legal ways to hopefully win their case.

'It's not what I, or the Judge believes mate, it's what the Jury believes.' I would try to explain to them.

'The prosecutor is just the Judges bitch, and the police are the prosecutor's lap dogs, and so, your only real hope is in convincing the Jury that a terrible injustice is at hand.'

I gave my personal verdict, and, they went away holding their bulky rolls of depositions as if they were hoping that someone else could give them a more positive adjudication to their trial of the century. I, *of course,* had at times felt sorry for many who were guilty of the crimes they were so charged with, but I could see where the false *'verbalised evidence'* had made the incident a lot more serious than it really was. The basic purpose of verbalization was to show; *serious intent to commit the crime in question,* and sometimes, the defendant had not intended to commit the crime, *or even be any part of it.* In fact, just to be in the company of an offender could get you put in prison for ten years, *or so,* and in one case in particular, I saw that there was a genuine travesty of justice waiting to happen.

Seemingly, the youth in question had been out with a friend that had accosted a pedestrian, and out of the blue, his friend had punched the poor man and then stole from the prostrate victim.

When his friend ran, *he ran too,* and a witness later described them both to police, *and of course,* they were soon apprehended some short blocks away. The only way the police could connect the younger man to the case of the idiotic robbery, was to deliberately create an unsigned confession. *And to tender it as evidence.* Legal aid did not like to take a case it could not possibly win, *that is due to a tight budget,* and so the foolish youth was soon left to the mercy of the court. *Hopefully the good Judge Taylor would take the bench.* That particular Judge, was said to hand out more bonds than any Sydney Insurance Broker. The good man was known affectionately by many older prisoners as; *Judge Bondy Taylor.*

The amount of men who were imprisoned wrongly, due to impulsive one off crimes, or, *being present when a new friend or current associate committed a crime,* was quite astronomical. For a few minutes of random time, they were a victim of their own mate's stupidity, *and usually,* out of some loyalty they had refused to tell the truth to clear up their innocent part in the offense.

Learned people had put it down to, *stupidity of arrogance, or ignorance,* toward the law, but I put it down to that ever deepening loneliness and alienation that younger people had suffered unfairly, *and consistently,* during their turbulent, and or confusing teenage years.

They of course would mature in time, but if the courts kept contaminating them with the wasteful lazy life of prisons, *addictive masturbation,* and any crude sexual contact with other sad lazy emotional men, then their maturity would take a great deal longer to arrive at. *'Much longer,'* I had decided, as I watched them act like high school boys that had at last made the top grade in the Boggo Road Remand Section for Men. *'You poor silly bugger's;'* I'd think with some serious concern as a tattooed toothless man listened attentively to a teenagers many alleged criminal deeds.

I actually took the case of that young man, *who'd ran,* and I carefully explained to him that telling the truth, was not dobbing, and that what he'd owed his mother, *and sister,* was more than he owed a teenager whom he had known only for a week prior to their incarceration. Somehow I'd succeeded, where his family had failed, and the boy did what I suggested, *and,* in his low court hearing his test case was heard in camera, *So it was, that the youth had apologized to the court, the police, and his friend.* In fact his friend had pleaded guilty and was certainly on his way to the old B wing and would be in a three out cell with the boys home toughs. Rough young men that would soon have his measure. *If not his young anus.*

My client, *who clearly had a fool for a lawyer,* gave evidence at his friend's committal hearing, and he respectfully told the magistrate the truth, *the whole truth and nothing but the truth.* So it was, that the false police version was dismissed, and I never saw. or heard from the lad, ever again.

In a minor way, I clearly understood why smart people took up the Law, *other than the money of course,* and a few men soon came to me who were, *it appeared,* in serious need of sensible advice. Over time, I personally began to view the unfairness of their untenable positions.

In full reality, a government lawyer had barely a few quick minutes, *or at the most,* one hour to consult with the accused men prior to a trial, *and,* at first glance they appeared guilty.

But, given more facts of extenuating circumstances, one soon determined that the lazy inept detectives were just as guilty of perjury, *as I was myself.* It certainly was not the type of career one would choose if he, *or she,* could be disillusioned at the fact that all men lied, *including their own colleagues.* I do indeed feel, that without a male or females practiced lies, millions of girls would never have married.

It appeared to me, that a criminal case could be lost or won on how *believable* any fabricated police evidence, actually was in a DPP criminal prosecution. It clearly had nothing at all to do with; *proof.'* Nor did it count for how many witnesses one called, and in my view, *the fewer witnesses called,* the better for all concerned. *For or against.*

Judges in the District Court, seldom made it to the high court, because of their obvious bias, and most would address the jury when summing up a case for the prosecution;

In a Judge's jargon;

'Gentlemen, I would ask that you draw on your worldly experience when you determine whether the defendant before the court, is being truthful in this matter?' Or, if, my highly respected officers are at all to be viewed as dishonest men.'

It was not a case if pointing out, that there was no sign of blood, lack of hair, no fingerprints, no recovered property, no images, and the only proffering was the alleged words of a prisoner, who had allegedly blurted out his guilt. Possibly because he just loved to give himself up. *What Bullshit.' I thought.*

Families with big money, *of course,* could hire a lawyer of great expertise, and if he destroyed the lies of the police, he'd also destroyed the Crown case. When some honest policeman presented his case, *minus the lies,* he could not be shaken by even the best in the land, and so, he soon made himself a name that a defense Barrister attempted to avoid at all cost. *In truth, I occasionally met such policemen, but in the 1970's, and 80's, they were as rare as hens teeth.*

I obviously had a lot of spare time to view all those facts, *or insights, that duty solicitors lacked,* or even knew of. I was also well aware of court procedure that could make a real difference. In fact, I was aware enough to throw a spanner into the sneaky works of a massive number of police committing perjury, with a legal impunity, *or fear of any further prosecution by their superiors.*

Or, of their legal cronies on the bench.

One old alcoholic that I had known, since my dormitory days, was at that time in his late seventies, and he was suffering a mild form of Alzheimer's disease, due somewhat to the intake of alcohol. *This man, respectfully asked me for my help.*

It was a sad case, where two old alcoholics going back to their boarding house had passed a Jewelry shop window, and one, decided to break the glass of that shop front with the intention of taking some of the glittering jewelry for their own personal use; *Possibly to trade for alcohol.*

Both were as responsible as the other, but old Snow swore to me that he had not confessed to that foolish crime, and he nervously explained to me how the police dog squad had later apprehended them.

'After, silly young Dick smashes the plate glass, we had quickly filled up our pockets with gold watches and rings. It was then we had hurried on back to the boarding house. We had another swig or two, when this fucking big cunt of an Alsatian dog on a fucking leash, drags a couple of coppers into our room. *Fuck me; I nearly had a fucking bloody heart attack.'* He had said to me, making me shake my head in amusement at their most amateur activity, *and,* habitual intoxicated street behavior.

It was truly amusing, but Snow said he could not handle a big sentence and he alleged to me that he had not admitted anything to the police. *Now,* it seemed that the police had deliberately credited him with an unsigned confession, and so, a genuine chance of any outright acquittal had seemed logically, *well out of the question.*

Snow's case had kept me up over half the night, but I did come up with a story of how he and his young friend had attempted to hail a cab outside of the jewelers shop window. The story was alleged to be, that the wary cabby having refused them a lift had then driven off, and Snow's friend, *in a much abbreviated condition,* had grabbed the brick out of the gutter and he intended to fling it after the disappearing cab. His supposed momentum, had, *it seemed,* carried him into a circle, and forgetting to let go of the brick, he had supposedly staggered off balance and into the glass.

I described it all to Snow and I inserted his excuse for leaving blood at the scene of the crime.

'You see Snow, old Dick goes into the window, *after the brick,* and you, being a friend, tried to lift him out of the window, and be buggered if silly Dick goes and drags jewelry onto the foot path. He refuses to let go of an armful and as you both staggered away he kept dropping things, and of course you being honest as the day is long, you had kept picking them up for what you felt was a future safekeeping. *Being an honest man, you had genuinely intended to return the property next day to the Jeweler.'*

'Remember, Dick was your first priority.' I warned the older man.

'What if they call Dick to give evidence? Dick already has his sentence, and he would be bloody scared of perjury to tell a lie to some big Judge.' said old Snow in a worried tone.

'Tell him to say he doesn't remember hardly anything, and he just did what the good policemen wanted him to do. So it was, he had signed what they had typed up.' I'd explained as logically as I could.

Within a few short days, Snow truly believed the new facts that swirled around in his head, and, he even became quite indignant that he could be held against his will for some crime that he did not at all commit. His charitable, or legal aid solicitor, *in an uncommon burst of energy*, had fought tooth and nail for old Snow and so it was he had also arranged a good Barrister in the District court. Snow, eventually had his day in court, and he was quickly acquitted from a lack of intent. *Happily for me, Snow never again returned to Prison.*

There were of course, quite a few different eye witness versions of his later experiences, and eventual demise, but I liked the one where he was boarding quietly with a caring sister in an outer Brisbane suburb. *It was said, he was trying especially hard to give up old man alcohol.*

To be locked inside an older prison, and actually forget you were there was as strange a feeling that anyone could ever at any time experience. It had become my only home, and it was my doing other people's cases, *or my writing pleas to the man on the bench*, that had kept me quite busy. As a man of twenty-six years of age, I had at last found my niche in life, and it seemed a little daunting, repressive, or even sadly depriving to others. *Especially to those that could not at all see that I was actually in my element.* I had grown accustomed to an easy lazy life of having all of my meals prepared, my clothing washed, as well as having popular music piped through an overhead speaker. This old time music reminded me of the long ago, and it had kept me dreaming of the impossible sweet dreams of yesteryear and a time that I felt could never come true for the prison rabble, or for anyone wearing that label of a criminal or thief. *'Sweet dreams baby, how long must I dream.'* Were the special words of my very favorite song of that long ago moment in time. *'Oh, Babette, I still love you.* I would murmur, and then shake my head and sheepishly look around in case someone heard me.

This appeared the best and the only system for men and children who had been sexually, or socially fouled up, *or,* in some serious cases, *mentally contaminated.* It was with this inhumane method of lumping us all in the prison yards together in such a close proximity that that we would eventually learn to create a brand new defacto type of family. *Which, was so very wrong.* Men that would learn to be a close knit temporarily staunch group of humans, that had soon learned to respect, to care, and to love one another. *Such as 'Bikers'*

Criticisms and condemnation would roll off all such prisoners like water from a ducks back, and those critics who would dare to say we were finished in the outside world of normality, were loudly jeered at. *Or punched in the head.*

In my own personal opinion, this pairing off of the male in prison was just an easier way of looking at life from the angle of the loser. *But a very real angle indeed.* This attitude was so real, that thousands of the younger prisoners paired off together and many became genuine success stories in the bigger and wider world, *as some of them shared and battled a cold cruel world of that lonely outcast,* or socially contaminated reject. Some rose above the cold harsh criticism to open up small store front businesses, cafes, and in a few occasions rich property development firms that would some day dwarf all of their former critics.

In comparison, those accepting civilian type of families who sat back on their laurels and criticised their foolish child, or their failed sibling, never once realised that they too had to face the future of old age with the same uncertain ignorance that they had once shown a brother, *or a friend. Loyalty and genuine support, had seemed to be the key to success, in any area of life.*

Without loyalty we were clearly equal to the lowest of all those weak human beings that forever begged others for charitable handouts. *Or pleaded for attention that no one liked to give without at first requesting some reward, or service, in exchange.*

Outside of the family, there was no free lunch, and no quarter given, so if men behind walls sought to create a family of their own, *then I would always support them.* Personally, when outside the walls, I soon learned how to manipulate employers into a friendly frame of mind by my hiring teenage prostitutes to go with me on my job interviews. It never failed, but I seldom stayed with any employer, usually because prison life had turned me away from ever obeying my superiors. My belief was, that having a loyal determined friend would give me all the ammunition I needed to create a business of my own, but my finding that special friend in my life, *was extremely hard.* Especially under those very precarious circumstances when uniformed people were paid large sums to find you, beat you, *and tell lies about you.*

I never ever gave up hoping that I would someday meet a loyal ally, even in that world of men that could not offer any person, *so much as a cigarette,* let alone the loyalty or realistic support that one needed to surmount a impossible social hurdle. True loyalty and support were indeed those enormous social hurdles that most uneducated men or women can never overcome, *on their own.* Like many prisoners who were lost in the system, I had never at that time realized that by my giving the same loyalty to a wife and children was the answer to my dilemma.

Personally I did not ever think that any self-respecting, or truly honest female, would choose to remain in my company longer than a selfish evening, mostly because of my past criminal ways, *as well as my hearing problem.* It had become apparent that I had many lessons to learn back then, but like any foolish property addicted, *or socially rejected person,* I quickly learned, or I soon got burned.

Still, the Boggo Road remand yard, *although physically much more dangerous and having less privileges,* had always held an aura of hope that one would meet a genuine friend and ally, while hopefully being released on the same day to seek unlimited success. I did feel I had a better chance than most to get one more crack at making good on the lonely street, *hearing difficulties or no,* but habits turn into addictions, and my addiction was, *my skimming those opportunistic rackets,* just like my piggish like opponents.

I also had been making future contacts, as well as sharing reliable information on places I could break into. *To hopefully afford the fundamentals of success, and a brand new start in life.*

My plan was to get enough cash in hand to rent a modern flat, and to hopefully buy a small car and alarm clock. I would then go back to work in some old factory for a month, *or seven,* and hopefully try to fit in where I could be an anonymous and every day person. It was obvious to all that such crims left without a kick-start, were left to the mercies of the law, *the queer folk,* and the ever supportive, Salvation Army. *And, each in their own way had a different humiliating effect upon anyone with higher hopes of success.*

CHAPTER 25

TROUBLESOME PRISONERS

Predicting the behavior of prisoners was quite impossible, back in the 70's, and even the old time warders never knew when a prisoner would erupt in wild anger, or object to personal property being taken by warders on a legal search.

Or, just a sudden whim.

One day when the siren went off in the old 1 Division, we went quickly to the cyclone fence to observe the warders tumbling out of the officer's mess. Rumors of escape, and or a riot, were soon quelled when one big German prisoner was frog marched onto the 1 Division Compound and taken by warders to the old surgery, *so as to get his needle.*

A prisoner that I knew well, *whose name was Bobby Stephens,* was being spoken to by the Chief Officer, and we simply surmised that the German and Bob had had a confrontation in the old yards. Later, we found that the German had attacked the warder, *namely Black Jack Baimbridge,* with a lump of wood, and we were further told that Bob had intervened with a hay maker that knocked the German completely out.

Bob of course had not intervened to save Black Jack, *simply because he liked him*, but it was mostly because if a warder was killed stone dead, then all the prisoners would be isolated and probably beaten by the special violent revenge squad. (*The Flying Squad.*) Furthermore, it turned out that Bob Stephens did the German a big favor, as he would most certainly have gotten life, *and in Boggo Road Gaol, life meant life, for screw killers.*

As it was the Kraut got a tap dance on his forehead, *while drugged to the eyeballs*, and the dormitories went back to normal, and then of course, everybody was as happy as Larry.

Ten years was a long time, and over a long period I would get to know Bob real well, and his rumored right hand punch was indeed as lethal as some victims had said. Bob, like me, had hit the streets early, *He never told me who or what had started him off in is career of crime, and prison yard life,* but we got on well, and I would have got up to a lot of mischief with him had we ever met beyond the prison walls.

Like me, Bob Stephens hid his age well, and whether those prison walls had somehow preserved us, or not, we used our youthful features to chat up young street girls on the outside. *Girls who should have been in High School.* Unfortunately, neither of us stayed out of jail long enough to establish ourselves, and we soon got the rightful name of *persistent troublemakers* and were obviously doing too much time for our own good. Worse still, *in Gaol,* prisoners who got the name of a troublemaker *or a name to be remembered,* were always gossiped about, or else they were never really noticed, but Bob, much like me, had thought that the streets and the prison were our oyster. *Although it was seriously hard trying to find a pearl that was sometime cast among the swine.* Meaning, we seldom got mail from females on the outside, but the warders still marked us for a future reference. Mainly because of the untrue views that were bandied about by the gossip mongers.

With never a dull moment for those gossips, *including me,* I had heard that one morning, Bob had simply walked into the main kitchen and began to fry a steak, *with onions on the side,* and he was happily buttering up his bread when the prisoner who was labeled the head cook, at that time, *(Billy Hess)* bellowed at him.

'*What the fuck do you think your doing Cunt?*'

Bob simply turned about and had knocked him out with one single punch, while continuing to making his sandwich. Bob then walked out the door and back to the yards as he munched on a succulent sandwich. Like me, Bob knew the warders, in key positions, *as well as the roster of the day*, and some prisoners needed to be shown that they were not screws with authority, but just ordinary inmates. *Just like we were.*

I found out over a period of time, that like a lot of men that did ten years or more, Bob was not against having sex with gullible boys. So it was, that one day when he found a youth named Susie Carr was in a full on relationship with a prison officer, *named Mr. Thomas,* he had chased the lad around and around the top tier of B wing until the lad gave in due to exhaustion he allowed Bob mount him with the lubricated use of a tube of Brylcreem. Susie's later complaint was, that Bob never paid him anything at all, and years later I explained to Susie that Bob descended from a Jewish background, and such men never paid for common prostitutes, unless of course they had actually married them.

'Well he had my ring on his finger.' Susie sniffed as indignantly as he could.

Stories and tales of past incidents followed some men around like a bad smell, and at time to come the tales were exaggerated way out of all proportion. But no matter who you were, you eventually paid in spades for having the name of a *'Heavy,* or *Trouble maker,* or even a *Smart Arse.* Of course Bob was in good favor, especially after having saved Black Jack from a well deserved hit on the head, and on the upside from that particular incident, Bob entered a new program called; *'Release to Work'* and he'd commenced to go in and out of the prison each day and he was able to earn wages prior to the parole he was expected to receive for doing a good act in saving old Jack. *Who in time retired at sixty five and died six months later from sheer loneliness. (Jack retired in 1975.)*

Unfortunately, when Bob was given his pay envelope on the first Friday on the Release to Work job, he went to a hotel, *got drunk,* and then later stole a brand new car. Police of course had upgraded their methods of finding stolen cars, *by the 70's,* especially by a thief who was drunk. Excitedly they chased him at high speed into a building site. *After that the prison received the wages of prisoners.*

Bob was shot in the right buttock and taken to hospital, where it took him many months to recover. Police of course gave a version of events that had convicted Bob of intended Grievous Bodily harm, *even though he was drunkenly running away from them at the time.*

Like me, Bob was virtually a part and parcel of prison life, and in the years to come we would laugh at each other to the point of making ourselves sick. *That is when reminiscing of days long gone by.*

Around me were the males that had, *totally hopeless lives*, with even less chance than I had at that time, and if sympathy for those poor men was a weakness, my hopeless sympathy for my self was even much greater. For even then I had not yet learned, *by that time in life*, that if you do not improve yourself, you will simply stay the same as you always have, *or were.*

There is of course always trouble behind walls, and one night an illegal Immigrant was bought into the Remand yard and he had commenced to smash up the cell he was in. It was then the water from the broken cistern and toilet base soon spread over the Remand yard as the man objected to be incarcerated for being an illegal immigrant. Sections of glass had exploded, and warders stood in the darkened yards attempting to talk to the angry man, *to no avail.* Eventually they used a mattress and batons to overwhelm the man. *They then had no choice but to drag him off to the underground cells.*

The down side was, that the warders turned off the water at the mains, and the cell taps were completely cut off, and the thought of having no water had made men thirstier than they were. Fortunately, I and a number of the other *'habitual'* criminals, never went to our cells without a plastic bottle full of water, *and a few slices of bread*, as we knew well from a vast experience that the unexpected always happens. *Even with warders suddenly going on strike and leaving us all in the cells for days and sometimes for a week at a time. That is, without any adequate food.*

Personally, my mind was never still, and I had suffered some serious mental disillusion as I had searched for a peace of mind from memories of my long ago child hood. This included my early teenage years when I had lived and suffered bullying humiliations in the township of Cunnamulla. The unexpected deaths of my loved ones, *siblings and friends*, had preoccupied much of my hours in the darkened cell, and I could see all their faces as clear as day. I saw the babies I had once cuddled, including the few good friends I had once wrestled with and taunted with childhood humor. I also recalled younger girls I had once cared for and I had seriously believed all were there together with my dear foster mother watching over them as one big family. In my personal preoccupation with death I saw us all together someday. *I saw us together in another time and place when a car smash, or a violent beating would hopefully take my life, abruptly and decisively.*

The ever present sympathy I had for others I had attempted to show in practical ways, without becoming up close or personal. *Or feeling for them in such ways that my interest could be misconstrued as rude and or sexual. Or emotional interludes of indecency.*

'What are you doing talking to that cunt?' my yard friends would say while wondering what my angle was.

In earlier chapters, I've spoken of the sexuality of young males and females in Queensland institutions, and here again I must explain, that even many irreproachable priests and school administrators had once allowed humane feelings to develop into something sexual, *that had in turn placed them all behind walls.* This is, in fact, *a terrible shame*, for deep down they were truly good men that had allowed their emotions to overpower their reasoning. *My view is, that stress and loneliness do tend to make strange bedfellows.*

I still believe this of such people, and regardless of their lack of control, I can still see them in a cell with uniformed men beating the living daylights out of them. They were simply non violent people and yet they'd suffered dismally whenever they were sent behind walls, *I found also, that the total lack of empathy by both the majority of warders, and prisoners, was a sign of the things to come.*

Strangely, such men had told me that although the boys were very young, they had permanent erections and needed little urging to go to a secluded room, *or the naughty room*, and after the initial oral seductions, those men alleged that the children would initiate further meetings. *Most men branded as 'Deviates' informed me that they were themselves seduced as children, and it came back to haunt them.* Such damaged old men did not see it as abuse, but had often observed such things as a form of emotional need to hold someone who truly wanted to be held. I, being a softie, was sympathetic toward them, mainly because they could not see that they were marking those boys down for a life of mental doubt, *and misery.* That is, when they grew up and regretted their actions. Men who were damaged as children, were prone to be sexually aligned with whatever form of sexuality they were introduced to. *Counseling and literature, is and always will be, the only solution.*

Whatever punishment the middle aged men deserved, it was certainly not in a prison surroundings, for as I saw it, what they would obviously learn in such places would only make them worse predators, *and, much more cunning ones.*

To me, such '*soft bellies*' needed to be put to work on distant cattle stations, *far from children,* and toughened up to be hardened workers, while well trained visiting counselors could explain to them the stupid error of their ways. The reason for my sympathy, was that an armed robber could shoot a woman in a bank holdup, *put her in a wheelchair,* and then be considered a good crim. *But the softies were seen as punching bags, for sucking a penis.* There simply was no real logic, considering that there were dozens of career crims that did the same thing to boys in the shower. But, in the remand yard, my having sympathetically devised a way out for so many educated men in such a quandary, had somehow made me feel extremely pleased with myself, *especially when they were released to get on with the lives that they had so suddenly lost.* Most were not career criminals, while few had even stolen a pencil or a cigarette lighter, yet there they were in the 'dog kennel' because of what some other person had done to them as a child. *Or for a non violent act of shared sex.* I would watch these men who were all the shapes and sizes, as well as citizens of the bigger fast paced world, *beyond our world,* and wonder of their inner feelings, their dreams, and their ambitions. Even a stupid young boy suffering attention deficit disorder, soon came alive under the full attention of such men, even in jail, and who somehow took the place of the father, or that early lover they never had back when they were incarcerated as children. '*Or even as a developing teenager quite unable to control urges that came as natural as masturbation, and or a aggravated ejaculation when a muscled man stepped into shower cubicle to wash him or her down.'*

Somehow I felt that society had lost the plot and that they felt a rude man was worse than a killer that had shot families in a home invasion. To me, all the critics really needed was a month in the Remand Yard, to get their priorities right.

But no, society would rather read about Ivan Milat, Hannibal Lector, or, watch reruns of the wholly exaggerated; *'Underbelly Series.'*

CHAPTER 26

A GENTLE GIANT, AND POLICE SNITCHES

In the Remand yard the sensible warders saw what I saw, and many were trying to drum some common sense into younger or dumber heads, but found it was nigh impossible, and so it was that all one could really do was simply shrug ones shoulders and look the other way.

My kitchenette associates would say.

'I don't know why you help these cunts Flex, they will never do you a good turn back, and they will forget you the moment they get probation. Or, a transfer to the farm.'

I would just shrug and smile.

'Life rewards those who try to save lives, and if I get anything in the future it will be because of good Karma. In any case I learn something from each person, and sometimes I learn things that just may get me out of a tight corner one day.'

It was the poor vagrant type prisoners and the mentally impaired that had received my greater reserve of sympathy, and, one lumbering giant of a man had soon drawn my curiosity. Mostly by his type of caring assistance. As well as that kindly softer helpfulness toward that older or infirm group of prisoners; *that is,* the older men who had great difficulty with their limbs, or having trouble in rising to their feet.'

One day, after I watched the big man assist an older man onto his feet, I had gone over and I spoke to him about his charges of armed robbery, and bodily assault, which he was obviously then facing without defiance. Or, the slightest remnant of opposition.

'The charge officially had the legal term of; *stealing with actual Violence. 14 years H.L.* This also included the serious charges of a grievous bodily harm, and to me, it seemed highly unlikely that the big gentle giant could do such a thing without any provocation. The younger man readily allowed me to peruse his low court depositions *and* the alleged confession, which he had innocently signed. Things just did not seem to add up, and I had gently queried his version of events over a few hours, *or so,* and with a little prompting on my part, this good and gentle giant had told me of his strange and most perturbing tale.

It appeared that he had worked for a builder who had offered him seven day a week work for a two year period, but who held back the overtime pay in a special fund for him, so that one day he would have enough for a block of land. Some years later this young man met a lovely young woman in a hotel bar, and after calculating the large amount of money owing to him, the very smart well in touch and quite attractive female, soon suggested they become intimate. In less than a week into their budding relationship that good caring woman sweetly suggested that he cash in his accumulated funds and take a holiday with her. *So it was that on his next pay day, the trusting gentle giant politely asked 'The Boss' for all of his overtime pay in one lump sum.*

The owner builder immediately sacked him and he threw his weeks wage at him and told him to get the fuck out. *'Or he would call the police.'* The good man went back to the waiting girl in her car and told her of the strange actions of his employer. She of course had told him to go and get that box of envelopes from the office. *Because it was rightly his.* When he had tried to do so, the manager, who was nearly as big as him had hit him with a piece of wood, and the young man quickly wrestled it off him and beat the construction manager quite soundly. *And with good measure to boot.*

Taking the box of envelopes, he had returned to the girl who promptly dropped him at a nearby hotel, and in the blink of an eye she had vanished into thin blue air. The police version of course, *was entirely different,* and their quickly typed up Record of Interview held so many legal discrepancies, that I had immediately begun a written amateurish legal brief to a sitting Judge. Seeing as that poor man was not at all legally represented.

When his big day did eventually arrive, I quickly gave him his final instructions and impressed on him that the truth would set him free. He went off to the Supreme Court and was released by the good Judge, *who incidentally had entered a plea of 'Not Guilty' on his behalf.*

It was during that period, I was called to the superintendent's office, and Jack Farrell introduced me to two bloated Homicide detectives who wished to question me over a threat to kill a prisoner with a large knife. *Supposedly it had taken place over in the remand section kitchenette.* My mouth dropped open in surprise, and then I shook my head in complete ridicule of the accusations as I peered at them with a mixture of feelings. Including that deeper fear of a well rehearsed police verbalization.

'You blokes honestly can't be fair dinkum?'

The two men were like weight lifters and they had hands so big and thick that I had felt quite dwarfed. *And strangely enough, a little intimidated by their aggressive manner.* Jack Farrell was not about to go anywhere, *as he was well aware of verbalization,* and mostly because the allegations in question had apparently involved those prison authorities. *As well as himself. Fortunately for me, Jack had remained quiet and he'd politely listened to what these allegedly honest officers of the law had to say to me.*

I was shown a photograph of the complainant, *and his face vaguely rang a bell,* but in truth, I could not in anyway recall the man ever at all speaking to me. I had cautiously asked for details, and I was then to be told that on the previous Friday at approximately ten in the morning, which was, *it seemed,* when this male person had falsely alleged that I approached him inside the remand yard, and where I had then supposedly threatened him about being an undercover brother, *or a police informant.*

My mind spun back ten days, which was not that hard to do when little much happened in our day to day life, and I had vaguely recalled that I had been in court on that particular day in question.

Due to the fact that remand prisoners who were going to court, had usually *or always* had left their cell and went straight over to the old reception area quite early. This meant there was no possible way I could be guilty of their trumped up effort to rail road me.

I had told the overweight offensive giants the same thing, *in a much cruder fashion*, and I also told them of my undeniable court appearance.

'Furthermore, I'll save you a lot of trouble and you can check to see if I really was in court on that day.'

This shocked even Jack Farrell, whom I knew had wanted to believe in me, but he also knew the powers of the police hierarchy, *even more than I did*, but he quickly, and hopefully, sent for my thick prison file. There, right on the top of the pile, was the last filed entry where it had shown to us quite clearly, that I had been taken to the District court for my most recent mention, *or stand over.* The two Homicide men looked at one another uncomfortably, in a stony silence, and then the good Jack Farrell had intentionally cleared his throat while scratching under his chin.

'Well, that's it then, gentlemen.'

I quickly added my verdict also, as the big men glared at me when I daringly showed them my jail house type of disrespect.

'Yeah, tell your rotten mates at Inala that I have all the time in the world, and that none of you mugs can even win a toad race around the block without belting up poor silly buggers in your filthy cop shops.'

One detective jeered contemptuously. He then had spoken coldly with a future promise of a harsh retribution.

'I don't see any complaints on your file about police wrong doing; *Campbell.* There are plenty of proper venues in which to make such unfounded and preposterous allegations.'

'I don't complain mate, I just put it all down to experience.' I said, staring calmly into his red veined and deadly green-blue eyes. My unexpected reply had made both of them laugh out loud, *with a genuine humor,* and in a flash they'd lost all their malice toward me and both respectfully nodded their defeat.

'You're okay Larry, I think we've misjudged you my old mate.' And so, in an instance, their whole manner had changed and they were friendly and sweetly jovial like big warm teddy bears wanting to hug me to death.

The obvious signs of street corruption were written all over them, and I for one knew such men ate four main meals a day, which those normal police wages could never possibly cover. Their two thousand-dollar Rolex watches and gold signet rings spoke of a lifestyle of gigantic proportions that had easily dwarfed the average honest workers. *Ordinary men who toiled for their wage.* The red veins in their noses told me they were addicted to expensive spirits, and excluding their expensive suits, and other apparel, I knew these big men were pocketing no less than a thousand dollars above their monthly wage.

I asked for and got two cigarettes, and then I swapped some news on that Tattoo King-Pin, *the infamous Billy Phillips,* and I had also laughed out loud when they said that he was out of the game. Jack Farrell was the only one who was surprised by this big sudden change of personality, or apparent about face. As it was, I had seen it all so many times before when a maniac detective had to beat men unconscious one day, and then go and buy them tobacco and or cold drinks the next. It was all a crooked puzzle where both the parties involved were simply seeking a fast closure, and once it had been sorted out to the satisfaction of all concerned, there was no hard feeling. *Until of course the next time around the merry go round of street to cell and then back again.* Once a person was marked as *'persistently active,'* the Merry Go Round never ever stopped. Even when you begged to get off.

Jack was torn between being an officer of the Crown, and seeing fair play, but he was officially by then just a small cog in the wheel of Government. Prisoners, and seemingly the ignorant taxpayers, were simply that social oil that made the greater society work, and like me, the superintendent was very dispensable in the final analysis.

If Jack did learn anything, it was that justice played no part in the criminal game, and that justice concerned only the poor victim, or the victim's family. The Government was never the victim, and, their part in the whole affair was simply to keep the victims voting for them. 'And in turn, for those officers who professed to uphold the law in the good State of Queensland.'

On the upside, Jack Farrell had spoken to me kindly, and he had allowed me to visit friends in the kitchen while I was loose in the main jail. After a fillet steak and fried eggs, it was soon back to another night in the cell, and of course, planning for my next to last trial. A trial which I had nervously hoped would be the Supreme Court appeal, that could in turn, lead to my eventual freedom.

I never stopped to think, exactly what sort of a person I *was* in the eyes of Superintendent Farrell, but looking far back into the past I now realise that he must have felt great sympathy for me, at times.

Jack Farrell had given me more leeway in the prison system, than any other official had in all my days as a common prisoner, and somehow he found it in himself to keep on giving me more.

It was as if this very down to earth countryman had sensed that I was my own worst enemy. Or that I could possibly spend the rest of my life in a cell, long after he had retired.

Had it not been for an amazing miracle in those later years, I do feel Jack Farrell may well have been right.

Maybe it was Karma, and to some it could have just been circumstances or unexplainable incidences, but in the year 2010, some forty years later, I know that there are things that only a few people get to understand about life and death. I do of course respect all people's views on spiritualism, as well as their choice of religion, and customs, but as a prisoner in a future time, I was beaten unconscious by warders and had experienced a spiritual awakening that gave me a view that there was something there for us all, after death. Including a complete understanding that we are all more than just flesh and blood.

Like all young men, I brushed it aside as just one of those things in life, but the feeling had stayed with me for all my life and I made a point of never putting the boot in. I also made a point of always helping out the underdog who helped others. But, in 2010 my brother Bruce had died during the night and around four in the morning I came out of a deep sleep and saw a strange dream like vision of my good brother who had seemed younger and looked about thirty years of age walking across a field bathed in a golden glow. He looked back at me and smiled. He waved, and then he was gone.

Later at nine o'clock in the morning the phone rang and I just knew it was about Bruce.

Sure enough my big brother was gone, but I had accepted the news quietly and I did not grieve, as I somehow knew or sensed he was okay, and that he had found a world of peace.

I flew Jet star Airlines to Brisbane to pay my respect to his children, and I delivered words to our extended family that I know Bruce would have wanted me to say on his behalf.

The message was;

Loyalty is our way of showing our inner humanity.

CHAPTER 27

THE APPEAL TRIAL

I was feeling the cooling end of our summer, once again, and I had considered going out into the cold mean streets. If of course I was indeed ever released from the remand yard life that was becoming like a second home to me.

My cell held all of my personal papers, and toiletries, along with my sugar coffee and tea as well as a large amount of jail tobacco that I'd used in bartering. I had grown quite accustomed to those sudden, or unexpected cell searches, especially by that muscle tough *Special Squad group* that I saw as a silent and lethal bunch of uncaring men.

Such men were friendly with no one, *except those that wore their insignia of the Vietnam Veteran*, or, to those troubled prisoners that had done their tour of duty overseas.

Regardless of such numerous and quite negative influences, the Boggo Road Remand section was home to hundreds of lost men, and sometimes, the possibility of release was even more daunting than their ongoing or expected appearance in a court of law.

The big day had at last arrived, and some of the men came to wish me luck, as if sensing that this trial could be my swan song. Cheerfully, I shook hands with them all while I was hurriedly sipping on a big mug of hot tea in the reception holding pen.

It was on these early mornings that I had often found time to contemplate my fate, that is, before the big Maria arrived to take me to court for my long awaited appeal trial. My feelings at the time, was that it looked a great deal harder than ever, to win a trial debate, especially now that I was not in control to play it by my method of using misleading acts. *While at the same time, sneakily grasping for a sympathy vote.*

Mostly any person, *much like my brother Bruce,* would know I was being deceptive, as well as seriously dishonest. So it was, I could easily understand him losing a confidence in me, while believing that the detectives were indeed completely honest men.

In my personal opinion, the detectives were nothing but manipulators and or the salesmen that searched for a bent dollar, just like any self-promoting man on the streets would, and if it came easily, *and without the normal legal complications,* then jolly for them. In truth, I would rather not have played out my stupid antics for the jury, *out of a self-pride,* but at that particular time, there had been no other way available to defeat their perjured verbalization in a Court of Law. It was the only area of life where it was said, that two wrongs made a right, and luckily for me it had worked both ways.

It was a gloomy and cloudy day as I was handcuffed and put aboard that old enclosed truck. A big lumbering truck that still spat the exhaust fumes into the rear cabin, and which, had assisted thousands of prisoners to die earlier from symptoms relating to bronchial and lung complications. In fact, all I had ever done was to stare at the turning differential under that grate at my feet and to imagine how those thousands of both men and women before me, *who had also breathed up carbon monoxide,* had survived the court-run gauntlet. That is, considering it our expected fate, or a written decree, that our lives were already lost? *'Not always from the carbon monoxide,* but from the all-powerful courts. In fact, the exact same courts that were often managed by the selfish and arrogant poseurs who had apparently forever cared more about the Law itself, *than in their upholding it.'*

I had time to speak to Mr. Bavington, prior to my entering the court, and this time the handcuffs were taken off outside, *which allowed me to appear as a less ominous type of man.*

I still gazed around like a very confused neutral human being who appeared quite fascinated at seeing for the very first time those daunting Queensland District Courts. I was not able to ignore the dock on that occasion, as Jack was there first and he held it open and smiled half apologetically at me, *and,* I smiled back as if his face had looked somewhat slightly familiar. The amateur play-acting was soon over, as Mr. Bavington quietly attempted to have the case dismissed, due to the lack of evidence. Obviously he was unable to reveal that Mr. Barbeller, *in the previous sittings,* had a similar charge dismissed outright, on much the same sort of evidence.

The Law was quite an idiotic ass when it had came to rules, *and of procedure,* although in my case, those prosecutors could not reveal I was an alleged, hardened criminal with many similar types of crimes to my credit.

On the same token, the fresh clean-skins had been convicted by their not exaggerating their lack of culpability. You were that person that you appeared to be, and any sudden glimpse of a criminal tattoo, or a badly broken nose, could possibly mean a guaranteed future of time waste inside a maximum-security prison.

The proof that I was not at all in control of my own destiny was that, I had found that the acoustics and voice level was unsuited for me. As it were, I had a very hard time trying to interpret a lot of exactly what was being said.

Still, to my great pleasure, Mr. Bavington soon had Stringbean squirming like vomit on a stick, but unfortunately, l was still unable to distinguish exactly what it was that had made Stringbean so uncomfortable. Later, during the short recess, Jack the warder had told me a little of what was at that time happening, and then he in his quiet way explained that it was the discrepancies in the police evidence, that appeared to be the crux of the defense rebuttal.

It appeared that because the police had not been present at the crime scene, they had unwittingly had my alleged truthful confession made from notes which had alleged that the back door had been entered, and not the front door, *as alleged by Stringbean.* Nor could they describe if it was a big building, low-set, or, if it was situated on some hill. In fact they had been too lazy to investigate the particular offence and they had simply copied the notes of other investigating officers. *They suggested I had shown them how I had wilfully broken through the front door, and confessed my culpability, due to remorse.*

Mr. Bavington recalled the owner of the said premises, who'd agreed that the back door had been jimmied, as well as it being an empty building. I could not by law, *or common sense,* reveal that when I broke into locked premises I always knew what it was that I wanted, *and would not ever enter an empty building.* There were ten other plain clothed government officials and detectives present, *on that day in the court,* and all of them had looked very uncomfortable as they saw their easy method of *creative detection* was surely under serious fire. *All looked very questionable, to any ethical spectators, that may take any undue notice of such going son.*

The Courier Mail was certainly not there at all to observe such goings on.

Now that I had been given a rough idea of what was actually being discussed, I could then easily follow the flow of things, *to a degree,* and I had felt a little more confidence in the eventual outcome. I knew that it was not at all a foregone conclusion, as I was shortly to find after the angry prosecutor went for broke.

The prosecutors only chance was to break me down when I was to be eventually called up to the stand, and with wet and sweating palms, I had saturated the Bible with running fluid from my moist right hand. *That is, when I was being sworn in.*

I was quite nervous and stressed, and I had obviously lost all of my inner composure, *while physically,* I had swallowed consistently. This was the big one that meant many years of my life, *and,* it rested on my shoulders to explain to that jury that I had no alibi, and that I could not even remember that day in question.

The prosecutor eventually had the floor, and he quickly began to cut into me and swirl his black cape onto his hip as if showing me who was now the top dog in charge. I'd gotten him angry time and again by my begging his pardon, *Sir',* which was quite genuine under the circumstances, and so it was, he eventually whispered to his young aide who'd immediately stood up and quickly left the room.

The dainty man returned in moments with two younger men from the Coopers Plains area, and who it seemed had been taken from both their respective working places in old factories in the Rocklea Industrial area. Both were wrongly detained, and were illegally and unethically bought into the court room foyer as visual witnesses, *but not as witnesses sworn in under oath,* or under any legal subpoena.

One was a supposedly good and loyal friend, named Alan Kelly, and the other I had known casually as, Paulie *'Dog Boy'* Flynn.

'Do you know these young men, Campbell?' asked the seething prosecutor in a booming voice, as his slit eyes stared at me coldly and contemptuously.

'I do indeed, although I know young Alan a little better. Both are decent young fellows and I feel they can do quite well in their future lives, if given a chance.' I replied gently, and respectfully.

It was not the answer or presentation the critical obnoxious man was at that time seeking, but I knew that he was searching for a guilty verdict by association, and to his credit, *by his creating an aura of friendship and insinuation of guilt by proxy*, he was making a slight progress.

The angry prosecutor had made his first mistake and then he, by throwing all caution to the wind, had began to then briskly question me and eventually he had flung words at me in an outright allegation that insinuated I had prior convictions.

'This is not the first time you have been in a Court of Law, is it Campbell?'

I could not believe he had made such a blunder, and nor could he, *that learned prosecutor himself,* for a fleeting moment, but Mr. Bavington quickly shot to his feet and a vicious and heated legal argument ensued.

During this argument two females had entered the courtrooms. I must say I was totally shocked to see my natural mother, Shirley Richardson, and her young teenage daughter, *my half sister, Shaarron Richardson,* walk into the daunting courtroom. Sitting high in the witness box, I must indeed have looked quite shocked, because, Judge McGrath, who incidentally was a very fine observer and a Judge of situations, had then quickly taken in those new arrivals and he sensitively, *and sensibly,* called for a short recess.

In moments, I was allowed to approach my two relatives and I silently shook my head in surprise, and to be truthful, I felt sick with amazement and total disbelief that any one would be on my side.

'What are you doing here Shirl? I thought you were living out west?'

Shirley gazed up at me like I was still her long lost son, and, being a little short sighted, she had stared somewhat curiously at me as if trying to see the many changes in my appearance. I had not seen her, *or her small troubled family,* for over ten long years or more. Ten years after a Longreach police force beat and harassed me for wearing red shirts, including for my street fighting, as well as breaking into houses all over Longreach. Shirley and her selfish husband had thrown me onto the streets of an ignorant and insensitive outback town, to survive like a destitute vagrant, while being forced to survive on the minor charity of strangers.

I had never ever at all ever forgiven her, for her cold and selfish act, but right at that particular moment I had very little choice but to accept her presence in the District courtroom. For, for whatever it was worth.

'Any support was better then none.' I had considered at the time. *'And all of us learn in time to come, that friends may come and go, but family will always return to you in a future time when you, or they, have learned the error of our ways.'* Such were my softer views of their sudden presence back into my hopeless life, and yes, even today in 2015, family are family no matter how distant, or spread out in all directions of our historical bloodlines, we so remain.

The young girl Shaaron was a pretty-faced blonde with that freckled washed out weather beaten complexion of the country people, and to me she was totally at a loss in that intimidating courtroom. Or, much like some gentle Bambi that is surrounded by hunters with big guns. *Or lawyers in black with gold edged law books that threaten to end a life, or two, with the closing of the pages.*

Along with the many observers who were looking on, I'd said a few kind words to the young girl, and, receiving no reply, I'd simply accepted a tailor made cigarette from Shirley, and then we all went outside for one last deep appreciative inhalation before the resumption of proceedings. Jack being Jack stood well back, and he allowed us to talk privately while knowing full well I would never run on him. *Due to my deep respect for him.*

It was the big turning point, *and the peak of the trial,* when Mr. Bavington argued, that *if a mistrial* could not be so ordered, then he under Law had every right to explain the wrongful and related charges against me. He'd felt that he should legally be permitted to describe the unlawful ordeal I had then experienced by my attempting to defend myself without any legal interpreter, *or of course*, any legal assistance. To show the jury, word by word the many similarities in police verbalization, and how no one could possibly be interviewed five, or even up to six times inside of one single hour. He'd demanded also, that he be permitted to explain exactly how twelve different and clearly honest juries, *had previously acquitted his client,* and that they too had obviously not believed a word that all the indecent conniving police detectives had so unlawfully uttered.

I looked at Stringbean along with his angry cronies, as they huddled in prayer, for a positive ruling from a Judge that they hoped was in full agreement with the feeble argument by the prosecutor. I did not feel sorry for them, one bit, but the one sure thing that was clear to all of us present, was that I had seriously educated them about their method of *verbalization,* and their presenting *their* perjury a whole lot better in a Queensland court of law.

The humiliations I caused for the corrupt police, had later been the means for the government to create the special crash course for Queensland detectives, *on,* how to present and deliver such verbal evidence to Queensland Juries. Unfortunately, for accused persons in those many long years ahead, they, *the perjured detectives,* would somehow avoid those extensive inquiries into police corruption, where the hundred or so of their fellows were duly convicted, or run out of the police force for taking money under the table. While, not paying taxes. *Like a good prostitute would.*

Not for one moment did I at all believe that men like Mr. Bavington or a Mr. Barbeller, were at all blind to what was really happening in the vast Queensland police force. Sadly, it seemed to me that even decent lawyers had felt that corrupt government ministers had long tied the judiciary's hands with a binding official red tape. *Or, by their withholding future financial funding for legal aid services to assist the many less educated people in our wider society.*

Little did I know then, that when I sat there in that witness chair waiting for a ruling by Judge McGrath, that the rusty old wheels of justice were in actual movement, and also, dedicated officials were gathering a very secret vital information to bring down the then Commissioner of police. *'In fact, Police Commissioner Terry Lewis eventually got fourteen years H.L.' And, Paroled in seven.*

It took time, but more than twenty years later I'd paid with honest money for a bottle of Chivas Regal Scotch Whiskey so as to cheer and salute the changing of the guard. Furthermore, I gave up mischievous crime completely, and set about being an honest husband and father; *to the relief of my very worried wife.*

One after one, an Inspector and commissioned officers, would eventually fall, and their counterparts, *brave and honest men and loyal women,* would eventually topple that incumbent corrupted Government. In turn, they would put that incumbent Premier of Queensland on trial for financial corruption. As well as criminal collusion, *and perjury.*

Had I known what was to happen back then in 1970, it could well have changed my life completely, but even then, at that time, I did not at all know if the presiding Judge was part of the prosecution department. *Or if he was his own man.*

As it was, all that I could really do, was to hold my breath as the Judge had prepared to give out his ruling on the matter before him. The Jury was bought in, and then, in a calm and precise voice, Judge McGrath ruled in favor of the defense.

Which in turn, allowed Mr. Bavington to totally desecrate the Crown case.

Mr. Bavington was a master of his profession, and he held the Jury raptly in the palm of his hand as he had described my time spent in the remand section fighting a losing battle against the might of the Queensland police force.

He spoke of how over a year and a half of wasted time had passed by, as one Jury member, after another, had totally refused to swallow the concocted creation of manufactured false confessions.

They were untrue and clearly fabricated confessions against a young man who could not at all hear properly, let alone answer to a questioning without the detectives realising, that the defendant was hearing impaired.

It was a long tale that bought the ordeal into the new fresh light of reality, and I felt the tremor of a shiver and of goose bumps at what I'd perceived as an end to my illegal troubles in the Queensland District Court. I'd felt it was; *all over Red Rover* at the very moment that the Jury looked over at me in genuine sympathy, and much later, *soon after the prosecution summary of that evidence had failed,* the good Judge spoke quietly, and in full favour of the defence.

The Jury filed out slowly, *and ominously*, as Jack the warder had opened the wooden gate to let me out for a cigarette, when all of a sudden the elderly Courtroom Bailiff quickly returned and said that the Jury had reached a unanimous verdict. In fact, that Jury had simply reached the hallway outside of their Jury room when they had, *as one entity,* decided on their verdict. So it was that they had quickly asked the bailiff to return with their decision.

Even that good man on the bench was curious at this sudden departure from formality, and he had bought that still sworn in Jury before him, and he lined them up across the courtroom to face him.

In actual fact, the people of Queensland had by their action spoken, and was legally questioning those one sided laws, and its due process of accepting verbal evidence as a legal tool.'

Judge McGrath explained Queensland law in relation to their abnormally *short deliberations,* and, he suggested that, as far as he had known, no other jury in living memory had ever reached a verdict as quickly as they had. In fact, *ten minutes,* was the required amount of time normally suggested in jury room discussions, and the good Judge had felt that it would be an appropriate amount of time, under the circumstances, to reach such a verdict.

It had looked seriously good for me, but in no way was it a predictable outcome, as some juries may well have agreed in the first hour, *on a defendant's guilt,* as well as be angered at the suggestion that a genuine police constable of the Crown could be unfairly accused of perjury. *A perjury that no Queensland policemen will ever be taken before a court, and sentenced to prison.*

This trial had seriously shaken even Jack the good warder, and he had nervously shared my very last cigarette, *although he did not smoke.* Still, Jack had wished me all of the very best of his Irish family's luck, *and,* of the very best of good fortune on a hopefully positive outcome.

'In explanation, Jack the warder was on the court run only because he could handle inmates with fairness and calm respect, and he was not suited as a stand over man in maximum security Division. Plus, he had previously rejected seniority so as to retain such an unwanted position.'

The police were in a big huddle, as were all the legal men *who were all friends by then,* were laughing about certain incidents during the trial. My sister Shirley, or my natural mother, had just kept staring at me in her curious bird like way, and I could see on her face the unfair ravages of her life of unabated alcoholism. Like me, her many brothers and sisters had turned away from her, as they in turn had scrabbled up that financial ladder of success. *While retaining the view that every human being was responsible for their own good, or bad fortune.*

In my own way, I truly did feel quite sorry for Shirley, and even the ignorant young girl dressed up in clothes that were obviously out of a bargain bin at some welfare outlet. A good looking and attractive teenager indeed, but it was obvious that she had not been spoiled, in all the days of her life.

I did not need, *or want them there,* at all, but I could not in any reality, tell them to leave. They were a problem in the sense that I had already made a decision on my immediate future, that is, *were I to be released,* and I had already had a possible break and enter lined up that had allegedly held more than an eight thousand dollar haul in coins. *Supposedly, a payment for a supposedly successful job I would then supposedly have to bail out my helpful supposed friend, and together we would supposedly skip over the Queensland border into the State of New South Wales.* Never, ever again, to return to a lying illegal Police State that could ever be reined in, by anyone, good bad or ugly.

Or so I thought.

The verdict was in, and I had quickly taken my place in the dock as Shirley mumbled a prayer. One juryman had looked over at me, *and he winked.*

I slowly let out my abated breath, with some quiet elation.

The verdict was, *not guilty,* and the tears had sprung to my eyes in grati-tude for these decent ordinary men who were not bound by rules or for-malities. Men who had given a fair genuine verdict from ordinary common sense, *and with the utmost of ease,* once all the facts were on the table to be seen in their correct light.

Jack, the good and decent warder, was the first to shake my hand and I'd nearly hugged him for his caring attitude. But sensibly I had simply thanked the good man for everything he had done, and I had wished him good fortune in the future.

The Judge then called us to order as those two charges of the theft of a two-way radio, *and of false pretences regarding the scrap metal,* was bought before him. The prosecution was seeking a remand date without the benefit of bail. It was obvious to me that those original charges had been held back by the prosecution, until the very last. *So that I would have no money for my defence.*

The Judge had allowed me a general self-recognizance bail, and I was free at last.

I sat down, *mentally exhausted,* on an inner aisle bench, and I then watched the detectives file out, *one by one,* and each glared at me as they had passed out of the courtroom. Obviously, they would not forget me in any short period of time, and I knew I had better get out of Brisbane City as quickly as I could. *And as fast as my skinny long legs would carry me.*

I was later informed that Stringbean had never lost another case in court, and that his foul verbalizations became quite renowned out in Western Queensland where he was sent to serve his penance. Aboriginal men had told me that he became an Inspector in Mt. Isa, *and* it was alleged, *quite lib-eral with the baton and the boot.* He continued to falsify all presented evidence, until of course he wrongly verbalised a prisoner into serving life, which was overturned by the Privy Council. *As it was the Queensland government had to later pay the aboriginal man $500.000 in compensation.*

String bean, of course, had laughed at such government incompe-tence, and he went onto doing dirty work for Jupiter's Casino, as a lackey and provider of the highly expensive prostitutes for Junket Gamblers. *Even today I still dream of coming out of retirement and waiting for him in the casino car park, just to say hello to him.* I mean, can I not dream of such a rebuke for a dog of a Queenslander.

But back then, I genuinely thanked my defence team that had used up a lot of precious government awarded funds on my case. It was a department that had relied heavily on the good will of those taxpayers, *and Treasury*, to keep them afloat. The government grant bestowed on them was not meant for a criminal like me, and as I shook Mr. Bavington's hand, I thanked him once again as he spoke kindly to me when giving to me, his best and caring advice.

'You have a genuine chance now to make something of your life Larry, so you just try seriously hard, and show yourself just what you can really do.'

'I will Mr. Bavington, thank you again.' I replied, more than attentive to his last words. That is, as much as most dishonest men were prone to do, especially after having a close brush with that law society and then being let off with a mere slap on the wrist. Or almost a slap, considering I would in hindsight have spent less time in prison had I pleaded no contest to the Sims Metal charges.

What was so amazing to me was that the lawyer had considered I was getting a chance, yet no mention was made of dozens of acts of perjury committed by dishonest policemen, and that under an honest system, charges would have been laid to imprison such men for their deliberate acts.

The lesson learned in the end, was that the court system of the twentieth century was nothing but a boys club for the wealthy as well as those established descendant's of old colonial families. But in the ranks were people that genuinely sought to make it a better world, even if their method of doing so, was somewhat questionable.

Females had been looked upon as a large joke, and were not even allowed to consider a verdict, *at that time,* or at least I never saw one either on the jury or in a legal position of being a solicitor or barrister. The perks and lurks had consisted of the chauffeur driven cars, all the way to that government paid working holiday with a family. *With hired help in attendance.* It did appear they had an open chequebook to practice English vernacular on the idiotic common people. *As well as many dumb blind and deaf felons.*

I would never really know just exactly how much they had wasted chasing those perjured convictions, on me? *Or attempting to legally incarcerate me?* But one thing was sure as butter milk, they did not at all reimburse me for my loss or my time inside their courtrooms.

The true fact of the matter, was that most Queensland police could allege fraud, even a carnal knowledge, vagrancy, indecent dealing,, without a true genuine witness to back up their lies. To actually win lose or draw, you had simply gone back onto the street penniless. All of your belongings were by then gone, and your place of abode was by then rented to another. Your motor car was either; *sold stripped or stolen*, and the courts had never once reimbursed you, for your loss.

Those lofty arrogant legal people, may well have sneered with contempt for the criminal who had stupidly gone straight out and repeated his crime within hours. But in reality, the released, *or then acquitted person*, had no real alternative but to help themselves; *'Especially at night.'*

Like most people released destitute by the courts, *that is, after the hour of five PM at night*, you took your chances on the street and had to decide if you would bash a stranger, or break into their house.

In this case, I went with the Richardson's to Woody Point and had suffered their unending selfishness, until I had received my charitable ear operation by a specialist on Wickham St. the city.

The good doctor booked me in at the Mater, and I soon went on drugs in a matter of hours.

I woke up during the operation and I heard a booming voice;

'Lie still. Mr. Campbell.' and then, I blacked out again.

The recovery was slow, *while I was full up of morphine*, but in a few short days I walked slowly into a area where religious statues blended into a big garden that was so serene, that I sat down and I genuinely pondered my life.

After awhile, I'd felt myself needing to reveal my innermost feelings and I had began to mumble to a grandmother...*long dead.*

I promised that if the operation was successful, I would be a *'Crim,'* no more.

Weeks later in the old doctors visiting rooms, on the old tree lined Wickham Terrace, the swathe of bandage was removed, and the sound rushed at me like a steel locomotive that was completely out of control.

I looked at the doctor, *in amazement,* and he... smiled.

His satisfaction heralded another human being who was whole again, and with as much chance as anyone else in the world of making good with their life.

Outside on the pavement I happily rejoiced by smiling at a pretty young woman and I said brightly.

'Good morning darling, *how are you going?'*

It was then that I had sauntered down Wickham Terrace with my heart on my sleeve...

For all the world, to see.

CHAPTER 28

FLEX'S LAW

In the State of Queensland, it is suggested a District court judge has the power to reimburse legal expenses, *but seldom does he use his discretion.*

In any case, an on the spot legal application for full compensation on my part would have revealed further charges of receiving, and of selling the stolen property of various habitual criminals in the south side area of Brisbane. On the other hand, all of the Crown evidence pointed to a blatant case of perjury, by those lying police officers and that the then Department of Public Prosecutions, which had apparently supported such illegal activity. It also had appeared that no records were available of any private prosecution's ever succeeding, against a Police officer. *That is, in the good State of Queensland.*

'Or for that matter, in the police force itself.'

Legally, there is an age old argument for an; *'On the spot compensation,'* in the area of common decency, especially for defendants released destitute late at night from the courts after many months on remand. It does, in a logical way; *or from an area of common sense,* demand under the law of human rights, that a Crown Law office in any state of Australia may give transport and accommodation costs to any defendant who is a prisoner released without immediate funds. *'Or, any acceptable abode befitting a released person.'*

No court in Queensland has ever at all been charitable to released persons.

I further believe that any person that is sworn in, and gives evidence in a court of law, should receive an *'Attendance Fee.'* This also includes the defendant, his witnesses, and compensation for transport costs and costs for refreshments during the trial. At present, this one sided privilege, only adheres to the Crown Witnesses.

Sadly, under the Justices act, there is no statutory right to compensations, no matter what the police, the D.P.P, or the courts do to any citizen, *felon or child*, who is proven to be innocent beyond any doubt.

The law of Queensland makes no provision for anyone who;

(A) Serves time, and later has it Quashed on appeal, *or;* (B) A person acquitted by a jury and discharged by the court.(C) A person detained on remand for one or more days, weeks, months or years, and is discharged with, or without a trial.

There are no provisions made for taxi fare, or bus fare.

There are no means to get them to their family, relatives or friends, even should they have such support, and it is reasonable to assume that if they had such support or help, it is clear that they would also have met their stringent or minor bail requirements in the first place;

Or, they may not have at all offended in the first place.

Under Queensland law it is nigh impossible for a man without funds, *property, or wealth,* to tackle the enormous challenge of seeking reimbursement, *via litigation.* This is, in every respect, wrong in law, or should be seen as wrong in law. That is, considering that the people of Australia pay for the process to give Justice for all.

The Justices, whether they be offended, or not, are clearly the servant, or are in the employee of the people, and not just employed for the benefit of a wealthy people who are so considered '*Society, Royalty, business, Public service, etc.'*

The concerns of lawmaker's, is that to reimburse a felon, *or an accused,* simply works against the good intention of 'Justice,' which is, in reality, the basic framework of all free thinking communities. To remove that immunity from the hand of a media outlet, by our allowing Police, prosecutors or the Court system, to actually be beyond any criticism or condemnation, is in their opinion, very unsafe in an area of control and correction of the general public. This means, that if they were subject to the same laws of the ordinary citizen, they themselves would be unable to operate safely without civil prosecution. *Or protection, for their wrong doing.*

In Rondel v Worsley (1969) 1 AC 191; Lord Pearce stated on page 268 that to prevent the Media, police or the courts, from denigrating a persons name, community standing, or employment prospects, would cause a great injury to Justice. *(Or, words to that effect)*

What it really meant; was that the courts would have to be more careful of making untrue, or defamatory statements against any citizens, should those illegal, or wrongful methods, be so disallowed;

[Such a ruling works both ways, but not for whistle blowers] To be prevented from denigrating any man, woman, or child, *with or without the lever of perjury*, the manufacturing of evidence, was to be so allowed to be used by the police, the courts, and the Courier Mail. *As long as that denigrated person had no means of refuting such allegations, in a public place.* **(The media, still controls all public opinions.)**

In a logical view, the Prosecution department should be forced to account for all moneys wasted. That is, on those unfounded or wrongful prosecution of felons, citizens, or children.

Especially those who are bought to trial on such contaminated evidence.

Under such a one sided ruling, had the courts been forced to give the unending masses of people that full right to automatic compensations, it would soon dilute that power of the police, and give an official degree of human rights to all citizens.

Such rights would then flow on to felons, considered lucky, *but guilty,* and that in it self, would constitute a serious injustice; *'In the eyes of the Powers that Be.'*

In perspective, it is only the much poorer citizen, *and the innocent victim of the courts,* who genuinely suffer from this imbalance,' for the felon, without a succour, or any immediate assistance, *has no choice but to re-offend'.* That of course means, that another citizen will inadvertently pay for the felon's immediate needs, that is if the coffers of the police, *or the courts*, 'will not legally be forced to assist', *or immediately help, or accommodate the acquitted person?*

It means that after 4pm, a non gratis Federal Centerlink payment by the then Sheriffs Office; could lawfully compensate the released person.

Without any Legal Fraternity reviewing this imbalance, the ongoing situation of injustice in the State of Queensland must eventually escalate to a most serious level of intolerance. In the eyes of homeless, and wrongfully victimised families.

I had also found, that there were later fresh projects to alleviate the pressure on the criminal courts, although, in our own State Government view, even they may soon be beyond a realistic control of manageable levels. Of the Department of Prosecutions.

In my case, I was viewed as; *morally guilty,* and was of no real consequence to any person, *but,* with a degree of hopeful expectation, I would have, under a different circumstance, been so forced to illegally accommodate myself, *whether it be that new motel in town, or a local watch house; for stealing from a locked premises.'*

In my opinion, a legal financial reimbursement, is not just a right, but a genuine necessity, and for a law society to place any individual '*Into that Vagrant State'* quite late in the evening, is not only wrong in law, it is wholly hypocritical, of all fair minded Australians.

In the area of verbalization, or of '*Verbal,'* we might well ask, if modern day lawmakers and their *many* enforcement groups, could feel that, if a '*Fear of Legal Retribution'* was removed, then, the true interests of Modern Justice would not be served.

I find this uneven, for all Australians are supposedly equal under the law.

The Verbalization had, *in fact,* allowed them to balance those uneven scales in full favor of a; *'Good against Evil,'* and so it was, could keep those foolish masses in a line. Sadly, such learned men and women, are unaware that *'Fear of Evil'* attracts more than it repels, and often it only encourages the young people who seek to challenge any form of Injustice; *As long as it is directed against an uneven and insensitive Authority.* 'Furthermore, when evil people, *such as Terry Lewis and his crew,* get to balance the scales of evil against good, *that then is when good men suffer, while many selfish men and women, do nothing.*

Enforcement, Prosecution, as well as Adjudication, are conducted by 'Servants of the Crown,' and each section washes the back of the other. There is no one to question this 'Union of Fellows,' for the 'media' is part of the sham that suggests that 'Officers of the Crown are above the law.'

Not one person has ever marched in protest down George St. Brisbane to prevent 'Perjury' being used as a legal tool to destroy the reputations of good and honest citizens.

Upwards of 14,000,000 accusations of perjury has been leveled at the 'Officers of the Crown,' since 1943, and yet no Officer of the Crown has ever been confined in a maximum security prison for perjury. Or, for fabricating evidence against a civilian defendant.

It took another twenty or so years for our Queensland society, to make minor changes to police procedures. *That is, dealing with the apprehension and the lawful questioning of all alleged wrong doers.* The Bingham Inquiry suggested that police personnel *should* tape-record criminal suspects the very moment they are apprehended, but the police workers, strongly resist this most necessary policy, and they suggest that such a *'tool'* may tend to reveal the methods that a police force uses to *'soften up'* the suspects. It was further suggested that; were audio recordings made of certain arrests, police may actually find themselves facing criminal charges themselves.

It is considered, that those unforgiving *'Court Adjudicators,'* are seen to be part of criminal wrongdoing, *or part thereof,* an illegal conspiracy so as to convict citizens charged by police workers. If this is so, then those unfairly and ill treated members of our society, may well feel quite justified in being disobedient in the future. *Or, even criminally rebellious, in the area of drug and or property matters.* In other words, if young people are led to believe that the justice system does not obey its own rules, *and regulations,* they then may feel quite justified in breaking the laws of the land.

To denigrate or not to denigrate, *was the question,* and while the good Lord Pearce did not suggest, that I, *as a prisoner,* could not expose or denigrate those who would imprison and or defame me, the police courts and News limited soldiered on together when the then authorities illegally stole or confiscated parts of this unfinished writing. *Over twenty seven years ago.*

Personally, I was quite unconcerned by their actions, and I began to rewrite the same words, *although not word for word.* Somehow, a Goss Government bent its palsy knee to the bullies of the Crown, and introduced a bill that states that a prisoner, *or ex prisoners writing,* will under Queensland law be deemed the proceeds of crime. In effect, the containment officers in the state of Queensland discouraged publishers of showing any interest in any material written by an ex prisoner.

As I well knew, I was the only ex prisoner they were then concerned with.

So, into the cupboard it went for another twenty five years, or more, until I wrote a freshly bound expose of; *Child Exploitation and the Criminal Element in the State of Queensland,* my views had remained hidden, from the people of Queensland.

In 2008 I sent the only copy available, **of Child Exploitation of Children by the Criminal Element in the State of Queensland,** to the Department Of Justice Librarian, and it somehow eased the rules concerning prisoners and their writing of Government Departments. I then registered, as a publisher and I had released '*The Real Boggo Road.*' in 2013.

Under law, because I was not challenged, I now may publish my views legally, under the High Court ruling, that such views are for a; *'Public Digestion.'*

The correct title for the child abuse writing is titled; *'The Male Harlot,* and someday the people of Queensland will get to know how my writings could well have saved thousands upon thousands of children being groomed by established pedophiles. *That is, to so enslave them as child prostitutes; (Long before computers became as popular with children, as they are today.)*

Finally, under my fresh new imagined Laws, the media in Queensland would have no say at all in determining the outcome of a trial. *Or legal decision in the State of Queensland.*

The media would not at all be permitted to force a Prosecutions Department in Queensland to review a case. *Or to shut down a case in which a media contingent did not at all agree with.*

The Media would not be considered a useful tool, by those who amend the law.

David Fagin, Editor in Chief of the Courier Mail took my advice and he created a section to the Courier Mail, *whereas the news of the courts was given a fair hearing in matters of Law.* I also suggested in my letter to him, that concerned independent writers should have a space to air their views.

That is, to speak of prison institutional news and events surrounding inmates.

David Fagin created *'Earsay'* but gave no thought to people who care for and choose to expose certain wrong doings in institutions. Or, for them to be given space to defend the rights of the less unfortunate in our mostly ignorant society.

(The Courier Mail still will not let ex prisoners have a say.)

The Courier Mail does not answer to any citizen, and it does not answer to the Law. It only operates when there is something in it for the Courier

Mail. *The Learning for Life Program has no space,* nor does the Armed Forces have any right to have their concerns aired in Public. And yet, the Courier Mail can clearly decide what case can be leapfrogged into the Supreme Court. That is, due to their belief that *'Public Opinion'* demands it.

Sadly the Legal fraternity acquiesces to the demands of the media, but clearly ignores the rights of people in the community who are of no real consequence to the eventual outcome.

It is not for public opinion, *that the media demands legal rights,* but simply it is the media's belief that they are the only voice in town and can sic their trained dogs onto anyone, whom they so choose to slander.

Under Flex's law, *the Courts of Queensland would accept that the media should get back in its box,* and 'Earsay' should clean the wax out of its ear-say, and listen to all that the people of Queensland suggest, *or wish to say.* Not just a portion of society that has always pleased the arrogant, and the pig headed.

Without writings from the horse's mouth, *instead of its butt,* governments in every area of Australia, are running blind. It is also said, that in the land of the blind, the ONE EYED MAN IS KING, and as far as Queensland is concerned, I do feel they should hope deep in their hearts, that the man with one eye, is a good decent man with one ear and an honest family supporting him;

Regardless of what newspapers so wish to selfishly sprout to ordinary people who foolishly buy their newspapers like loyal obedient subjects, I AM STILL A CITIZEN IN THE SUBURBS. AND, A HUMAN BEING.

I respect the law, but not the many liars and thieves that have an almost total control of such laws.

There is a better system than this. *Trust me*, I know what it is.

CHAPTER 29

QUEENSLAND JUSTICE & I

The Queensland Department of Justice; *or The Office of The Attorney General,* have been considered, by myself, *and by others,* to be little more than a type of watch dog organization. That is, of a many University type of trained legal people.

Educated people that appear to plug leaks, when, or wherever they crop up.

I may of course be wrong in my many first hand views, but in the midst of their enormous, *mountains of paperwork,* there are many good people who try extremely hard to do exactly what is right. That is, by as many people as humanely possible.

I could even say, that if they could pass, *or create a law to prevent bullying, and abuse in all areas of Queensland life,* I feel they would do so immediately.

However, their being a well paid Government Department, employee, *they* have priorities that must be dealt with before they can at all move on into the public arena and institute a modern law, that may tend to embarrass any Government Departments.

Of course, the desire to right a serious wrong, *is there,* but obviously protocols must be clearly adhered to, and even I, *as a convicted felon,* can understand where their; *'Indecisive Position,'* actually derives from.

With my writings of those old Prison Institutions in the 20th Century, I am in no way attempting to create dissent, but I am attempting to explain a real need for change in the area of a modern Corrective Services. An ignorant all powerful group, that are using old 20th Century rules, and or methods, to hopefully lower rising crime rates in Queensland. *Possibly to assist a Federal Government at the same time.*

Because our Queensland Public Servants, *and media,* have a policy of, *not at all communicating with convicted felons,* there is no way to explain to them, that there is *real* need to review the methodology and classification policies in dealing with modern prisoner containment. *(See my 'Book of Projects.')*

In just four important areas alone, there has been the need for an Inquiry to ease the pressure on all aspects of prison life; *and,* I will name them as follows.

So that there can be no mistake of my intent to do the right thing.

(1) The greater influx of inmates charged with Drug offences.
(2) The greater influx of citizens charged with crimes affecting Children.
(3) The greater influx of people charged with murder and personal violence.
(4) The verbal, and or a fabrication of evidence in the State of Queensland.

What is quite apparent, to numerous interested parties, is that many offenders of today, are today considered to be a flight risk, *(because of drugs)* and so it is that our Remand, *or our modern Stand-By facilities,* are abounding with personalities that will not, *or cannot at all,* be classified. *(Behaviorally, or mentally.)* That is, until they have been examined by the court. *Then it is, that hopefully, he or she will be processed into containment areas as wholly sentenced prisoners. Possibly more suited to their own personal personality.*

It is my clear, and honest view, that the *mix of personalities* that are eventually formed in any containment system, *that we have at this present time,* is that, *officially* under the now jurisdiction of the arresting police, *and also the Department of Public Prosecutions,* such forced haphazard 'Consorting of Offenders,' are going to become a social threat.

To almost every community in the State of Queensland.

Therefore, I have no choice but to write of, or to speak of my own experiences, so that citizens of the future, will have a genuine perspective to work with when they seek to ease the ever mounting crazed burden of criminal behaviour, on an inadequate Corrective Services regime. *And ultimately, upon our general communities.*

My role is not to simply sell books and make money, but to hopefully leave my writings in the hands of ordinary caring people that may someday seek to observe, *or to comprehend,* that *we as citizens* have to clean and rake up societies pig pens, *or fowl yards,* from time to time.

Mainly so that our own descendants, *such as our personal future children and grandchildren,* will not be made scapegoats out of, *or by,* such arrogant Legal Eagles, and their bullying armed up enforcers.

Magistrate Bias;

A serious problem, where *'Justice' is concerned,* is that the Society of Law, *or the Bar association,* permits soldiers, Warders, Policemen or those *armed security people,* to conveniently be awarded positions as a *'Stipendiary Magistrate.'*

Such men, *and now women,* are trained to break down, and to humiliate their opposition, *or enemy,* and for us to allow such varied people to have the position of an independent; *Adjudicator,* is a travesty of law, in itself.

It would be like allowing a Klu Klux Klan supporter to sit on the High Court of America. Or allowing a Bullock Driver, to be a Justice of the Peace.

Why? Our Queensland Magistrates, have not at all been previously investigated for finding *consistent* PRIMA FACIE cases, *without any physical evidence.* Is in my view, clearly suggesting that thousands of these inadequate legal persons, have passed uncountable life changing decisions, *wholly based on bias,* and, not on law.

Bias; is why we have 'Recidivism,' and to allow a prior policeman, magistrate, *or a judge,* to refuse me bail, *for one and a half years,* even after ten acquittals by his old cronies, certainly gives us proof enough, that the arrogant police workers, have had more than enough power than is necessary to complete their duties.

To get writings, such as *'The Dream Breaker' Or the Boggo Road Connection,* published, *legally,* so that more and more modern students in University, *Criminology Social Sciences Penology and Anthropology,* can see a clearer picture of what they are facing, is tremendously hard for a pensioner. Which is, that a new modern Department of Justice, and the modern Attorney General, need to pass fresh new laws. *Laws that not only legalize such writings of those who today live and work behind walls, but to financially support any writings, or manuscripts by prisoners, for the good of all our future citizens, who are yet to be ostracized.* 'Or verballed.'

Personally I genuinely feel, that the many issues mentioned, need to be studied independently of policing, or, containment officials.

After some thought, I decided to not end the story of my legal fight with the Law Society, *as well as the Queensland government,* mainly because history has today decided to allow *'Historical Societies'* to unfairly humanise police and warders in their treatment of prison inmates. *While in turn, dehumanising men and women who were, or are, locked in societies concrete containers.*

'Most parents do consider, that there is two sides to every story.'

Although I should, *not,* I decided to give my version of how I had long coped with a changing world, and how, *like the reader,* I handled a mundane life of day to day struggles to deal with what is on our plate, *on any given day.*

What I have added, in various; *book writing exercises,* is an honest appraisal of why I did not go on to lead an honest, and successful life, *much earlier than I did.*

But at the same time, I do feel that I was not a demon, or a bully, but a simple man with an immaturity problem. A behavioural trend that had been damaged by a series of events that can lead only to the streets. *Or, to a prison wall.*

Possibly also, to a point in ones life when suicide appears the only alternative to our being able to socially breathe the same air that you do.

As for bail pending trial. If a defendant is refused bail, and is duly acquitted of the crime so charged, he or she must immediately be paid the same amount that a jury member is paid for his or her attendance. An order made by the residing judge, or Justice, that payment be forthcoming and that travel arrangements and lodging be arranged before the defendant has LEFT THE COURT PRECINCTS.

CHAPTER 30

THE BALANCE OF LIFE

*B*efore everyone actually dies, there is a small fleeting and magical moment, when they would like to pass on a message. Or just a little wisdom that they have learned about; *'Life'* in general.

Seldom, do any of us ever do it.

So, now, *today,* because of the words I have already written, *and sometimes published*, I too would seek to pass on a very important message.

I do know, *the media will not listen to what I have to say*, and nor will the cold self centered legal fraternity, for there are those among them who see God, *as having to make a appointment to see them, personally*. But there are men and women that are maliciously locking horns with other men and women, *and so it is,* I seriously want to extend them a message of great importance. *That is, before they grow much too old to care about anyone, but themselves, as they today lay dying with cancer.*

Policing Authorities, *and prisoners,* have always tricked and manipulated each other, *and,* in every generation, there are more and more of them that will do anything that they can, just to have the upper hand.

For both contestants, the message is crystal clear, and that is; *To not disregard the 'Balance of Life.'*

Like many people in our world, I once believed that you cannot put brains in statues, and that society had to educate children before they were set in their ways. So it was, that I once wrote a Children's Book I had titled *'My Amazing Family'*

Although I never published the small sweet inadequate writing, *mainly because I could not afford an illustrator?* that writing made it clear to me that I had to help other human beings, *as some sort of inner atonement for my irresponsible past.* I did of course understand, that police workers would not at all listen to me, but I did find out, during my prior; *'Lifetime as a prisoner,'* that many of those troubled prisoners would, and *'did listen to me'* as I had spoken in a type of language that only they could at all interpret, *and understand.* It is not to say, that police workers do not need help, *for I know they do,* and alcohol is something that decimates whole families.

Simply because they do not understand the balance of life.

The many sayings of prisoners today, *do suggest,* that *what goes around soon comes around,* and that *Karma* itself, is something to be respected. Others suggest that if the crocodile does not get you, the alligator will, or even, *he who dares wins.* But the truth of the matter is; *'Life holds true balance over all things great and small. And a balance for all people, who today believe they are far beyond the penalty of day to day repercussions. That is, for what they do.*

Or, of life's unrelenting retaliation for being selfish greedy and bullying human beings.

There is balance in our lives, *whether we like it or not,* and the more we choose to think that we can rudely *unbalance* other peoples lives, *or foolishly think,* there will be no violent reprisal at all, from destiny, *or of 'Life,'* then we should seriously think again.

In this writing, the *'Dream Breaker,'* I have given various examples of many men in prison, *and of course in legal circles,* who believed there was no boomerang for; *hitting people, verbal abuse, tongue raping foolish young men, or girls.* Or, of striking people with a ladle wrapped in a tea towel.

Or again, even their abusing a Downs Syndrome youth by believing there was no *tit for tat* in their own personal world.

Police also, were arrogant enough to actually believe that there was no *counter stroke* for illegal activity, *or that,* they had no need to ever at all reciprocate to anything, or anybody, simply because they were atheists, or agnostic. Then one day, like many others have done, they will arrive home from the late shift only to find that their good spouse had left with the children. *And are not coming back.*

Or a Doctors report explains to them, that they have bowel cancer, due to the drink, and take away foods they have consumed over thirty years.

Millions of people, do not believe in; *'life's payback,' the ricochet,* and a retro-action of unseen reverberation of **'square up,'** *for all that we do in all the years of our lives.*

Believe me, repercussion of; *Life,* is not racist, nor does *'Life,* pay any homage to wealth or power, and yet, all I know is, that I have seen thousands of instances in my lifetime, where the arrogant, *or those totally selfish people, who have no fear, and no religion,* have received their deserved come-up-pence.

Trust me, *I had received mine,* and today I continue to fully pay my dues so that hopefully my two decent and normal living sons will not at all be affected by my past deeds. I do feel, that a lot of people choose not help others in distress, *simply because they believe that what goes around, does indeed come around.* But I totally reject that, and I do feel, that if we stand by and let a gang of bullies terrorize a lone teenager, then someday we too will also be shocked and angry when years in the future, your twelve year old grand daughter is held down and sexually fingered by four or five aggressive girls. It is then, that your mind will wander back to a time in the long ago, when you too could have assisted, *or helped another child.*

But you did not.

Serious as it is, your beautiful granddaughter will tell no one of her ordeal, and her whole demeanor soon changes as she stays in her room flinging hateful insults at other girls on Face Book.

Or listening to, what you refer to as the 'Devil's music.'

The sweet child will then lose all interest in her up-coming exams, and your own daughter comes to you for parental advice, *about the child you all had so much hope for.* Somehow you know, *with your lifetime of wisdom,* that it is payback time, *and also,* that prayer will not help, for now you must pay your dues, or simply watch on helplessly as the child you dearly love, quickly spirals out of control.

Hiding, *and retreating from life,* is not going to make things better, and the courage you lacked in the long ago, *to at all help a youth forty years before*, is now needed today, *even more,* so that both, *I and you,* can save someone that means the world to you.

Rather than your being worldly, *and full of useless advice,* you must go to your granddaughter, and you must say with true blue humility, *and sincerity.*

'Do please forgive me my child, for it is my fault that you have experienced pain, and I want to tell you a story and ask that you help me face what I should have dealt with, so many long years ago.'

To say to her; 'What I did not deal with, was my own cowardice.'

These are the down to earth words, that children have to hear from you, *and if she can forgive you,* she can also forgive those that have hurt and humiliated her. Just as I too learned to forgive my many oppressors.

Of course, *alternatively,* I may easily, like others, have angrily chosen to suffer hatred, and anger, *for the rest of my life.*

I am surely hopeful, *that you and I,* do not wish to destroy a child's life, for it appears to me, that the ingrained nature of human beings are quite busy doing *exactly that,* in every way and manner known to man. But, what I do know for sure is, that all negative things are related to other incidences and actions in our lives, and if we do not balance things in life, we may not at all survive the drive, or even stay alive to create something truly good for ourselves, *Or, for our little ones;*

That is for ignoring another parents pain when their teenager dies in a car accident. Meaning, that we too could find our loved ones may suffer the same fate.

If we are not careful.

Something amazing can give us an all-powerful courage, knowledge, fortitude, and a genuine wisdom, to help others overcome imbalances in *their own* lives.

If you do not believe in religion, *or Christianity,* or of any other giving and or a caring faith, then remember to give a little goodness back, *or I promise you,* that you will truly suffer, even much worse than I have in my most confusing life.

Balance violence with kindness, greed with charity, or trust me, all will be lost, much sooner than you may think.

Without humility, and *'our'* *deeper inner substance,* we are nothing. While our life, *which we hold so dear,* will mean nothing at all. *At the end of our days.*

One thing is certain, 80% of adult Queenslanders believe, that Justice is rigged against the average *'Joe'* on the street, and that court procedure is *biased and unfair* to the civilian class of citizen.

Most feel, *that there is no clear transparency,* especially with the biased media reporting only what ruling political parties want the public to hear.

Courts, *and prosecution hard heads,* do today use cruel intimidation, threats, as well as *mischief-making,* so as to reach their most desired outcome.

Mediation for the upper class, and ongoing prison time for the *'No Hopers.'* is the procedure that is well practiced in the State of Queensland.

Without reasonable, and open accounting by our *'shifty'* legal system, we cannot at all ever expect any reasonable change in the years ahead.

As far as I am concerned, *'Justice should not hide behind closed doors.'*

Whether they like it or not, the *Scales of 'Life'* do a much better job than the; *Scales of Queensland Police Justice.*

Introduction to a Poem;

The following is a small poem that I wrote in the long ago and I present here to put a smile on the faces of those of us who have not always been treated fairly, and justly, by our legal fraternity. A poem, which I feel, suggests that even when we win, we actually lose. But it also shows that the uneducated poor among us sometimes have very useful and surprising talents. Acknowledging the booklet; 'How to Win a Trial.'

The Court Jester

The policemen, the lawyers, the old bailiff, and the
Judge,
all sat around, while deciding my fate.
'Ten years, if not twenty!' said the policemen red faced,
and the lawyers, all agreed, with distaste.
The Bailiff served tea, and he'd tended to agree,
but the Judge, with a frown, he did state:

'The defendant has won it, and I want you to know it,
and I want you to know, what I know
'It appears this fool, is no fool, though he acts like a
fool,
I must say, he's put on an extraordinary, show.
Though be as it may, I must have my say, of matters,
that I do know, I know.
Dear colleagues it is cruel, but rather, than be fools,
we must let, this, scalawag go

The policemen all choked, knowing it wasn't a joke,
and those lawyers all cringed, as if sacked.
The bailiff agreed, as he sipped on his tea,
but he did make one statement, of fact.

'The fool may be a fool, and he may appear, as a fool,
but by Jove, the young wastrel, can act.'

Larry Denis Campbell. 1970. Boggo Road

TO THE READER

For the many caring people of the world, that genuinely want a change in your community, you simply have to stop buying newspapers, or advertising your goods in them. That is, until they stop destroying poor peoples lives.

Choose to advertise in computer networks. *And, on line. I Pad etc.... Or even in letter box drops that clearly work for me.*

Remember, back in the 1970's, when established American based Hells Angels conveniently discovered Queensland, it was an extremely corrupt State, and, in moved their lawyers, the business people, money men, and their high blown advertising scams. Then, had followed the bikers, who sold our kids drugs and drew attention away from the money men who had our politicians, *and our coppers,* in their hip pockets.

What a time they have had, turning clubs pubs and tattoo parlours, prostitution, pornography net works, *into houses of hell.* Worse still, they turned hundreds and thousands of our kids into drug affected derelicts.

Not a peep from the self concerned journalists, *but,* when some idiotic Egyptian Court, in 2014, sent one of their own lads to prison for seven years, for supporting, *by his reporting terrorism,* they screamed the *bloody* roof down.

In the 1970's, the media did not scream when a deaf man was railroaded into defending himself against trumped up charges by the official Bullies buggers and the professional Liars. The then so called Courier Mail said nothing at all, about the verbal evidence, or, the business people, who were putting their own *'scum bags'* in our; State Parliament.

Everyman and woman in the free world, can easily make great humane changes, by voting out ruling politicians, that will not, shall not, *or cannot,* get the rot out of the containment system.

Nor of those in power, that will not live by the rule of *'Fair Play.'*

Today, the poor, are speaking electronically, and sooner or later, they too will come to learn that; *'Mass Voting'* can get them everything that those greedy people had once had in the 20th Century.

For me, life has been a roller coaster of many ups and downs, and I never once stopped attempting to change the laws that were dead set against helping the poor people in the back blocks. *(So, my own publishing firm of; 'Dead Set Publishing.')*

Today the bully boy Governments are back in power, and once again we must get set for a roller coaster ride of greed, power, and unwarranted injustice.

I must say, I am only warming up. For what I need to do, is introduce to you a new system of containment. A humane, **but restrictive system,** that allows our young to sort out their lives without costing them, *or our society*, tons of money and time.

Serious time, that leaves everyone losers.

Should you, *the reader,* wish to know of my projects and ideas to help kids, *and stop the rot*, then pop up to the old Boggo Road Markets this Sunday, and look at my writing on USB key, *or novel.*

In fact, there should be ten *'true blue'* writings, by the end of 2016'

At the end of the day, you will know that you have a lot more *knowledge,* than you ever had before, and now that you have this knowledge, it is up to you to learn more.

Or forget about it.

Three hundred people attempt to commit suicide in Australia every single day of the week, and believe it or not, 2500, *or more*, actually succeed over the following year.

People like myself, *never give up*, for I found the secret to a long life, and that is that while you are helping others to survive, you do not have any time to think about dying, taking drugs, or getting as drunk as a skunk.

larrycampbell09@gmail.com

LAST, BUT NOT LEAST..

I thank you for reading this writing, *and or*, getting thus far, so as to consider the words I have so written.

I believe all readers have a sense, of when something is true, or if it is just plain hogwash? *Or again*, exaggerated nonsense so as to put a few tickets on a writer looking for a few back yard sales.

What I have written, *is the truth*. Not so much for good people at the beginning of the 21ˢᵗ Century, *but*, for those at the end of the Century, who well may be in serious need of a true writing that explains just how our laws of policing, became so tangled.

I hope to leave ten more writings to the State Library, so that my views can be compared to other struggling authors.

Caring authors who were not at all, and never will be, criminals.

If such comparisons find a new solution, then I shall be happy. *Wherever I am.*

But, remember, *always*, bullies truly hate being beaten at their own game.

Larry Campbell. 2015.

Boggo Road Books can be acquired from, www.createspace.com

Or at the Old Boggo Road Gaol site, each and every Sunday.

1. *Concrime, Publisher and Author. 'Dead Set Publishing.'*
larrycampbell09@gmail.com

www.ingramcontent.com/pod-product-compliance
Lightning Source LLC
Chambersburg PA
CBHW051858170526
45168CB00001B/151